CM

Kerala: The Development Experience

Kerala: The Development Experience

Reflections on Sustainability and Replicability

Edited by Govindan Parayil

ZED BOOKS
London & New York

Kerala: The Development Experience was first published by
Zed Books Ltd, 7 Cynthia Street, London N1 9JF, UK,
and Room 400, 175 Fifth Avenue, New York, NY 10010, USA in 2000

Distributed in the USA exclusively by St Martin's Press, Inc.,
175 Fifth Avenue, New York, NY 10010, USA

Editorial copyright © Govindan Parayil 2000
Copyright © individual contributors 2000

The rights of the contributors to be identified as the authors of this
work have been asserted by them in accordance with the Copyright,
Designs and Patents Act, 1988

Typeset in Monotype Garamond
by Lucy Morton & Robin Gable, Grosmont
Cover designed by Andrew Corbett
Cover photographs by Rajesh Parayil
Printed and bound in the United Kingdom
by Biddles Ltd, Guildford and King's Lynn

A catalogue record for this book is available from the British Library

Library of Congress Cataloging-in-Publication Data
Kerala's development experience : reflections on sustainability and replicability /
editor, Govindan Parayil
    p. cm.
    Includes bibliographical references and index.
    ISBN 1–85649–726–7 (cased) — ISBN 1–85649–727–5 (softcover)
    1. Sustainable development—India—Kerala. 2. Income distribution—
India—Kerala. 3. Social justice—India—Kerala. 4. Kerala (India)—Social
conditions. I. Parayil, Govindan, 1955–
HC437.K4 K476 2000
338.954'83'07—dc21   99–051632

ISBN 1 85649 726 7 (Hb)
ISBN 1 85649 727 5 (Pb)

Contents

Preface

Govindan Parayil

Kerala is a small state within India. Although the population of Kerala is greater than that of several OECD (Canada, Australia, Denmark, Sweden, for instance) and Third World (Sri Lanka, Malaysia, for example) countries, when compared with such large Indian states as Uttar Pradesh, Bihar, and Madhya Pradesh, Kerala looks small. However, being small within India in terms of population and geographic size has not prevented Kerala from attracting attention both within and outside India. Kerala is the only state in India that has been declared fully literate. Uttar Pradesh, India's largest state with a population of nearly 150 million, remains the least literate with an adult literacy rate of about 40 per cent (Sen 1997). Kerala also has the lowest infant mortality and highest life expectancy rates of all the Indian states. It is the only state where females outnumber males in the population. Kerala has the largest per-capita circulation of newspapers and magazines in India. Furthermore, it benefits from a thriving literary and film culture.

In the pre-modern era, Kerala was an important source of spices for the world and an entrepôt for trade between East and West. All modern martial arts of Asia can be traced back to the ancient Kerala martial art of *Kalarippayat*, which still survives there despite the efforts of the British colonial government to destroy it. Pre-modern Kerala was a cauldron of caste oppression, aptly described by the nineteenth-century Hindu reformer Vivekananda as a 'mad house'.

In more recent times, Kerala attracted attention when in 1957 it elected a Communist government to rule the state. A combination of public action and popular mobilization led to the electoral success of the Communist Party, although it represented the culmination of an almost century-long struggle by the oppressed classes and castes for social justice. The first democratically elected government of Kerala was dismissed by the Congress-led central government two years later, for ideological reasons; nevertheless, during its short claim on power, the new government tried to enact legislation to reduce social and economic inequalities through such measures as land and educational reforms. What we call 'Kerala's development experience' or the 'Kerala model' of development – the central focus of this book – is a unique pattern of social and economic changes that have been taking place in Kerala as a result of initiatives, both governmental and non-governmental, based on public action.

One particular aspect of the Kerala experience that has caught the attention of development scholars is its high social indicators of development – manifested by the state's near First World levels of infant mortality, population growth, literacy, life expectancy, and so on, which came about without the usual trappings of 'rapid' economic growth in per-capita GDP and corresponding increases in throughput. While a few scholars tried to explain away this apparent counter-intuitive state of events as an enigma or a paradox, most saw something of great significance. It was clear to many that Kerala's development experience demanded further investigation, so that lessons could be learnt by other developing states within India and elsewhere. The purpose of this book is to explore these possibilities.

The book examines such questions as the replicability of Kerala's development experience, as well as the constraints that operate. It also appraises the question of sustainability, which is addressed on two fronts: how the social advances can be sustained over the long term while working within limited financial and economic resources, and how environmental sustainability can be achieved by learning from the limitations on growth and by living with minimal natural and physical resources. Particular attention is paid to the issue of how the development experience can be made more enduring, and how it can be renewed within Kerala itself. This has become significant in light of the recent attempts by the government to decentralize and democratize the whole process of development. Although Kerala has not yet evolved into the ideal model of development for raising the masses from poverty and deprivation everywhere, it nevertheless has several important lessons to offer other developing states. This is important given the failure of competing models of development to deliver. The book thus identifies Kerala as a positive 'model' of development, and challenges those who attempt to malign it as an 'anomaly' or a 'riddle', or even – as some neoliberals choose to portray it – as a 'debacle'. There are many lessons to be learnt from Kerala's development experience; these may provide solace to those development scholars and practitioners who have been disappointed by the prevailing alternatives.

Kerala has been a favourite discussion topic among the academic development community for decades now. Numerous books and articles have been written about Kerala's history, economics, politics and culture in the effort to understand the state's particular pattern of development and change. In response to the unprecedented level of interest being shown in Kerala's development, an International Congress on Kerala Studies was held in Thiruvananthapuram, the capital of Kerala, in August 1994. The conference drew some 1,600 participants, of whom 700 were academic scholars, from India and twenty-three other countries (Thomas Isaac and Tharakan 1995). The conference discussed Kerala's successes and shortcomings, as well as the challenges that lie ahead in the future. Two years after the Thiruvananthapuram congress, another conference on Kerala's development experience was held at the Institute for Social Sciences in New Delhi. This meeting also attracted several hundred national and international scholars with an interest in Kerala's development. In the light of this growing international forum, particular attention has been paid in the selection of contributions for this book, which in consequence presents the work of Kerala experts from around the world. Furthermore, this is the first book that has tried to present a balanced account of Kerala's development achievements and shortcomings, focusing on sustainability and replicability as the key factors of the development experience.

What makes Kerala distinctive as a subject for study and analysis is the optimistic conclusions that are drawn. This is significant because development studies is awash with research that points to the problems of the field – how the development project itself has gone awry or failed to deliver. For the fact is that poverty, deprivation, social conflict and environmental problems in countries of the South have not really abated since the development project began, following decolonization. Indeed, such conditions have worsened in many places. One of the major objectives in putting together this volume is to show that things are not unremittingly bad: glimmers of hope exist in an apparently hopeless world. Kerala, despite its shortcomings, is one such place where hope remains alive.

Following the publication in 1996 of an article on Kerala in *Third World Quarterly*, I received numerous reprint requests from scholars around the world with an interest in the 'Kerala model of development' that I had tried to articulate. I could only deal peripherally in the article with the immense issue of what it is that makes Kerala such an important subject for development practitioners and theorists. It was clear that there was a need to bring together as a single resource the best theoretical analyses and empirical studies of Kerala's development experience by experts in the field. I therefore mooted the possibility of such a volume to my friend Sundar, who without hesitation agreed that it was a great idea. In 1998 I began to give serious thought to putting an edited volume together. To this end, I contacted several scholars who had published books and articles on Kerala. The response was overwhelmingly positive: contributions were promised from Richard Franke, Barbara Chasin, K.P. Kannan, John Kurien, M.P. Parameswaran, Patrick Heller, Olle Törnquist, René Véron and Rex Casinader. Some suggested contacting other scholars in the field; Wesley Shrum, Sundar Ramanathaiyer, V.K Ramachandran and Will Alexander subsequently came on board. Although unable to contribute due to prior commitments, Amartya Sen expressed his support for the project and posed some important questions concerning the nature of its subject. I elaborate on these in the introductory chapter.

The next step was to contact the publishers that I thought might be interested in a book on Kerala. The most enthusiastic response came from Robert Molteno of Zed Books. Robert believed in the project as much as I did; indeed, from the beginning there was a meeting of minds on its intrinsic worth.

I would like to thank Robert Molteno for his knowledge and advice in helping me put this volume together. My gratitude also goes to all the contributors. I thank especially Richard Franke, Sundar Ramanathaiyer and René Véron for their early support and encouragement. I found out the hard way that editing a book is, indeed, a much more difficult task than writing one. Nevertheless, the effort was worthwhile and rewarding. I am confident that this will be a useful book and that it is an optimistic one. It is at once a timely scholarly addition to the literature and a valuable resource for university students and teachers of development studies. Finally, I dedicate this book to the memory of my parents, whose own life stories of struggles in Kerala during pre- and post-independence India inspired me.

1

Introduction: Is Kerala's Development Experience a 'Model'?

Govindan Parayil

An Enigma?

The Indian state of Kerala, with its population of nearly 30 million (larger than that of Canada, which has a land mass more than 250 times greater), has become an 'enigma' and a 'paradox' to many economists and development experts.[1] Kerala has confounded the widely accepted principle that improvement in the standard of living of ordinary people can come about only after the achievement of rapid economic development (Thomas Isaac and Tharakan 1995). According to Bill McKibben (1996), Kerala has in fact proved the development experts wrong. Over the past fifty years or more, Kerala has been transforming itself from an extremely poor state, ridden with caste and class conflicts and burdened by high birth, infant-mortality, and population growth rates, into a social-democratic state with low birth, infant-mortality and population growth rates and a high level of literacy.[2] Kerala's indicators of social development are comparable to many so-called developed nations, although its per-capita income is a mere fraction of theirs (see the chapter by Parameswaran for a comparison of the development indicators of Kerala and the USA). Yet this transformation occurred without the rapid economic growth character-istic of the East and Southeast Asian newly industrializing economies (NIEs) (that is, until their spectacular crash in 1997). Most importantly, the change has taken place peacefully and within a democratic framework by enfranchising most of the formerly dispossessed groups and com-munities of Kerala society. However, as K.P. Kannan argues in this volume, Kerala's development record should not be perceived, in common with most analysts, as merely the achievement of a high quality of social life, despite low economic growth. Instead, as he shows, enhanced social conditions, including alleviation of poverty, have been attained, along with a reduction in both spatial and gender gaps (between rural and urban areas, and between males and females) – two regressive trends that characterize most developing societies. Most significantly, Kerala's economic and social transformation took place without outside help.

Those who perceive Kerala as an enigma believe that a state or society can 'develop' only if it follows the neoliberal nostrums preached by the International Monetary Fund (IMF), the World Bank and their development experts. They maintain that a state's social development and improvement in material conditions of living can come about only by first achieving economic growth, and this by opening itself up to 'free trade' and the linking of its economy to the network of globalized financial systems dominated by the Western industrial nations. The belief of most modern economists that the only way to practise development economics is to accept the tenets of neoclassical economic doctrine – which was modelled on Newtonian mechanics, and developed to modernize the nations of Europe and North America – must be reconsidered if Third World states are to achieve genuine social transformation and economic development. Specifically, the convergence principle encoded in the neoclassical development orthodoxy – that there is exclusively one path to modernization, and that is to follow blindly the tenets of globalization and liberalization as postulated by the industrialized nations – needs to be turned on its head if the states of the South are to extricate themselves from their unsatisfactory present course. That is, they need to leave the uneven path of convergence and unequal exchange practices that has been dictated from without. Modernization can be pursued in different ways. It is not incumbent on the states of the South to occupy passively the predetermined positions on the periodic table of nations that the dominant economic and political powers have specified for them. Indeed, what Kerala has done is to defy the status quo by charting a new path of development and modernization on its own terms, and in many respects despite the constraints within which it has had to operate. It should be remembered that Kerala is only a state within the federal structure of the Indian union. The development experience of Kerala is not an enigma to those able to see the world in the light of a new development paradigm that has emerged from within the Third World. The question remains: How did Kerala achieve indicators of social development that are comparable to those of the so-called First World countries?

The main objective of this book is to understand the nature of Kerala's achievement through the work of leading scholars from around the world. Kerala has long attracted the attention of development scholars. A study sponsored by the United Nations in the early 1970s on the state's economic and social development, conducted by K.N. Raj and his colleagues at the Centre for Development Studies in Thiruvanathapuram, recognized the policy implications of Kerala's development record (CDS 1975). Although Raj did not use the term 'model' in the study (Raj 1994) of Kerala's alternative development path, he nevertheless assured it special status in international development debate. In a later study, John Ratcliffe (1978) showed that the causative factor underlying Kerala's social achievements was social justice. Amartya Sen and Jean Drèze have, for their part, long championed Kerala's development experience in their numerous works. Many other scholars have examined different aspects of the state's progress. What is unique about the present volume is that it brings together contemporary works that take stock of Kerala's achievements and shortcomings by focusing specifically on questions of sustainability and replicability (see, in particular, the chapters by Franke and Chasin, Ramachandran, Véron, Parameswaran and Alexander). The book also looks at the future of the so-called 'Kerala model', particularly the new development initiatives such as participatory and local level planning (see especially the chapters by Franke and Chasin, Törnquist, Véron and Parameswaran).

What Kerala has achieved with very low per-capita income and economic growth is remarkable. Hence, other developing states have a great deal more to learn from Kerala than from the growth models of First World states. According to Amartya Sen (1997) India does not need to look elsewhere for development pointers; yet there is much that India can learn from Kerala's development experience. Sen writes: '[T]he average levels of literacy, life expectancy, infant mortality, etc., in India are enormously adverse compared with China, and yet in all these respects Kerala does significantly better than China.' 'In some respects', he adds, 'Kerala – despite its low income level – has achieved more than even some of the most admired high-growth economies, such as South Korea' (Sen 1997: 7–8). It follows that Kerala's experience can stand as a 'model' for emulation, with all due caveats acknowledged. In what follows, I defend the claim that there is indeed a 'Kerala model' of development, and that it should be analysed and debated in order to discern its normative claims and the potential for emulation. I will first present a brief socio-geographical sketch of Kerala to place it in the Indian and global context.

Kerala: A Sociogeographical Sketch

Kerala is one of the twenty-five constituent states of the Indian union. It occupies 1.18 per cent of the total land area of the country. It has a population of 30 million, which was about 3.44 per cent of the total population at the 1991 census (Prakash 1994). The state of Kerala as a political entity came into existence in 1956 by integrating the Malayalam-speaking former princely states of Travancore and Cochin with the Malabar district of the former British colonial province of Madras. Kerala is a tropical land of some 38,850 square kilometres (about 15,000 square miles), situated on the southwestern tip of the Indian subcontinent; it has a lengthy coastline. The region has a long history of commercial and cultural contact with the outside world. In antiquity, Arab, Greek, Roman and Chinese traders came to Kerala to buy spices, for which it developed an international reputation. Along with commerce and exploration came several world religions. Over the past several centuries, Kerala has been influenced in varying degrees by several world religions: Hinduism, Christianity, Islam, Buddhism, Jainism and Judaism. Modern Kerala is one of the most religiously diverse regions in South Asia. The current population distribution of Kerala according to religion is: 57 per cent Hindu, 23 per cent Muslim, 19.5 per cent Christian, and the rest Buddhist and animist. With a population density of 740 persons per square kilometre, Kerala is one of the most densely populated regions in the world.

The population growth rate in Kerala during the 1950s was the highest in India, but by the 1970s it had fallen to become the lowest of all the Indian states (Kannan et al. 1991): from 44 per 1,000 in 1951 to 18 per 1,000 in 1991 (lower than China's 19 per 1,000). Kerala's population as a percentage of India's fell from 3.88 per cent in 1971 to 3.44 per cent in 1991 (Prakash 1994).[3] Kerala has an adult literacy rate of over 90 per cent, while that of India stands at around 50 per cent. In terms of female literacy, Kerala stands out among all the Indian states, and is way ahead of China. Furthermore, almost 100 per cent of children of school age and youths are literate. According to Amartya Sen, 'The distinction of Kerala is particularly striking in the field of gender equality' (Sen 1997: 13). The female-to-male ratio is 1.04:1, in contrast to India's ratio of 0.93:1 and China's 0.94:1 (Sen 1993). Kerala's ratio is similar to the ratio in North America and Europe. (See the chapter by Kannan for details on women's role in making Kerala both healthy and literate.) Observing the state's excellent gender development indicators, Alexander argues in this volume that it is in fact Kerala that is 'normal', and India that is 'abnormal'. While Kerala's infant mortality rate (IMR) is 13 per 1,000 live births, India's rate is over 80 per 1,000. Again, Kerala's figure compares favourably with many so-called developed states, notwithstanding its very low per-capita income.[4] The chapters that follow provide a fuller picture of Kerala's achievements.

A 'Model' or Just an Alternative Development Experience?

If Kerala's radical reductions in infant mortality, population growth, illiteracy, and crude death rates, along with the elimination of acute poverty, without significant erosion of the ecological balance, are justification for positing a new development paradigm, then there are grounds for comparison with the ideal model currently in vogue – sustainable development. Indeed, Kerala's development experience may help articulate, and offer an alternative examination of, the sustainable development (SD) paradigm popularized by the United Nations World Commission on Environment and Development (WCED 1987), notwithstanding the vagueness of its definition and its dependence on controversial concepts such as economic growth, borrowed from neoclassical economics (Parayil 1996 and 1998). That is, rather than postulating *a priori* how SD ought to be practised, a practical, reflexive approach can be adopted: by considering the paradigmatic case of a society in which rudimentary components of the SD thesis have seemingly been put into practice. Such an examination of Kerala, as presented in this volume and elsewhere, will in turn help the people and government of Kerala to address the state's shortcomings and to face the challenges ahead. That is, we need to show how the Kerala development experience can be improved and reformulated in conformity with the spirit of SD promulgated by the United Nations and other organizations.

Conventional development models, legitimated through quantitative growth measures like GNP per capita, fail to account for indicators of social development. The experience of Kerala is that sustainability measures must be sought not in quantitative indices alone, but also in qualitative indices. The meaninglessness of income and GDP per capita as measures of socioeconomic development becomes obvious when we compare these figures with those of other states within India and elsewhere (see the chapters by Kannan, Ramachandran, Shrum and Ramanathaiyer and Parameswaran in this volume). States with a per-capita income higher than that of Kerala fared very poorly in terms of social indicators of development, which clearly shows the inadequacy of economic growth as *the* measure of 'development'. Alternative indicators of development, such as physical quality of life index (PQLI), human development index (HDI), and gender development index (GDI), measure 'development' more usefully than do economic growth indicators like GDP per capita (Parayil 1996; Kannan, this volume). In 1991–92, the state of Punjab, whose per-capita income is more than double that of Kerala, rated 23 PQLI points fewer. In the same year, Kerala's PQLI rating was 53 points higher than the all-India average (EPW Research Foundation 1994b). Franke calculated that in

1981 Kerala rated a PQLI of 82, compared to a USA index of 96 (Franke 1996: 2). In 1994 the HDI of the USA was 0.925, while Kerala's index was 0.775, with a per-capita income about one-eightieth of that of the former (Parayil 1996).[5]

Until July 1997, the 'miracle' economies of East and Southeast Asia were the shining examples within the ambit of the Third World of free-market capitalist development and its attendant globalization and liberalization. The World Bank's development experts advised the rest of the developing world to emulate the 'tiger' economies as the model for rapid development of their economies and societies (World Bank 1993). Although no real measure has yet been made of the human suffering that followed the spectacular crash and meltdown of the economies and financial markets of these 'miracle' economies, early reports indicate that hundreds of millions of people have been pushed below the poverty line in countries such as Indonesia, Thailand, Malaysia, South Korea and the Philippines as a result of losing their jobs in the manufacturing and service sectors. More are losing their jobs in Russia and Latin America as the financial crisis spreads from Asia to other parts of the developing world. In Indonesia alone, nearly half of the population has been affected by the crash. It has become painfully apparent that the 'free market' economic model constructed and imposed by the IMF/World Bank and Western industrial powers on developing nations is unravelling as the wealth produced by the workers is expropriated by speculators and greedy 'investors' from the West, as well as by crony capitalists and corrupt government officials in the countries themselves.

Now that the perils of globalization and predatory capitalism have been exposed at such tremendous cost to the people at the bottom of society, it is time to look for alternative models of development and social change, and in particular new forms of production in which the vulnerable members of society will not stand to lose everything through no fault of their own when things go wrong. With the disappearance and metamorphosis of the Soviet, East European and Chinese economic systems into a kind of proto-'free market' capitalism, the so-called planned state-capitalist model has largely disappeared. The question, then, is whether an alternative economic model exists that can deliver equitable economic development and truly participatory industrial democracy. It is in this context that the development experience of Kerala – now encoded as the 'Kerala model' – gains significance.

The 'Kerala model' of development and sustainability is characterized by public actions carried out through popular mobilizations and governmental interventions within a democratic framework, with the aim of transforming a poor and restive society marked by very low economic growth. In the annals of development theory, such a 'model' is counter-intuitive and contrary to the nostrum preached by the IMF/World Bank and other international development agencies that a state's social development and material conditions of living can improve only after it has achieved economic growth. Whereas the growth-based economic development model practised by most developing countries has nowhere made a significant contribution to reducing poverty, ecological devastation and population growth, or lessening inequalities in the distribution of income, wealth and social status, Kerala for its part has demonstrated that the quality of life of ordinary citizens can be radically improved in the absence of high economic growth and without consuming excessive energy and other natural resources. What it shows is that growth is a necessary but not a sufficient condition for genuine development.

Although Kerala's achievements are in many respects laudable, some concerned commentators have drawn attention to the model's short-comings by highlighting the conditions of excluded communities. For example, Joan Mencher (1980 and 1994) and Richard Franke and Barbara Chasin (1996) have examined the lives of female agricultural labourers in parts of the state. John Kurien, in this volume, assesses the poor circumstances of the large number of traditional fishermen, describing them as the 'outlier' of the Kerala model. What is more, there has been a trend recently, including among certain supposedly sympathetic commentators, to portray such shortcomings as a disaster. The neoliberal scholars Joseph Tharamangalam (1998a and 1998b) and K.K. George (1993 and 1998) represent this trend. The main complaint is that, unlike the East Asian 'tiger' economies (now, ironically, clawless paper tigers after the 1997 crash), Kerala failed to 'grow' economically while it developed socially. This, though, is an example of how readily critics can lose sight of the wood for the trees, lapsing into neoliberal nostalgia for economic growth. These analysts claim that the sub-national entity of Kerala is a 'mirror-image' of the authoritarian developmental states of East and Southeast Asia – a hackneyed notion that I deconstruct below – and that it passed up the opportunity for 'miracle' growth in favour of redistributive development programmes. Tharamangalam's (1998a) thesis, then, is that the social, political and cultural attributes of the 'Kerala model' are a recipe for failure. That is, the explanation for the failure of Kerala to attain rapid economic growth and other trappings of capitalist or statist modernization is inherent in the model itself. Therefore, he argues, it would be a mistake to recommend the Kerala model of development to other states in India and elsewhere.

Tharamagalam presents several arguments to explain Kerala's failure to grow. For example, he asserts that the people of Kerala, Malayalees, were an enterprising people before the state began to mobilize redistributive development programmes after the first democratically elected Communist government assumed power in 1957. In what he describes as the 'development debacle' of the past several decades (the period that saw impressive social development), Malayalees became unproductive and uncooperative welfare dependents, relying on the patronizing state for 'land, rice, jobs, roads, schools, and other varieties of welfare' (1998a: 29). He further points out that during the British colonial era, under the patronage of the benign rajas of Travancore and Cochin (the southern half of present-day Kerala state), Malayalees enjoyed the largest number of banks per capita in India and boasted a thriving commercial agriculture and the rudiments of an agrarian-based industry. What is more, he claims, by working through communally organized enterprises, the Malayalees built cooperative banks, hospitals and educational institutions. However, after the creation of the state of Kerala, when the redistributive development programme started, this communal and entrepreneurial spirit disappeared, stymieing economic growth and industrial expansion.[6]

One of my objectives in putting together this volume was to assess whether these allegations have any substance. It is my view, and that of other contributors to this volume, that much of this criticism remains unsubstantiated. This is not to suggest, though, that the model doesn't have genuine shortcomings.[7] There is no claim that Kerala has found the panacea for the masses, and will deliver them from misery and deprivation. Indeed, this volume contains several critical chapters that look at various problems and challenges that Kerala still faces (see the chapters by Kannan, Shrum and Iyer, Kurien and Véron). Nonetheless, the objective is to show that, despite the problems, Kerala has more to offer other developing states than do the competing models championed by Tharamangalam and others.

If sociological theory can show unequivocally, with ample empirical evidence, that Malayalees were historically an entrepreneurial people and that their innovative nature (for developing and running business enterprises) and communitarian spirit have since disappeared, then there would be a serious cause for concern. In fact, the merely anecdotal claim that community spirit has vanished in Kerala is untrue. A summary survey of the past several decades shows that Malayalees have ventured into community-based banks, hospitals, educational, and light industrial enterprises. The evidence is in the proliferation of rural and urban cooperative banks, milk producers' co-ops, vegetable growers' co-ops, cottage and light industry co-ops, as well as the establishment of cooperative hospitals – built by different social groups all over Kerala. The democratic mobilization of thousands of unemployed industrial workers (made redundant when the tobacco company which employed them moved to the neighbouring state of Karnataka) to form what became a very successful industrial cooperative employing 35,000 men and women is an example that attests to the existence of community-based ventures in Kerala.[8] In fact, in terms of cooperative ventures per capita, Kerala state remains unsurpassed in India (see the chapter by Heller). As many authors show in this volume, community-based and decentralized development programmes initiated by both non-governmental organizations and the state government are thriving in Kerala today (see the chapters by Törnquist, Franke and Chasin, Véron and Parameswaran in this volume).

Comparing Kerala with Southeast Asian NIEs for the purpose of showing Kerala's failure is a favourite device of Kerala's critics. Following Peter Evans (1995), Tharamangalam (1998a) asserts that the 'redistributive' developmental state of Kerala can be viewed as a 'mirror image' of the 'growth states' of Southeast Asia. It is difficult to see in what sense this is the case.[9] In historical, political and economic terms, Kerala's development experience has no parallel with that of these authoritarian 'growth states'. Kerala's transformation was based on peasant and worker mobilization conducted within a social-democratic framework, whereas the Southeast Asian states have mobilized around private and foreign capital in an authoritarian framework without worker or peasant participation, and without their involvement, directly or through representatives, in the political and economic distribution of power.

What of the assertion that Kerala, unlike the NIEs, frittered away its comparative advantage in human resources for inducing economic growth? The first obesrvation is that those critical of the Kerala model pay no attention to the political, economic and environmental cost to the ordinary people of the East/Southeast Asian 'miracle'. As Frederic Deyo (1987) and others have shown, the dark side of the 'miracle' is the 'extreme political subordination and exclusion of workers' and the suppression of political dissent. Another claim is that the rapid growth of many of the East/Southeast Asian NIEs is directly accounted for by the ready availability of a large educated populace. This notion, too, is wanting. It was in fact the availability of a large number of unskilled rural workers (mostly peasants) who could be mobilized to work in the factories and on the assembly lines of multinational firms at very low wages and under appalling working conditions that attracted the flow of multinational capital to these states, the products of which are exported to the markets of Western industrial nations. The growth is not directly attributable to the relatively high level of education of the workforce.[10] Recently, of course, thousands of these workers have been forced back to their villages and abandoned rice fields, having lost their jobs in the wake of financial meltdown. As

Samir Amin puts it, the pattern of industrialization of the Asian NIEs 'resembles a gigantic sub-contracting enterprise controlled from countries of the centre' of the world system (1997: 148). Another suggestion re-quiring rebuttal is that a poor work ethic and labour militancy caused outside capital to shy away from Kerala. Patrick Heller, in this volume and elsewhere, shows that, on the contrary, the mobilized nature of the working class, and the part it plays in electoral politics and indeed the government – what Heller (1995) describes as 'class compromise' prag-matism – has created an ideal investment climate in the state. Any reluc-tance on the part of outside capital to move into Kerala can be put down to persistence of the fear of organized labour and to the inadequacy of Kerala's infrastructure.

Critics of the Kerala model tend to view all those who have written favourably about it as naïve romantics. Interestingly enough, most of these 'romantics' are identified as 'outsiders': these include Amartya Sen, Richard Franke and William Alexander (George 1998). Although argu-ably some admirers of the model have gone overboard in their encomia on Kerala's achievements, most serious commentators are a long way from being romantics determined to sing a paean to a poor state's heroic struggle to liberate itself from the shackles of imperialism and capitalist exploitation. Such forms of criticism are the wrong way to go about focusing attention on the deficiencies and problems of the development path Kerala has chosen.

It is true that the course of Kerala's development needs to be clarified and re-energized in order to maintain the high social standards the state has already achieved. Indeed, there is an urgent need to improve further the material conditions of the people and, in particular, to address the problem of acute unemployment and other failings. Yet there are still many lessons that other states in India and elsewhere can learn from Kerala's development experience. The most important lesson – that public action through democratic means (which includes both popular move-ments and progressive governmental intervention) can radically trans-form a society – is as relevant today as it was a generation ago. What Kerala has achieved during its struggle to chart a bold new develop-mental trajectory is in many respects exemplary. It is therefore not un-reasonable to suggest that other struggling and oppressed peoples – whether they are in Chiapas or Orissa, in Indonesia or Sudan – may advance their causes by creatively replicating aspects of Kerala's develop-ment experience or model of development. As Samir Amin has noted while reflecting on the Kerala model of development, 'It is incorrect to think that nothing can be done until revolution, and that until then "the worst is the best"' (Amin 1991: 28).

Many renowned scholars who have written about Kerala's development experience, including some contributors to this volume, voice concern about the term 'Kerala model', fearing that use of the word 'model' might imply an excessive normative baggage, given the numerous problems Kerala still faces. Such concern generally expresses itself in one of two arguments. The first follows from the observation that Kerala's achievement is unique – a paradox that defies the norm and that can easily be explained away. As such, it is ineligible as a model that others can emulate. The argument is that Kerala's apparent uniqueness derives from the state's particular history, geography, culture and politics. However this argument is unpersuasive: after all, it is an easy matter to ascribe uniqueness to any society or state in the world. Moreover, as many of the contributors to this volume and elsewhere have shown, there is in fact nothing unique or abnormal about Kerala's development experience that cannot be explained analytically. For example, by looking specifically at the gender-related development indicators, Alexander in this volume aptly characterizes Kerala as 'normal' within 'abnormal' India. Although the data may appear to be extraordinary, the causal factors behind Kerala's achievements are in fact rather ordinary and well within the realm of the possible for any other people, provided they possess the will and the commitment to demand and win their rights. Indeed, Ramachandran, in this volume, shows how Kerala's achievements can be readily replicated elsewhere in India, provided the political will exists. One variant of the uniqueness argument, that the southern part of Kerala (the former princely states of Travancore and Cochin) was unique because of its comparatively high literacy and health indicators compared to other regions in India during the same period, loses its force when we look at the way the northern part of Kerala (formerly the Malabar district of British India) has successfully bridged the gap in development indicators with the southern part. By public action and popular mobilization, Malabar indeed not only matched the south's achievements in only a few decades but, in fact, surpassed some health and economic indicators.

The second argument about the inappropriateness of the term 'model' derives from Kerala's low rate of economic growth, which is viewed as a compromising feature of the model. As we have seen, a key argument of some critics is that Kerala failed to achieve the 'miracle' growth that the East/Southeast Asian NIEs exhibited – a failure that is put down to the state's refusal to embrace the tenets of liberalization and globalization. Ironically, what some other scholars mean by the term 'Kerala model' is the inverse of the above argument. For them the very specificity of the Kerala model is its great social achievements despite a very low economic growth rate (Thomas Isaac et al. 1998). Amartya Sen, although a great admirer of Kerala's development experience, does not use the term 'Kerala model of development'. In correspondence he explained his reason thus:

> The so-called 'Kerala model' has many features of excellence, and I believe these features could be understood and appreciated without endorsing the 'model' altogether. In particular, Kerala's failure to have economic growth can be seen to be a compromising feature. Bearing this in mind, I have been persistently chary of using the word 'Kerala model' since it carries a stronger normative baggage than would be carried by a more discriminating description, such as 'Kerala's experience of development'.[11]

It is possible, however, to view the fact of Kerala's low economic growth rate in a normative perspective. That is, poor societies are able to improve the conditions of living of their people without first waiting for economic growth to materialize, regardless of whether there is potential for this growth. This, in my view, is the critical argument for retaining normativity as the endorsement of the model. The economic growth argument may in fact be a red herring. For Kerala did grow during the period in which the spectacular changes in social indicators occurred. Furthermore, K.P. Kannan (1998) argues that since the 1990s Kerala's growth has been on a par with or better than any other state in India. Significantly, if Kerala did not redistribute income and spend on social programmes, its economic growth statistics would have been impressive, like those of the admired growth states such as Punjab and Maharashtra – which, for all their great strides in economic growth, exhibit an appalling record on protection of infants, keeping people healthy, improving the status of women and eliminating the scourge of illiteracy (see Franke and Chasin 1998 for related arguments).

Finally, what does it mean when we invoke the term 'model'? And what is in a model? A model is invoked in an effort to see if there are identifiable features and causal relationships from which others states can benefit if it is emulated. A model is a means of representing with the intention of intervening. The normative stress should not be on representing, but rather on creatively intervening. The rationale for putting together this volume is to show that Kerala can indeed be looked upon as a 'model', in the sense of a normatively circumscribed description of an entity that can be emulated and features of which can be replicated by others, taking into account their own specific contexts. By failing to see or to accept this simple point, many well-meaning scholars are, in my view, being caught in a regressive positivist trap and misconstruing what a 'model' ought to be. It seems that many social science scholars perceive the notion of a model in the same way as neoclassical economics, which borrowed it from Newtonian mechanics (McCloskey 1985). Although the notion of what a model is has since changed, particularly since the emergence of the post-Newtonian quantum mechanical world-view, many in the social sciences, including economics, hold on to a view of representation as simply a process of mapping on to a picture theory of knowledge and reality. Since the old distinction between observation/ theory and normative/descriptive has been blurred by historicist thinking, particularly in the wake of the onslaught on the rational foundations of modernization theories, it is time to move on and understand a model, at least in the social sciences, as simply a construction of the human mind to represent social reality. To worry about the normative aspect of models out of a fear of not being representational is to wallow in the metaphysics of a pointless realism/anti-realism debate. The argument concerning intervention and change should be taken as the basis for the normative, and not the nature or structure or 'inner constitution' of the subject being modelled. Our intentions and sense of fairness and justice should become the basis for the normative. Emulating a model does not imply blindly following everything the model represents.

Models in the social sciences are social constructions to explicate and represent grounded social reality. The assumptions and boundary conditions we invoke circumscribe any model's explanatory power or predictive potential. The fact that a model is unable to explain everything does not mean that it is false. The objective here is not to romanticize and take out of context the so-called 'Kerala model' of development. As many in this volume and elsewhere have pointed out, Kerala's development is only just beginning. A lot more has to be done to make it enduring and work to the benefit of all. It is an undeniable fact that industrial and agricultural production needs to be boosted if the material standards of living of many Malayalees is to improve. As E.M.S. Namboodiripad – who as veteran Communist leader and the first democratically elected chief minister spearheaded many development initiatives, including the recent campaign for development through decentralization from below (see the chapters by Franke and Chasin, Törnquist, Véron and Parameswaran) – remarked, a state cannot prosper without industrialization, modernization of agriculture and the 'development of modern secular and scientific education' (Namboodiripad 1995). P.K. Vasudevan Nair, another former chief minister of Kerala and Communist leader, while duly acknowledging the major positive indicators of the state, concedes that the Kerala model of development needs follow-up to make it more enduring (Vasudevan Nair 1995).

The case being made here is that the 'Kerala model' of development is not based on any one existing model of development and modernization. Cuba, Costa Rica and Sri Lanka (see the chapter by

Casinader for a comparative account of Kerala and Sri Lanka), and other countries might profitably be compared in certain respects; however, Kerala's development experience bears no resemblance to that of the East/Southeast Asian NIEs. These lattter are special cases of export-led development, brought to prominence by the industrialized West during the Cold War. The sustainability of these economies, if they can recover from the crash of 1997, is dependent upon the benevolence of the West. As I pointed out earlier, the 'development' of these states has been achieved at the very high cost of deteriorating environmental conditions and inadequate civil and political rights for ordinary citizens.

The Third World is littered with failed development models. Kerala's development experience, encapsulated in the so-called 'Kerala model', requires careful scrutiny with an eye to its possible improvement and to the viability of its replication. A relatively successful model that has emerged from within the Third World might be said to be more appropriate for other developing societies than models derived from a historically different political and economic tradition. There is nothing *sui generis* about Kerala that makes its experience unsuitable as a model of development for other states. Indeed, it provides them with a valuable lesson.

Notes

1. Paul Wallich (1995: 37) claims that 'the Indian state of Kerala has been one of economists' favorite anomalies'.

2. In fact, the struggle to rid the majority of the people of Kerala of caste oppression started at the beginning of the twentieth century. See the chapters by Kannan, Ramachandran, Alexander and Casinader in this volume.

3. Given that the population growth rate of Kerala has fallen considerably since 1991, the state's percentage share in India's population is likely to have dropped further accordingly.

4. Survey data among certain groups in Kerala have shown an IMR of 6 to 7 per 1,000 (see the chapter by Ramachandran). For further details of IMR and other social indicators, see the chapters by Franke and Chasin, Kannan, Ramachandran, Alexander and Parameswaran in this volume.

5. One-third of the HDI composite index is made up of per-capita income, while the other two indicators are life expectancy at birth and adult literacy. The PQLI composite is made up of infant mortality, life expectancy and literacy. For more details, see Parayil (1996: n. 17).

6. Tharamangalam's assertion that it was the culture of dependency created by an all-encompassing welfare state that snuffed out the entrepreneurial spirit of Malayalees echoes those neoliberals and conservatives in the West who claim that the welfare system makes single mothers lazy and unproductive and perpetuates a culture of dependency and ghettoism among the underclass.

7. For a spirited commentary on Tharamangalam's article, see issues 3 and 4 of *Bulletin of Concerned Asian Scholars*, 30 (3 and 4), 1998 (which includes Parayil 1998).

8. See Thomas Isaac et al. (1998). For a review essay of this book, see Parayil (1999).

9. See the chapter by Casinader in this volume for some geographical and cultural similarities between Kerala and the Indonesian islands of Bali and Java. Beyond these rather superficial similarities, there is little economic or political common ground.

10. Typically, the multinationals prefer young women from rural areas; they are less liable to unionization and relatively easy to manage. For a cogent analysis of gender and exploitation in the modern 'homework' economies of transnational capitalism, see Donna Haraway (1985). For a news story about how thousands of young rural women are housed in camps to 'cut the soles, sew the seams and run the machines' to make training shoes for the multinational Nike, which employs nearly half a million workers in Asia, see Keith Richburg and Anne Swardson (1998).

11. From Amartya Sen's letter of 30 June 1998 that he wrote to me in response to my letter concerning this book project.

2

Is the Kerala Model Sustainable? Lessons from the Past, Prospects for the Future

Richard W. Franke and Barbara H. Chasin

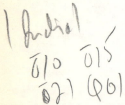

Is the Kerala model sustainable? To answer this question adequately we must ask some questions: What do we mean by sustainability? What is the model to be sustained? What forces brought the model into being? Why is the question of sustainability being asked now? What principal forces are threatening the model's sustainability? What resources are available to sustain the model? Can the forces that created the model in the first place be used to sustain it, or will new forces be necessary? To respond to these questions we will propose a formal definition of sustainability and of the Kerala model. We shall then elaborate the definition of the Kerala model to identify those elements that are most critical to the question of sustainability. Then we consider the model's major failures and shortcomings that threaten its sustainability – what many scholars now call the 'crisis of the Kerala model'.

Sustainability

Sustainability is one of the most widely discussed concepts in development at present.[1] Most proponents see it primarily in ecological terms. We suggest a broader conceptualization. We consider a development model sustainable to the extent that it:

- Improves or at least maintains the material quality of life of the population.
- Expands or at least maintains access to any entitlements necessary for economic security and personal dignity, particularly of vulnerable groups.

- Expands or at least maintains the number of people obtaining access to production resources adequate for a decent life or employment at reasonable wages.
- Reduces the level of social and economic inequalities, or at least does not exacerbate them.
- Expands or at least maintains basic political and individual rights.
- Improves or at least maintains productive resources including land, water, flora and fauna.[2]

For many years the Kerala model has met most of these criteria. Few models elsewhere have come so close to fulfilling all the demands of sustainability. This results from the features of the Kerala model.

The Kerala Model

We define the Kerala model as:

- A set of high material quality-of-life indicators coinciding with low per-capita incomes, both distributed across nearly the entire population of Kerala.
- A set of wealth and resource redistribution programmes that have largely brought about the high material quality-of-life indicators.
- High levels of political participation and activism among ordinary people along with substantial numbers of dedicated leaders at all levels. Kerala's mass activism and committed cadre were able to function within a largely democratic structure, which their activism has served to reinforce.

Quality-of-Life Indicators

The Kerala model can be viewed as a set of quality-of-life indicators that put Kerala closer to high-income developed countries than to the rest of India or to its counterparts in the low-income world. Table 2.1 presents the most recent figures we could locate, which are from 1991 to 1997.

Kerala continues to lead low-income areas and the rest of India. Recent criticisms of the Kerala model suggest that Kerala is losing its lead within India. K.K. George (1993: 119) cites figures indicating that Punjab spends more per capita on education and that both Rajasthan and Punjab spend more per capita on health than Kerala. He also compares Kerala un-favourably with Maharashtra, Haryana, Madhya Pradesh, Nagaland, Rajasthan, and Uttar Pradesh in terms of pension payments to destitutes.[3] These weaknesses should not be overlooked, but they remain minor compared with Kerala's continuing overall ability to deliver a high material

Table 2.1 Comparison of quality-of-life indicators, 1990s

	Kerala	India	Low-income countries[a]	United States
Per-capita GNP in $US	324[b]	390	350	28,740
at purchasing power parity (PPP)[d]	1,371	1,650	1,400	28,740
Adult literacy rate				
as % of total adults				
males	94[c]	65[f]	65	96
females	87[c]	38[f]	41	96
scheduled caste females[h]	74	24	–	–
scheduled tribe females[h]	51	18	–	–
Life expectancy in years				
males	67[e]	62[f]	58[f]	74
females	72[e]	63[f]	60[f]	80
Infant mortality per 1,000[e]	13	65	80	7
rural[h]	15	82		
urban[h]	7	45		
Birth rate per 1,000	18[e]	29[e]	40[g]	16[g]

Notes: We used the most recent figures we could locate in all cases. Figures with no superscript are for 1997 unless indicated by a year marking in the left column.

[a] Low income refers in 1997 to 54 economies with per-capita GNP of $785 or less. With India excluded, it refers to 53 countries, including the 37 countries used in Franke and Chasin (1989: 11) for 1986 data and the 38 countries used in Franke and Chasin (1994: ii) for 1991 data. The additional countries in the 1997 list are former Soviet republics and former regions of Yugoslavia. The addition of these countries tends to improve the quality-of-life figures for the low-income category, diminishing Kerala's lead.

[b] We estimated the US dollar figure for Kerala by dividing the State Government's 1996 per-capita State Domestic Product figure of Rs. 9,066 (GOK 1998a: 3) by 35, the approximate number of rupees per dollar during that year. To this figure of $259 we added 25 per cent, the maximum estimate of the value of overseas remittances added to the Kerala economy. See Thomas Isaac (1992: 79) for estimates of the ratio of remittances to the SDP from 1970 to 1989, showing that the highest was 19 per cent for the year 1980–81. The figure of $324 thus represents an estimate of the likely per-capita income with remittances and therefore does not exaggerate the difference between Kerala's income and its quality-of-life achievements.

[c] Kerala's adult literacy rate for 1991 is taken from the 1991 Indian Census (Bose 1991: 69), prior to the literacy campaign. By the end of 1991, Kerala's rate was near 100 per cent, but weaknesses in the follow-up may have reduced the rate again.

[d] Purchasing power parity (PPP) reflects local prices and makes the income figures more directly comparable: one PPP dollar has the same purchasing power over domestic GNP as a dollar in the USA has over US GDP. See World Bank (1999: 234).

[e] Figures are for 1996.

[f] Figures are for 1995.

[g] Figures are for 1993.

[h] Figures are for 1991.

Sources: GOK (1995b: 3; 1998a: 11, 101); Bose (1991); World Bank (1999: 187, 190, 192, 202; 1995: 162–3, 212–15).

quality of life to its people, as the indicators show. Oommen and Anandaraj's (1996) district-level profile found nine of Kerala's fourteen districts among the top twelve in all of India on a composite of literacy, life expectancy and several economic variables. Kerala's lowest district, Malappuram, was thirty-first on a list with 372 entries.

Kerala's performance on the basic indicators has continued to improve since the early 1980s. Generally, the rest of India and the low-income countries have made only sluggish progress. Kerala's infant mortality rate dropped from 27 in 1986 (Franke and Chasin 1994: 11) to 13 in 1993 where it stabilized up to 1996 (see Table 2.1). This is a 52 per cent drop. By contrast, the all-India rate went from 86 in 1986 to 65 in 1996, a decline of 19 per cent.[4] The Indian state closest to Kerala was Punjab, with an IMR in 1992 of 56 (GOK 1995b: S14), more than four times the 1993 Kerala rate. Furthermore, Kerala continues to maintain a nearly even distribution of indicators when compared with the rest of India. Table 2.1 shows that female scheduled caste literacy in Kerala in 1991 was 79 per cent that of males overall (74 vs 94) whereas in all-India it was 37 per cent (24 vs 65). For scheduled tribe females the figures for Kerala are 54 per cent vs all-India 28 per cent. In 1996, Kerala's 990 villages and 63 municipalities had 956 primary health centres, serving an average of 30,346 persons each, compared with an all-India average of 38,618.[5] Health subcentres numbered 5,094, serving 5,695 persons each, compared with an all-India rate of 6,358. Kerala offered 147 hospital beds per 100,000 people compared with the all-India average of 96 (GOK 1998a: 102). In Kerala, leprosy, filaria and tuberculosis have been reduced to levels below 1 per 2,000 (computed from GOK 1998a: 103). The all-India malaria rate in 1992 was 240 per 100,000 (UNDP 1996: 161) compared to a Kerala rate of 36 for 1997 (computed from GOK 1998a: 103 and S240). Nevertheless, Kerala faces many medical problems, including a serious shortage of blood in hospital blood banks, a possible resurgence of malaria, the threat of AIDS, and a high reported disease (morbidity) rate.[6]

Kerala's continuing ability to improve health services, literacy, birth rates, infant mortality and life expectancy means that the Kerala model is still valid and relevant as an alternative to growth-only development strategies. This important fact should not be overlooked when assessing the sustainability of the Kerala model.

Redistribution Programmes: Case Study of Nadur Village

Behind Kerala's statistical indicators lies a century of struggles for the redistribution of wealth and expansion of public services to benefit most people rather than a small elite. In 1986–87 we conducted research in the central Kerala village of Nadur ('Centreville') to ascertain the effects of these struggles at the local level.

Nadur village has many features typical of Kerala, historically, geographically and sociologically. Nadur lies in the former princely state of Cochin. In terms of land reforms, Cochin lies between the former princely state of Travancore, now southern Kerala, where many changes took place in the nineteenth century, and Malabar, now northern Kerala, where the most protracted and bitter land struggles occurred. Nadur was the scene neither of intense battles between tenants and landlords in past decades nor of land occupations by radical peasant groups in the late 1960s, as took place in some other villages. Nevertheless, Nadur has had its share of land reform militants and Communist organizers, so it represents a kind of mid-way point in terms of land reform struggles in Kerala.

Geographically Nadur is in the lower foothills of the Western Ghat Mountains and contains intensive wet-rice paddy fields typical of the lowland areas of Kerala, as well as cashew and coconut gardens and hillside fields more common in the central midlands. It also contains some upland rubber and forestlands more like the parts of Kerala in the higher elevations to the east. In both history and geography Nadur is thus in the middle of the range of types found in Kerala.

Nadur's 5,000 plus residents include representative numbers of all the major castes of Kerala except the Christians. Like many Cochin villages, Nadur has a higher than average percentage of Nambudiri Brahmins, one of the most important former landlord groups in Kerala. It also has Nair caste members in several occupations, craft castes, Ezhavas and Pulayas. The Nadur sample in 1987 contained only two households with workers sending large remittances from the Persian Gulf states. The near absence of such households in Nadur makes it a controlled case in which the redistribution of the land reform should show up more clearly than in areas where remittances have flooded the village economy.

Field research

Nadur had been studied by Professor Joan Mencher, who kindly made available to us copies of her 1971 household survey. Although the Kerala land reform was enacted in 1969 and went into effect in 1971, land titles in 1971 were still held by landlords and several households were paying rent. The 1971 survey, with a few assumptions, can be taken as pre-land reform, while our 1986–87 survey describes the situation fifteen to sixteen years later, after all land reform transfers had been completed. By comparing the two surveys we could ascertain how the land reform affected land ownership, income distribution by caste and class, and upward and downward income mobility of selected households.

The findings

In the Nadur sample, abolition of rice land tenancy resulted in the transfer of 52.25 acres of land from 10 large landlords (6 per cent of the sample) to 47 tenants (29 per cent of the sample), who became fully entitled smallholders. The former tenants received on average 74 cents each. One hundred and three landless households (64 per cent) were not affected by the rice land reform.[7]

The abolition of house compound tenancy benefited 92 per cent of households. Rights to 47.87 acres were transferred from 7 households (4 per cent) to 156 households (92 per cent). The average tenancy in 1971 was 51 cents while the average owned in 1987 was 54 cents. The poorest labouring families gained title only to small and often inferior plots. Rents and interest dropped from 7 per cent of total sample income in 1971 to 1 per cent in 1987 (Franke 1996: 110).

Declining land and income inequality   We used the Gini Index to measure inequality. A decline in the Index means a decline in inequality. In Nadur, the Gini Index for rice land ownership inequality dropped 13 points. For house compound land, the Gini dropped 39 points between the two surveys. During the same sixteen-year period, the Gini Index for income inequality declined by 5.3 points. Although forces outside the land reform pulled both towards greater and less inequality, land reform must have caused much of this decline in income inequality. The 1974 Kerala Agricultural Workers' Protection Act may also have played a role in these figures.

Declining caste inequality   In Nadur, a reduction in caste inequality is one of the clearest consequences of the land reform. The Nambudiri Brahmin hold on land and high incomes was broken. In 1971, 12 Nambudiri caste households had incomes that correlated 0.86 with rice land and 0.89 with house compound land owned. In 1987 the figures changed to −0.09 and −0.19. Nambudiri incomes rose far less rapidly than those of other castes. Nair and Mannan caste households gained the most while the lowest caste Pulayas raised their relative position slightly. Mannans and Pulayas probably gained more from programmes other than the land reform such as the reservation policies. The political conditions for these programmes, however, included the power of tenants and their allies in the land reform movement. Land reform struggles reinforced the leverage for these lowest caste groups to move upwards economically.

Class inequality Nadur's class structure was altered dramatically by the elimination of landlord and tenant classes. Former landlords dropped from garnering 6.5 times the sample average income in 1971 to 1.5 times the average in 1987. Former tenants did not gain much on average, but several occupational groups slightly improved their economic positions. Households depending primarily on farming raised their relative share of income from 60 per cent of average to 90 per cent. Land reform played an important but not determining role in these class changes.

Social and economic mobility In Nadur, upward mobility occurred in 16 households that gained land but only one that lost land. Downwardly mobile households included 2 that lost land and 5 that gained. Overall, changes in income levels correlated 0.19 with changes in rice land ownership, and 0.21 with changes in house compound land. Both associations are statistically significant. Many other factors interacted with the reform. These include access to highly paid wage labour, age and health of household head, number of wage earners in the household, and access to reservation and targeted development programmes. Land reform in Nadur helped foster upward mobility in conjunction with other social and economic processes.

Exploitation One of the most effective components of Kerala's land reform was to end the threat of eviction of tenants by their landlords from either rice land or house compounds. The success of the land reform, however, has produced new tensions. In place of the struggle between tenants and landlords, former tenants are now at odds with their hired agricultural labourers. Where once the poor were pitted against the rich, now the poor are pitted against the slightly less poor. This development may present an obstacle to progressive forces in Kerala in rallying small landowners to their programmes.[8]

Landlord response to the land reform Nadur's Nambudiri caste landlord households adopted various strategies to prevent the land reform from depriving them of high incomes and good futures for their children. One strategy was to send their children for higher education, thereby making professional employment the chief landlord response to the reform. This response has benefited Nadur because formerly parasitic landlords have become teachers, administrators and small business people who contribute to the economy in ways their ancestors did not. Kerala's high unemployment of the educated, however, threatens the former landlords' escape route and could result in impoverishment for some.

Other redistribution programs in Nadur

Our Nadur study found that other Kerala programmes also had measurable effects. School and nursery lunches added 3 per cent to the incomes of the poorest households with children in school and raised their calorie intake by 5 per cent. The lunches improved the distribution of calories and income by caste, class, income, and land ownership groups (Franke 1993: 360).

Nadur's ration shop effectively reduced income inequality by 5 per cent in 1987, providing 10 per cent more income for the bottom two quintiles, which include mostly labour and agricultural labour and low-caste households. The lunches and the ration shop became particularly important in July, near the end of the long lean season before the August harvest. By making available subsidized food, they probably reduced the need for borrowing by many poor households. Even so, 11 per cent of Nadur sample households reported food shortages so severe that, at least once during the reference year, they had to reduce food intake. Altogether 46 per cent reported eating less, borrowing money, or borrowing food at least once in the year (Franke 1996: 176).

Agricultural labour pensions played a small but significant role in reducing inequality and bringing up the income levels of the poorest groups. Our research showed that 91 per cent of Pulaya caste households received at least one pension, and that the pensions raised the average incomes of all households receiving them by 17 per cent. The ration shop, school lunches and agricultural labour pensions benefited female-supported households more than male-supported households. They thus contributed to reductions in one aspect of gender inequality (Franke and Chasin 1996: 628).

Literacy in Nadur rose from 60 per cent in 1971 to 74 per cent in 1987. Among members of the age cohort 15–29 years, the average years of schooling was 8.1 for males and 7.6 for females. The age cohort 61+, by contrast, had below 2.5 years of schooling (Franke 1996: 228). Every caste and class group experienced increases in the percentage literate and the average years of education between 1971 and 1987. Muslims and Pulayas experienced the greatest increase in years of education, thus tending to improve their position vis-à-vis the other castes. The rate of passing the SSLC (secondary school examination) also improved, but remained low, with only 14 per cent of the cohort 15–29 having passed. Those included 75 per cent of Nambudiris but only 5 per cent of Pulayas, 14 per cent of Nairs, and no Muslims in that cohort. The challenge for Nadur's educational system is clearly the creation of conditions favourable to real school success for those groups most disadvantaged in the past. The Nadur sample displays the same characteristics as have been noted in other parts of Kerala with regard to education, late marriage and declining birth rates. After age has been controlled for, age of marriage and years of education play statistically significant roles in accounting for the number of births to females (Franke 1996: 239).

Overall, our research in Nadur strongly suggests that redistribution has been beneficial to the lowest castes, lowest income groups, agricultural labourers, and female-supported households. During the sixteen-year period between the two surveys, several poor households experienced upward social mobility (Franke 1996: 241–64). The percentage of tiled roofs increased from 59 per cent to 91 per cent, and the average number of rooms per house increased by one (Franke 1996: 267). The provision of electricity rose from 8 per cent to 23 per cent of houses (Franke 1996: 270). Nevertheless, Nadur residents have few household furnishings or consumer goods (Franke 1996: 270–71). Only 22 per cent had enough cots for all household members; the average household income was Rs. 6,871 ($529) in 1987 (Franke 1996: 112), an increase of about 10 per cent over 1971 when adjusted for inflation. Most people remain very poor by international standards.

Political Participation and Activism

We believe that the Nadur study supports the contention that Kerala's quality-of-life achievements result from redistribution. But why has redistribution occurred in Kerala? Enlightened nineteenth-century maharajas provide part of the answer; Christian missions provides another part. We would argue, however, that the main factor is Kerala's popular movements that have sustained themselves for nearly a century.[9] These movements have gone through many stages, from caste improvement associations to trade unions and peasant associations to Communist parties to the Kerala People's Science Movement (KSSP). Whatever the stage, popular movements in Kerala have displayed a combination of characteristics that – taken together – make them especially powerful and enduring.

Kerala's movements have often contained very large numbers of members overall. Kerala's activists have shown an ability to mobilize very large numbers of people for a variety of causes. In 1957 the membership of the Kerala Karshaka Sangham (Kerala Peasant's Organization) reached 190,000 (Sathyamurthy 1985: 189). With just 3.5 per cent of India's people, Kerala had 20 per cent of all the unions in the country (7,836) in 1984. Kerala's union membership accounted for 7.5 per cent of total Indian union membership (Thampy 1994: 291). In 1983, 44 per cent of workers in Kerala's factory sector were trade-union members (Thampy 1994: 291).

In 1988, Communist Party of India–Marxist (the dominant party in the ruling Left Democratic Front) or CPM-organized events in Alleppey involved 750,000 participants (Franke and Chasin 1994: 27). The 1989–91 Total Literacy Campaign recruited 350,000 volunteer teachers.

Kerala's movements have often achieved nearly total representation in strategic geographical or economic areas so that their influence outweighed their numbers. During the period 1935–40, the All-Malabar Karshaka Sangham (Peasants' Organization) had a paid up membership of 5,000 in Kasargod, and 10,000 in Chirakkal (Sathyamurthy 1985: 156). The Shertellai Coir Factory Workers' Union in 1946 had 98 per cent of the workers as members. Six other unions in the area had above 80 per cent membership (Kannan 1988: 118). Similar concentrations existed in recent years for toddy tappers in Thrissur (Kannan 1988: 145–92) and agricultural labourers in Kuttanad and Palakkad (Kannan 1988: 249).

Kerala's movements have often been very militant and creative in finding ways to challenge authority. The birth and success of the Kerala Dinesh Beedi Workers' Cooperative in Kannur depended on the concentrated union membership, militancy and history of mobilization of the beedi workers in the area, and the class solidarity of other workers across Kerala who became the cooperative's initial market (Thomas Isaac, Franke and Raghavan 1998). The workers' creativity in sending out marketing teams to other unions and to community organizations was matched by their capacity to set aside party disputes and focus on the cooperative's survival. The KSSP in Kerala is known for its innovative communication style, which includes street theatre, puppet plays, songs, and an emphasis on making political struggle interesting to make it more effective.

Kerala's movements have thrown up an unusually large number of dedicated and self-sacrificing middle and top leaders, thereby creating a cadre structure of unusual strength, endurance and ability to generate new ideas and actions to adjust to changing local, national and international circumstances. It seems unlikely that movements with the features described above could sustain themselves for so long without a strong and viable cadre of leaders who for the most part do not succumb to corruption and privilege. Why did popular movements develop this set of characteristics in Kerala?

Kerala's location might play a role. As a transfer point on many ancient trading routes, Kerala has experienced influences from many other cultures, for the most part peacefully. This has led to a cosmopolitan outlook on the part of many of Kerala's people (Franke and Chasin 1994: 23–5). Today, Kerala maintains national and international ties of extraordinary strength: 50 per cent of the gross output of the primary and secondary sectors of the economy is exported to other parts of India and overseas, while around 65 per cent of consumption expenditure goes for imports (Thomas Isaac 1994a: 368). In the 1980s, over 682,000 of Kerala's people worked overseas (Franke and Chasin 1994: 69), with as many as 187,000 in the Gulf States in 1980 alone (Nair 1994: 104), possibly contributing as much as 19 per cent to the state SDP in 1981 and remaining above 12 per cent through 1989 (Thomas Isaac 1992: 24).[10]

Kerala's ecology might play a role (Cohn 1971; Fuller 1976; Mencher 1966; cf. Sreekumar 1993). The undifferentiated access to water led to an evenly dispersed settlement pattern that makes it easier to protect against water-borne bacteria and parasites. This means Kerala starts with an advantage in combating infectious and parasitic diseases – the main diseases of underdeveloped areas. Another advantage is political: rural and urban workers can more easily interact and support each others' struggles. Furthermore, Kerala's elected progressive governments could more easily supply public services to a population fairly evenly distributed: there were few special costs associated with isolated, distant, politically weak groups (Franke and Chasin 1994: 22–3).

Another probable factor is the set of historical conjunctures that produced a modern rural proletariat in Kerala. Cool, well watered, and close to ocean transport lanes, the Western Ghats were ideal for the tea and rubber plantations that British colonialists set up in the late nineteenth and early twentieth centuries. Coir mat-weaving factories, cashew nut processing, tile factories and sawmills were added. In a parallel process, the supply of cheap labour in northern Malabar seems to have stimulated the rise of beedi production under the direction of Indian capitalists (Thomas Isaac, Franke and Raghavan 1998: 23–5).[11] More sharply than any other part of India, Kerala experienced a rupture of traditional ties of kinship, caste and locality, creating the potential for intensified class consciousness.[12] The dissolution of traditional ties in Kerala coincided with one of the most radicalizing periods of world history: the Russian and Chinese revolutions, the class struggles in Europe, and the independence movement in India and other colonies. The combination of these several factors and their timing may be part of the answer to Kerala's apparently unique constellation of radical movements with power and endurance.

Crisis of the Kerala Model

Since the late 1970s, scholars and activists within Kerala have been sounding an alarm: the Kerala model faces a crisis (Thomas Isaac and Tharakan 1995: 1995). In 1990, the *Economic and Political Weekly* devoted two issues to the theme 'Kerala Economy at the Crossroads' (EPW 1990a and

1990b). 'The Crisis of the Kerala Model' was the major theme of the August 1994 First International Congress on Kerala Studies, held in Thiruvananthapuram. In our view, the crisis of the Kerala model has eight major components:

1. Kerala's economy has grown at a much slower rate than the Indian national average for most years since the late 1970s (Thomas Isaac and Tharakan 1995: 1995). Between 1988 and 1994, Kerala rebounded with an annual growth rate of 6.4 per cent compared to 5 per cent for all-India (Heller 1998: 35) before slipping again in 1996–97 with a rate of 7.5 per cent vs 14.2 per cent for the Indian national economy (GOK 1998a: 11).

2. Stagnation in agricultural production until the late 1980s coincided with a decline in the area planted in rice. This led to increasing vulnerability to outside sources for the major food crop – rice – which was already substantially dependent on the outside.

3. Price increases for raw materials and competition from cheaper labour sources in other areas have sent traditional industries such as coir, cashew and hand loom into a tailspin (Thomas Isaac and Tharakan 1995: 1995).

4. Industrial growth since the mid-1970s has been sluggish in general and even negative in some years (Mohan 1994; Subrahmanian 1994; Thomas Isaac and Tharakan 1995). By 1996–97, however, it had managed a comeback to 7.4 per cent (GOK 1998a: 11).

5. Unemployment – already high enough to be the major blight on the Kerala model – has remained at about three times the all-India average (Prakash 1994: 22; Thomas Isaac and Tharakan 1995: 1996).

6. The state government has experienced a series of fiscal crises that threaten to undermine many Kerala model redistribution programmes (George 1993). Threatened programmes include the agricultural labour pensions, educational and health spending, and the public distribution system for food. The prices of ration shop rice and wheat have been rising relative to the open market price. From 1991 to 1994, subsidized supplies declined by 31 per cent, but in 1997 increased to 94 per cent of 1991 levels (GOK 1998a: 21). Prospects for maintaining Kerala's extensive public distribution of basic foods depend on both state-wide political trends and which parties hold power at the national level. Increasing local productivity and local output is essential to Kerala's being able to exercise choice over its public distribution policies.

7. Up to 15 per cent of Kerala's people may have been left out of the model. These include fishing people (Karuna 1994; Kurien 1994), female stone cutters (Ukkuru et al. 1994), female domestic servants

(Subramony 1994), some female agricultural labourers (Mencher 1994), at least some tribal peoples (Devi 1994; Corrie 1994), migrant workers from Tamil Nadu, and many head-load and other casual labourers (Pillai 1992 and 1996).[13]

8. Finally, Kerala – like most places on earth – faces an environmental crisis of large proportions. Kerala's environmental damage directly threatens the quality of life and reduces the resource base that must be tapped to sustain the main elements of the model. The best documented component of Kerala's environmental destruction is the loss of forest cover, down from 44 per cent in 1905 to 27 per cent in 1965, 17 per cent in 1973, and 10 per cent in 1983 (Kannan and Pushpangadan 1988: A125–6; Chattopadhyay 1985). Loss of forest cover has resulted in soil erosion in the highlands and waterlogging of lowland areas. Additional environmental problems include water and air pollution, and possible overfishing of some offshore regions (Kurien 1991). Repairing environmental damage is among the costliest of human endeavours, adding difficulty to a stagnant economy with little surplus to invest in renewal. Kerala's ecological problems are exacerbated by the state's high population density and its intense land use, which make it difficult to set aside protected areas. Poverty drives settlers onto hillsides too steep for sustainable cultivation and forces people to cut the dangerously depleted forests for firewood to sell.

Sustainability in the Present World Situation

At the beginning of this chapter, we asked what forces threaten the sustainability of the Kerala model. Clearly, the several components of the crisis of the Kerala model described above threaten the model. So do outside forces. Sustaining the Kerala model requires surmounting several important national and international obstacles.

The New World Order and structural adjustment

One of the strengths of the Kerala model has been the (limited) power of the state government to meet some of the demands of the poorest groups. The collapse of the Soviet Union led to the emergence of a one-power world in the early 1990s. The New World Order means: (1) the protectionist policies that helped today's capitalist economies once develop will be denied to today's underdeveloped nations; (2) public expenditures are considered inefficient and inflationary – pressure is being exerted to reduce them; and (3) inequality is accepted as a natural result of market forces and seen as beneficial to development. Advocates of the one-power New World Order seem to have accepted Simon Kuznets's 1955 paper on the need for an entrepreneurial phase of development in which inequality increases in order to raise production, followed by a period of increased output, leading to eventual better lives for all with reduced inequality. Kuznets's scenario takes about one hundred years to unfold.[14]

Structural adjustment is new to India, but its effects have been experienced in other parts of the world. Much of Africa and Latin America have been in structural adjustment programmes since the 1980s. Between 1984 and 1990, average per-capita incomes in Latin America dropped by 9.1 per cent; in Africa they decreased by 12.5 per cent (Pinstrup-Anderson 1993: 87). Official poverty levels in Latin America rose from 25 per cent in 1980 to 31 per cent by the end of the decade (Pinstrup-Anderson 1993: 88). In Costa Rica between 1971 and 1983, the poorest 10 per cent of the population lost 20 per cent while the richest 10 per cent gained 15 per cent relative to prices (Pinstrup-Anderson 1993: 88–9). In Chile, in the decade between 1980 and 1990 the poorest half of the population saw its share of the national income drop from 20.4 per cent to 16.8 per cent. At the same time the richest 10 per cent experienced an increase in their share from 36.5 per cent to 46.8 per cent (Bello 1994: 45). In Ghana, a long-term trend of falling infant mortality rates was reversed by a 20 per cent increase from the mid-1970s to mid-1980s (Pinstrup-Anderson 1993: 105); in Abidjan, Ivory Coast, neonatal mortality rates went from 37 per 1,000 in 1977–81 to 81 per 1,000 in 1982–86 (Pinstrup-Anderson 1993: 106). In Brazil, 60,000 'extra' child deaths are attributed to the 1980s' recessions. Brazil had previously been labelled an economic miracle. The Third World generally absorbed more than 500,000 excess deaths in 1988 than might have been expected. War-related deaths are not included in these estimates (*New York Times*, 20 December 1988: 1; Grant 1989: 1). Despite a long-term trend of declining child deaths, 13 million children died in 1993, 98 per cent of them in the Third World. At least 8 million of them could have been saved by oral rehydration therapy, vaccinations and public-health actions to prevent diseases such as malaria, meningitis, respiratory ailments, and certain kinds of diarrhoea (Kane 1993: 96). To the best of our knowledge, no study has yet shown that structural adjustment or any other programme of the New World Order has benefited the poorest groups. Nor has any study shown that the policies of the New World Order fit logically, theoretically or empirically with the concept of sustainability.[15]

In the context of such statistics and trends the Kerala model is still valid and relevant as an alternative to growth-only development strategies. As the brutality of the New World Order imposes itself on societies unprepared or unable to defend their most vulnerable groups, Kerala, for all its shortcomings, might become even more of a model.

The survival of the Kerala model is in question, too, however. Structural adjustment threatens to undermine past achievements, replacing them with policies favouring affluent consumers and freewheeling investors. Fewer restrictions on investment may lead to more investment going out of the state – the precise opposite of what people from all political persuasions seem to think is necessary. Abolition of subsidy protections to domestic agriculture could undermine Kerala's spice, cashew and other cash-crop exchange earnings, thereby worsening the subsistence base that depends on such earnings. Small firms might lose government protections – a potentially catastrophic blow to an economy with high unemployment in which hundreds of thousands who are employed work in cottage industries. A market takeover of health, education and social welfare could price out the poor. M.A. Oommen (1994: 15) has characterized these trends as 'euthanasia' for the Kerala model.[16]

The international environmental crisis and the problem of sustainability

Structural adjustment and New World Order domination are not the only perils to the sustainability of the Kerala model. International environmental developments also pose serious hazards. The twentieth century has generated so much output that 'evidence of mounting stresses can be seen on every hand as more and more sustainable yield thresholds are crossed and as waste absorptive capacities are overwhelmed' (Brown 1998: 4). At current levels of abuse, any area can be affected by another area's practices. Freshwater tables are dropping all over the world. The demand for grains in many areas is outstripping supplies. In 1996, international grain stocks declined to their lowest recorded levels. Even with exceptionally good harvests in 1996, there were only 55 days of reserves, 15 days fewer than are required as protection against a bad harvest (Brown 1998: 15–16.) Nearly every one of the world's fisheries is in decline (Brown 1998: 5–9) and one-third of all fish species are at risk of extinction (Brown 1998: 11). Atmospheric warming from massive developed-country carbon emissions – with the USA by far the worst offender – has probably brought on local weather changes all over the world.[17] High winds, floods and droughts threaten food production in many areas.

Kerala could be influenced by international grain decline, fish-catch losses and climate irregularities. With no direct bargaining power in international forums, and dependent on India's limited influence, Kerala has few options for sustaining its model.

So Is the Kerala Model Sustainable?

Kerala's internal problems combine with several international threats that we have described. What are Kerala's strengths in the current situation?

The old Kerala model still matters

The old Kerala model fostered a literate, healthy, motivated population with a sense of purpose, involvement, commitment to ideals, and a generally optimistic future orientation. These achievements – along with the expectation of high material quality-of-life indicators and willingness to organize and carry out mass actions – give Kerala significant resources with which to build a new model appropriate to today's circumstances. How can such resources be effectively mobilized?

Let us return briefly to Nadur Village. In 1971 Joan Mencher found that only 25 per cent of sample respondents believed that the village 'had made progress'. Following the radical reforms, we found in 1987 that 59 per cent believed their lives were better than their parents', and 71 per cent thought life for their children would be even better (Franke 1996: 273). Several respondents volunteered observations about the importance of community actions in making life better. Eight years later, Thomas Isaac and Tharakan (1995: 1997) observed in their report on the First International Congress on Kerala Studies that 'It is the consciousness and struggles of the masses and not the manipulations of the politicians that will ultimately determine' if the Kerala model survives and is renewed.

Redistribution still matters too. A study by Cereseto and Waitzkin (1988) found that for any given level of average per-capita income, countries with more equality provided better education, longer life and lower infant mortality. In other words, the Kerala model holds cross-culturally. But does redistribution work at cross-purposes to production? Economists Bowles, Gordon and Weisskopf (1990: 223) found that among advanced industrial countries, both productivity growth and investment performance are strongly and *positively* correlated with equality. The *New York Times* (8 January 1994: A39) reported that 'many economists … [have] begun to see greater income equality as compatible with faster growth – and perhaps even contributing to it.' The US magazine *Business Week* led its issue of 15 August 1994 with a story entitled 'Inequality: How the Growing Gap between Rich and Poor in America is Hurting the Economy'. Among the studies cited in the article was one showing that in twenty-six US cities, those with the least inequality between suburban and inner-city incomes had job creation significantly greater than those with greater inequality. Another study cited was a summary of fifty-four other studies from which the author, Harvard economist Richard B.

Freeman, argued that market strategies and privatization tend to raise inequality while government programmes are essential to reducing it.

The exact mechanisms leading to the correlation between equality, productivity, investment performance and job creation are not spelled out in these reports, but surely they deserve closer attention. Taken together, they imply that Kerala's strategy of redistribution is not the likely cause of the state's high unemployment and sluggish economic growth. The gains made in Nadur – that we cited earlier – are not an outmoded left-wing chimera but rather a reasonable basis from which to launch new initiatives for sustainable development.

What initiatives would these be? In their review of the First International Congress on Kerala Studies, Thomas Isaac and Tharakan (1995: 1997) pointed out that 'the Left needs to draw up a new agenda that is more responsive to the changed reality of contemporary Kerala'. At the same Congress, veteran CPM leader, the late E.M.S. Namboodiripad, pointed out the need to 'accelerate economic growth without sacrificing the welfare gains and the democratic achievements of the past' (Thomas Isaac and Tharakan 1995: 1997).

A new Kerala model?

The left's 'new agenda' is the People's Campaign for the Ninth Plan. This was drawn up on the basis of discussions at the First International Congress on Kerala Studies and at several follow-up conferences in 1995 and 1996.[18] It is also based in part on the New Democratic Initiatives of the 1987–91 Left Democratic Front (LDF) Ministry. These included elected district councils (which were brought back to life for the new campaign), the Total Literacy Programme, some unrestricted funds to local panchayats, and the People's Resource-mapping Programme.[19] Each of these programmes had met with modest success in 1987–91. The Congress-led United Democratic Front (UDF) victory in the 1991 elections brought the programmes to a near halt (except for the panchayat unrestricted funds), but forces had been set in motion that could be reactivated after the LDF election success of April 1996. The New Democratic Initiatives had mobilized many activists and had given them experience, and LDF leaders and middle-level cadre may have learned lessons about the potential for grassroots development action aimed more at community integration and increasing production than at class struggle to spread existing wealth.

The People's Campaign: an overview of the first two years

Immediately after assuming power in May 1996, the new LDF ministry made a decision to allocate 35–40 per cent of the state plan for projects to be designed and implemented by elected local governments – village panchayats, municipalities, and the block and district panchayats.[20] The emphasis was on the village panchayats and urban neighbourhoods. India's nationwide ninth five-year plan was about to be formulated; in 1992 the national constitution's 73rd and 74th amendments had been adopted, requiring states to delegate twenty-nine general administrative functions to lower-level bodies. For the newly elected LDF ministry, it was an ideal conjunction for an experiment in democratic planning. But how does a government delegate administrative functions to lower levels? LDF activists decided that a mass mobilization would be needed. The constitutional administrative reforms became a people's campaign, drawing on the strength of Kerala's history of mobilization; its literate, activist population; and the political will of the LDF leadership to make things happen. The campaign was based on five main ideas:

1. Local people often understand better than outside bureaucrats or experts what their communities need. With assistance from bureaucrats and experts working directly with them rather than in power over them, ordinary people can make more efficient use of resources and can choose more appropriate priorities.
2. The use of a mass campaign mode would draw in people who might not come forward in a bureaucratically structured reform. The experiences of the Total Literacy Campaign, the People's Resource-mapping Programme, and many KSSP projects were applied to the new campaign.
3. A mass campaign mode would make it easier to ensure transparency and accountability, reducing corruption and hopefully reducing the cynicism of people towards government.
4. A mass campaign mode held out the best hope for bringing about changes in attitudes, creating a greater sense of community, a greater sense of optimism, and a lessening of party political identification in development activities – necessary elements of what activists called the 'new development culture'.[21]
5. Local planning and local participation offer the greatest hope for attention to the environmental aspects of development – sustainability of the resource base.

LDF activists moved quickly. They set up a High Level Guidance Council under the chairpersonship of E.M.S. Namboodiripad, Kerala's veteran communist leader who enjoyed wide respect from all sections of the public. The Council was intended to create the highest possible degree of consensus for the campaign: it included all living former chief ministers from all parties, vice chancellors of the universities, cultural leaders, and leaders of mass organizations.

The People's Campaign was set in motion on 17 August 1996, New Year's Day that year in the Malayalam calendar. The High Level Guidance Council presided over a two-hour ceremony in the Senate Hall of Kerala University in Thiruvananthapuram, which was broadcast live on state television. Simultaneously, inaugural ceremonies took place in every panchayat and urban municipality. Hundreds of thousands of people participated or watched. Immediately after the ceremony, the High Level Guidance Council remained in the Senate Hall to hold its first formal meeting: the People's Campaign was under way.

Phase 1: The grama sabhas or ward assemblies   On 15 September 1996 the first grama sabha was held at Nandiyode Panchayat, a politically active panchayat governed by the Opposition in Thiruvananthapuram district. During the next three months, 14,147 wards in Kerala's 990 panchayats held these assemblies. An average of 180 people attended each assembly, about 10 per cent of the population. Written invitations were delivered to each household requesting their participation. Street theatre and coconut-oil lamp processions created a festive atmosphere: democracy was to be enjoyable as well as necessary. Across Kerala, a thousand artists performed several thousand *janathikhara kalajathas*, 'power-to-the-people processions'.

The grama sabhas typically began at noon. After short introductory speeches, people broke into twelve topic groups where trained facilitators encouraged them to speak up about the problems in their ward: what organizers call getting at the 'felt needs of the people'. The topics were: (1) agriculture and irrigation; (2) fisheries and animal husbandry; (3) education; (4) transport, energy and markets; (5) industry; (6) housing and social welfare; (7) public health and drinking water; (8) culture; (9) women's welfare; (10) cooperatives; (11) welfare of scheduled castes and scheduled tribes; and (12) resource mobilization.

Phase 2: Development reports and development seminars   Topic group participants elected representatives to gather local data and prepare a local development report. In the period December 1996–February 1997 the topic groups discussed the development reports at village-wide development seminars and made lists of projects in response to the needs expressed in the grama sabhas. The development reports are among the greatest achievements of the ninth plan campaign. Each of Kerala's 990 panchayats and 63 municipalities produced a report, running to between seventy-five and one hundred pages. Much of the information for the reports was gathered by activists from local government offices. Never before had such a systematic compilation of data from different sources been undertaken. The reports offer overviews of their respective panchayats/urban areas, give brief histories gathered from elderly residents, and provide detailed information on each of the twelve topic areas discussed at the grama sabhas. Many include the results of a 'transect walk', in which a local committee chose a pathway through the community with the greatest geographical diversity, cross-cutting it and making a simple map to indicate the major ecological zones. It is hoped these maps will become a basis for careful attention to environmental issues in future years of the planning process; full-scale resource mapping is also planned.

Phase 3: The task forces The development seminars elected task forces to draft project proposals. These proposals were to include appropriate technical, cost–benefit, and time-frame considerations along with an assessment of the resources of the community to carry out each project. An estimated 120,000 persons drafted 100,000 project proposals by March 1997.

Phase 4: Finalization of the annual plan In March of 1997, the state budget was approved with 36 per cent, or Rs. 1,025 crores (one crore = 10 million Rs.) earmarked for local projects. At this point, power shifted from the assemblies and the task forces to the elected panchayat officials, who became responsible for approving overall local plans and for prioritizing projects. Each panchayat submitted a formal written plan up to the next level, the block (a group of two to thirteen villages), and from there to the district. Each plan included a brief description of the local development challenges, a statement of the local development strategy, estimates of the additional local resources that could be mobilized – volunteer labour and material contributions – a list of projects drafted by the task forces, a discussion of the possibilities of integration among the projects, a statement about the special programmes for scheduled castes and scheduled tribes, a statement about the gender impact of projects with a list of special projects for women that were supposed to employ at least 10 per cent of the total funds, and a plan for monitoring the implementation to avoid corruption and ensure effective use of funds towards the intended ends.

Phase 5: Annual plans for the block and district levels From April to September 1997, block- and district-level panchayats prepared plans based on the village plans submitted to them. A novel innovation was the idea of evaluating the development problems in each locality according to a four-point severity scale – using information from the lower-level plans – and making a similar matrix of ratings for the relative importance of the different types of project for each lower-level panchayat. The block and district panchayat plans were supposed to identify weaknesses in the lower-level plans and fill in the gaps that seemed to require higher-level action. Due to delays in the first round of local panchayat plan preparation, this phase did not work very well; nonetheless the concept holds promise for future years.

Phase 6: Plan appraisal: the Voluntary Technical Corps In their first year local communities experienced many problems in drawing up project descriptions and keeping track of technical issues. Planning Board activists attempted to overcome these problems by issuing a call for a 'Voluntary Technical Corps' (VTC), of retired technical experts living in Kerala's villages. The campaign took up the slogan 'Life Begins at 55', referring to Kerala's retirement age and the excitement and rewards of making life better in one's own community. More than four thousand experts answered the call, committing themselves to at least one day a week giving advice to the task forces and helping to evaluate local projects and plans. Expert committees were formed at the block and district levels, drawing on VTC members and government officers. These committees were expressly forbidden to alter the priorities set by the local bodies, but they were allowed to make suggestions on how to make individual projects more feasible.

Training for empowerment

In its first year the people's campaign trained hundreds of thousands of persons in seven rounds of training. In the initial three stages, training was provided to 660 at the state level, 11,808 at the district level, and 100,000 in the villages and municipalities. Training included sessions on what the campaign was about, how to lead an effective discussion, how existing government regulations would affect local planning, and how to draft project proposals. Each training session included a handbook, and an appeal for continuing self-study after the session. Lectures were supplemented by group discussions and, in some stages, 'project clinics'.

We witnessed the three-day training of local volunteers for the fourth stage of the campaign that took place in Calicut on 10–12 January 1997. The 4,500 volunteers came from all over northern Kerala. They received meals, lodging and transportation, but no other payment. They attended lectures, workshops and project clinics from 10 a.m. to midnight in several buildings of the Zamorin High School, which was borrowed for the weekend.

At the project clinics, panchayats with interesting or advanced projects presented seminars giving detailed descriptions of their work. The emphasis was on how to do it. Topics included: 'The Chapparapadava People's Bridge', 'The Thanalur People's Health Programme', 'Kunnothuparambu's Water Conservation Societies', 'Peelicode's Total Sanitation Programme', and Kalliasseri's experience in overall planning.

What has been accomplished?

The people's campaign has experienced numerous difficulties, delays and disappointments. Despite large-scale participation, the majority of Kerala's people did not attend any of the meetings or discussions. Despite tremendous energy and sacrifice by dedicated persons at all levels, the entire process was significantly delayed: a campaign originally conceptualized for one year has run into its third year. Corruption, incompetence and political haggling marred the campaign in some places. Women, scheduled castes and scheduled tribes participated at much lower levels than had been hoped. Opposition representatives and even some supporters of the LDF worked openly or surreptitiously against the campaign for their own political purposes.

But the campaign's achievements were also substantial. The initial 14,147 grama sabhas took place without any violent incidents. Plans *did* emerge from the local level and the planning process showed signs of taking off: plans that took more than a year in the first phase were completed in four months in the second year. People were learning by doing. Local communities supplemented government allocations with voluntary labour and donations that raised the value of the projects by 10 per cent. Mechanisms were put in place to reduce corruption and increase the level of public monitoring and government accountability at several levels. More funds than ever were made more directly available to scheduled caste and scheduled tribal communities – for more transparent projects than previously.

Most importantly, people are experiencing a new sense of optimism about their communities. And government bureaucrats are seeing the value of coming out from their offices to work more directly with the people.

Is the Kerala Model Sustainable?

It is too soon to say whether the people's campaign can sustain the Kerala model. But we think it offers the best hope for the future. By arranging government from the bottom up and by inspiring ordinary people to contribute more fully to developing their communities, the People's Campaign for the Ninth Plan constitutes a giant experimental alternative to the multinational corporate domination of the New World Order. It offers democracy in place of domination, empowerment in place of submission, environment and community in place of profit, and action in place of passivity. Having learned their lessons from the past, Kerala's people are creating prospects for a sustainable future.

Notes

This is a revised and updated version of a paper with the same title presented at the International Conference on Kerala's Development Experiences: National and Global Dimensions in New Delhi, on 9 December 1996, sponsored by the Institute of Social Sciences. We gratefully acknowledge support from the Montclair State University Global Education Center and the Geraldine R. Dodge Foundation of New Jersey.

1. A subject search of the Harvard University Library Union catalogue brought up 180 books with (nonmilitary) 'sustainability' as one of the key words. Most were published since 1993.

2. These are adapted from Franke and Chasin (1983: 11). Daly (1996a: 195) gives a more detailed and technical definition: 'An economy in sustainable development adapts and improves in knowledge, organization, technical efficiency, and wisdom; it does this without assimilating or accreting an ever greater percentage of the matter-energy of the ecosystem into itself but rather stops at a scale at which the remaining ecosystem can continue to function and renew itself year after year. The nongrowing economy is not static – it is being continually maintained and renewed as a steady-state subsystem of the environment.' Daly goes on to specify how particular elements of the economy should operate, but does not directly take up the questions of distribution of wealth, political rights, and material levels of living.

3. Based partly on George's criticisms, Tharamangalam (1998a) has launched a full-scale attack on the Kerala model. Our reply to his attack appears in Franke and Chasin (1998) along with other responses, both critical and supportive. A further set of responses appeared in *Bulletin of Concerned Asian Scholars* 30(4), 1998.

4. The figure of 65 comes from the 1998–99 World Bank report. Other sources give higher IMR rates for India as a whole. It should also be kept in mind that a small portion of the all-India figure is influenced by the Kerala figure that makes up a part of it.

5. For simplicity, we are grouping together fifty-nine municipalities, three municipal corporations (Thiruvananthapuram, Ernakulam and Kozhikode) and one township (Guruvayur).

6. See Franke and Chasin (1994: vi–vii) for a discussion of the problems of interpreting the apparently high morbidity rate in Kerala. Kerala's suicide rate in 1994 was the highest in India at 28 per 100,000. The all-India rate was 10; Karnataka was second to Kerala with 19 (Halliburton 1998: 2341). Police surveys indicate that the reasons for suicide in Kerala are the same as for the rest of India (Halliburton 1998). We do not wish to downplay this important failure of Kerala society, but one should keep in mind that the suicide rates are per *hundred* thousand, while the infant mortality and birth rates are per *one* thousand.

7. See Franke (1996: 121–92; 1992) for details of the land reform analysis that follows. See Chasin (1990) for an interpretation of the land reform's effects on gender inequality.

8. Thomas Isaac and Tharakan (1995: 1996) see this conflict as a possible reason for the heavy election losses of the LDF in 1978 in Palakkad and Alappuzha, two of its traditional strongholds. Herring (1989 and 1991) surveys many aspects of the conflict with reference to Palakkad.

9. Jeffrey (1992) appears to agree with this point, though his explanation for how the movements grew differs somewhat from ours. Casinader (1995) offers a view similar to ours in the context of a comparison between Kerala and Sri Lanka. Herring (1983) argues that mass movements and their level of militancy were the keys to the enactment of the Kerala land reform.

10. Our note to Table 2.1 explains that we took the exceptionally high figure of 40 per cent to make sure we did not exaggerate the difference between Kerala's quality-of-life achievements and its per-capita income. Some observers in Kerala have suggested the 40 per cent figure on the assumption that government data would surely underestimate the effects of the remittances, some of which might not be traceable.

11. The location of beedi production in northern Malabar is otherwise difficult to account for since none of the raw materials is available there.

12. Jeffrey (1992) has suggested that the decline of the *marumakkathayam* system and the breakup of the Nair *taravad* may also have played a role. His point is well argued, but we think larger forces also had to be at work. Nairs make up only about 14 per cent of Kerala's population, and, while many Ezhava households also practice *marumakkathayam*, this hardly seems enough to produce such widespread mobilization as occurred in twentieth-century Kerala.

13. Pillai (1996: 2099) reports that about 4,600 head-load workers are covered by a Kerala-model scheme to regularize their work relations and create a modern benefits structure. These workers represent about 2 per cent of the total estimated head-load and casual labourers in the state.

14. Franke (1996: 9–10) summarizes the Kuznets approach in terms of the international development literature.

15. Mander and Goldsmith (1996) provide a full-scale critique of the New World Order.

16. The other elements mentioned in this paragraph are also taken from Oommen's paper.

17. US emissions in 1997 were 23 per cent of the world total, ahead of second-place China, which accounted for 14 per cent. The average US citizen accounts for twenty-one times as much carbon as the typical Indian (Dunn 1998: 66).

18. Our paper on female-supported households was prepared for the follow-up conference on women's roles and empowerment.

19. Brief overviews of the People's Resource-mapping Programme are available in Franke and Chasin (1994: xvii–xviii) and Thomas Isaac, Franke and Parameswaran (1997: 42–4).

20. Village panchayats in Kerala average about 25,000 in population. Two to thirteen villages are grouped into development 'blocks', which also have elected councils or panchayats. The blocks are combined into the districts, which now have district councils.

21. For more details of the concept of a new development culture, see Thomas Isaac, Franke and Raghavan (1998: 71, 213).

3

Poverty Alleviation as Advancing
Basic Human Capabilities:
Kerala's Achievements Compared

K.P. Kannan

It is now widely recognized that poverty alleviation is not just a matter of having adequate consumption of food or other necessities of daily life, but should also include other dimensions such as education and health. The former is usually referred to as the 'entitlement' aspect of poverty and the latter as the 'capability' aspect. It is only when these two aspects are combined that one can move towards a more holistic definition of poverty. It is in this sense that the current literature talks about human development, which is the sense understood in this chapter. Even though the term 'human resource development' is widely used, we prefer to employ the term 'human development'. The former takes into account only the instrumental value of human development, viewed as a resource for furthering the economic welfare of either individuals or collectives or both. The latter has a more fundamental connotation as it takes into account human development for its instrumental and intrinsic values. In the latter sense, the human condition of being educated and in good health is valued in itself.

The objective of this chapter is to highlight Kerala's success in alleviating poverty, as defined above, to an extent that is considerably beyond what is warranted by its per-capita income. For this reason, the experience of Kerala, along with a few other countries, has now received considerable attention in the development literature. Here we intend to highlight Kerala's achievements by comparing them with the performance of six Asian countries. Although the achievements in poverty alleviation will be highlighted, the focus of the discussion will be on education. This is not only to examine the role of education in human development but also to assess the crucial part education has played in alleviating poverty in Kerala. The first section examines the significance of Kerala's achievements. The second section discusses Kerala's record in relation to six selected Asian countries. The third section briefly deals with Kerala's achievements in relation to all-India since the Indian experience in general is one of slow progress and the task ahead is quite considerable both in absolute terms and relative to most other countries. The fourth section discusses the social process by which Kerala has achieved the considerable reduction in poverty. Here we identify education as the central process through which other changes in society, especially for the poor, were brought about. In this process, the importance of historical factors in poverty alleviation has been investigated. The fifth section briefly deals with the impact of the historical process in which education played a crucial role. The final section is an attempt to draw some lessons from the Kerala experience by focusing on the role of public action.

The Significance of the Achievements

Kerala's achievements are considerable. From an international development perspective, they are, despite the state's low per-capita income, comparable to or even better than such countries as Sri Lanka, China, Costa Rica, and Cuba (Drèze and Sen 1989; Ghai 1997). But in our view the significance of Kerala goes beyond the 'low per-capita income and high human development' thesis. This is because the Kerala experience has also demonstrated that poverty alleviation can be achieved along with a reduction in spatial and gender gaps, the two important gaps that are quite prominent in the development experience. The former refers to the gap between rural and urban areas; the latter refers to the gap between men and women. As we shall see in this chapter, the Kerala experience shows that while the rural–urban gap is quite narrow, there are a number of indicators wherein women perform as well as men, or even better.

There is, however, another kind of significance. Most of the countries that are selected here for comparison, in spite of their high achievement in human development and in lowering human deprivation, cannot claim the kind of freedom of political choice for their people that is present in Kerala and in India at large. In the Indian case, this freedom of political choice in terms of a pluralistic democratic polity has been criticized for its lack of political will to alleviate poverty. What the Kerala record shows is the feasibility of poverty alleviation without denying the freedom of political choice to the people. In East and Southeast Asia, poverty alleviation took place with the active intervention of a strong state, the price

Table 3.1 Selected profile on population and economy, 1994

Country/state	Area (1,000 km²)	Population (million)	Density /km²	Urban pop. (%)	GDP per capita		Economic/employment structure					
					PPP$	1994$	Income			Labour force		
							Agri.	Ind.	Serv.	Agri.	Ind.	Serv.
1	2	3	4	5	6	7	8	9	10	11	12	13
Kerala	38.8	30.5	786	26	1618	380*	33	27	40	47	18	35
India	3287.6	918.6	279	27	1348	317	31	28	41	64	16	20
Sri Lanka	65.6	18.1	276	22	3277	646	26	26	49	48	21	31
Thailand	513.1	58.2	113	20	7104	2461	12	38	50	64	14	22
Malaysia	329.8	19.7	60	53	8865	3586	19	40	41	27	23	50
Indonesia	1904.6	194.6	102	34	3740	897	20	40	40	55	14	31
China	9561.0	1208.8	126	29	2604	420	22	44	34	72	15	13

Note: Agri., Ind. and Serv. stand for Agriculture, Industry and Service sectors.

* $380 is actually the GNP figure because it includes remittances from abroad. I have taken the estimate of Krishnan (1994) of around 26 per cent of the state domestic product as the share of remittances for 1986–87.

Source: UNDP (1997); for Kerala, GOK, *Economic Review* (1994); Column 8 to 13 for the Asian countries, UNCTAD (1997).

Table 3.2 Kerala's position in relation to selected Asian countries, 1994 (Kerala = 100)

Country/ state	Area (1,000 km²)	Population (million)	Density /km²	Urban pop. (%)	GDP per capita		Economic/employment structure					
							Income			Labour force		
					PPP$	1994$	Agri.	Ind.	Serv.	Agri.	Ind.	Serv.
1	2	3	4	5	6	7	8	9	10	11	12	13
Kerala	100	100	100	100	100	100	100	100	100	100	100	100
India	8473	3012	35	104	83	83	94	104	103	136	89	57
Sri Lanka	169	60	35	85	201	170	79	96	123	102	117	89
Thailand	1322	191	14	78	439	648	36	141	125	136	78	63
Malaysia	850	65	8	204	548	944	58	148	103	57	128	143
Indonesia	4909	639	13	131	231	236	61	148	100	117	78	89
China	24642	3963	16	112	161	111	67	163	85	153	83	37

Source: Based on Table 3.1.

of which was limited freedom of political choice for the people.[1] The Kerala experience is, therefore, significant in the sense that there are only a very few examples in the contemporary developing world where poverty alleviation has taken place within a framework of unrestricted political freedom of choice and low per-capita income. But for the suspension of civil rights and the disintegration of its democratic polity for prolonged periods arising out of its internal ethnic conflict, Sri Lanka would be the next best example in this regard.

Although Kerala is only a sub-national entity, its experience is taken out of the national context to demonstrate what can be achieved, notwithstanding the limitations of such an abstraction. At the same time, taking it out of the national context is not insignificant analytically or quantitatively. First, issues that fall under poverty alleviation in the Indian federal system are the responsibility of state governments. Second, the size of Kerala in terms of population (around 30 million in 1991) is much larger than that of many developing countries. The significance of Kerala's development experience is brought out here in terms of a comparison with selected Asian countries. Apart from India, which provides the national context for Kerala, the selection is guided by the fact that the countries are all high achievers in human development and in reducing human deprivation compared to their per-capita income levels. These countries (India and Sri Lanka are in South Asia; Thailand, Malaysia and Indonesia are in Southeast Asia; and China is in East Asia) also represent the most populous regions of Asia, or, for that matter, the world.

Tables 3.1 and 3.2 present some basic demographic and economic indicators of Kerala along with the selected Asian countries ('Asian Six', hereafter). We immediately observe that Kerala is bigger than two of the countries, Sri Lanka and Malaysia, in terms of population size. But population alone is not an adequate indicator to measure the carrying capacity of a country in terms of resources, such as land. If this is taken into account, we find that the population density of Kerala is the highest among all the countries listed, which suggests a higher inherent burden even if one were to make allowances for the quality of land and so on. It may not be an exaggeration to state that Kerala is one of the most densely populated regions in the world.[2]

When it pertains to per-capita income, whether measured in terms of purchasing power parity (PPP) or official exchange rate in US dollars, Kerala is the lowest along with India. In official Indian statistics, the per-capita income of Kerala is shown to be even lower than that of India. This is because such state income calculations within India do not capture the flow of remittances. Since the flow of international remittances to Kerala is quite significant, we have made some adjustment to this factor.

Even then, Kerala and India are the lowest in terms of per-capita income. In terms of income generation, it is evident from Tables 3.1 and 3.2 that Kerala has a relatively higher proportion of income generated in agriculture compared to all the other countries while its share of income originating from industry is the second lowest, above only Sri Lanka. As we pointed out earlier, this is because of the low level of modern industries and the dominance of low value-adding and labour-intensive agroprocessing activities in the industrial sector. Concomitantly, the sectoral distribution of the labour force in Kerala is more balanced than in the other countries except in Malaysia. Along with Malaysia and Sri Lanka, Kerala's labour force during the 1990s was more non-agricultural than agricultural. This is not the case with all-India, China, Thailand and Indonesia.

The Record

In terms of the record of poverty alleviation, let us first take the composite index of poverty, the Human Poverty Index (HPI) as measured by the UNDP in its Human Development Report 1997 (UNDP 1997). This index takes into account (i) the survival deprivation in terms of people not expected to survive to age 40; (ii) deprivation of education and knowledge indicated by adult illiteracy rate; and (iii) a composite index of deprivation in economic provisioning indicated by (a) population without access to safe water, (b) population without access to health services, and (c) underweight children under the age of 5. The value of HPI for Kerala is only 0.15; that is, only 15 per cent of the population is deemed poor by the HPI measure. As we can see in Table 3.3, only one country has a lower value than Kerala – namely, Thailand. All other countries have values higher than Kerala's. (The value for Malaysia has not been reported.) In terms of the seventy-six countries for which the values of HPI have been worked out and published in the Human Development Report of 1997, Kerala would rank 12th followed by China (18th), Sri lanka (22nd), Indonesia (23rd) and India (47th).

Now, if we turn to the Human Development Index (HDI), given in Table 3.3, which is an indicator of 'achievement' of a country, Kerala's value of 0.628 is considerably higher than India's (0.451) but lower than that for other countries.[3] It is closer to that of China's 0.650. The low level of per-capita income is partly reflected in the income measure of poverty for Kerala. Even in the 1990s, the proportion of people below the nationally determined poverty line was around 25 per cent in Kerala as against 22 per cent in Sri Lanka and considerably lower in all the other countries. The all-India estimate is the highest. What this suggests is that Kerala's achievement measured in terms of human capabilities is far higher

Table 3.3 Human development and deprivation: indices and indicators

Country/ state	HDI value 1995	HPI value (%) 1996	GDI value 1995	Population below poverty (%) 1989–94	
				poverty 1985 (PPP$/day)	national poverty line
Kerala	0.628	15.0	n/a	n/a	25.4
India	0.451	36.7	0.424	52.0	36.0
Sri Lanka	0.716	20.7	0.700	4.0	22.0
Thailand	0.838	11.7	0.812	0.1	13.0
Malaysia	0.834	n/a	0.785	5.6	16.0
Indonesia	0.679	20.8	0.651	14.5	8.0
China	0.650	17.5	0.641	29.4	11.0

	Adult literacy rate 1994 (%)			Gross enrolment ratio 1995			
				Primary		Secondary	
	total	male	female	total	f/m (%)	total	f/m (%)
Kerala	89.8	93.6	86.3	102	96	103	102
India	51.2	64.0	39.0	100	82	49	64
Sri Lanka	90.1	93.2	86.9	113	98	75	110
Thailand	93.5	95.6	90.7	87	n/a	55	n/a
Malaysia	83.0	88.2	77.5	91	101	57	107
Indonesia	83.2	89.4	77.1	114	96	48	85
China	80.9	89.6	70.9	118	98	67	89

Note: GDI = Gender Development Index; HDI = Human Development Index; HPI = Human Poverty Index. Adult literacy rates for Kerala refer to 1991.
Source: UNDP (1997); HDI for Kerala from Srinivasan and Shariff (1997). Education data for Kerala from GOK (1998a).

than its achievement in reducing income-poverty. Thus the adult literacy rate in Kerala is one of the highest and on a par with Sri Lanka and Thailand. Although all the other countries except all-India are high achievers, the gap between male and female literacy is small, as in Sri Lanka and Thailand. Relatively higher gaps are reported for other countries, the highest being for all-India followed by China.

Table 3.4   Indicators of Human Deprivation Index

Country/ state	Survival deprivation (% not reaching age 40)[a]	Deprivation of education/ knowledge (% adult illiteracy)[b]	Deprivation in economic provisioning		
			% without access to safe water[c]	% without access to health services[d]	% under-weight children below 5[c]
Kerala	6.0[e]	8.0	19	n/a	29
India	19.4	48.8	19	15	53
Sri Lanka	7.9	9.9	38	7	38
Thailand	8.9	6.5	11	10	26
Malaysia	n/a	n/a	n/a	n/a	n/a
Indonesia	14.8	16.8	15	7	35
China	9.1	19.1	33	12	16

Notes
[a] 1990.   [b] 1994.   [c] 1990–96.   [d] 1990–95.
[e] Computed from the West Model Life tables based on life expectancy at birth. I am grateful to my colleague K. Navaneetham for this computation.
Sources: UNDP (1997); CMIE (1996); Srinivasan and Shariff (1997).

The record of school enrolment in Kerala is quite impressive (see Table 3.3). Almost all the children in the relevant age group attend school. Enrolment at the secondary level seems to be the highest for Kerala among all the Asian Six, with the number of girls marginally exceeding boys. That only two other countries, Malaysia and Sri Lanka, show a higher percentage of girls than boys at the secondary level is interesting although the total enrolment is less than 100 per cent. In the Kerala context, the convergence of social changes with physical access perhaps explains the high enrolment ratio for the entire school-age population. The ten-year period of school education roughly corresponds with the age group 5 to 15 years. The demand for school education for boys and girls has been adequately met by physical access. By the 1990s, 94.4 per cent of the rural population was served by primary schools within a distance of one kilometre, 97.96 per cent within a distance of two kilometres, and 96.2 per cent for upper primary schools within a distance of three kilometres (GOK 1998a: 96).

One may decompose the HPI, as we do here in Table 3.4, in order to find out the record of human deprivation in some detail. Kerala's value for the percentage of 'people not surviving to age 40' has been found to be sixth, placing it at the top among the Asian Six (data for Malaysia were not available). Similarly, the latest figures for adult illiteracy indicate that it is the second lowest in the group, after Thailand. In terms of population without access to safe water, it is somewhere between the high achievers such as Thailand and Indonesia and the relatively low ones such as Sri Lanka and China. It is interesting to note that the all-India figure is the same as that of Kerala in this respect. We have every reason to believe that the percentage of population without access to health services is perhaps one of the lowest for Kerala, as both rural and urban areas are covered by at least primary health care services. In terms of the number of health-care institutions, rural areas reported a higher share as early as 1987 (Kannan et al. 1991), although this does not mean that the number of medical professionals employed are loaded in favour of rural areas. On the contrary, it is due to the concentration of secondary and tertiary care institutions in urban areas.

Further insights into the achievements in poverty alleviation can be gained by examining the demographic situation, which has a significant bearing on the health status of the population in general and women in particular. Some selected, but basic, indicators are reported in Table 3.5. It is here that one can appreciate the tremendous achievements of Kerala when viewed in the context of its very low per-capita income. Life expectancy is considered the most robust measure of health status. By the early 1990s, Kerala's life expectancy of 71.7 years was on a par with Sri Lanka's 72.2. Most importantly, women have a higher life expectancy in all countries, and it is also the highest in Kerala, Sri Lanka and Malaysia. One must remember here that Malaysia's per-capita income is more than five times that of Kerala measured in PPP terms and close to ten times when measured in official dollars. Sri Lanka's per-capita income is twice that of Kerala in PPP terms and 1.7 times in official dollars. Yet their achievements in life expectancy are the same for both men and women. Population growth is a major concern of policy in all these countries except perhaps Malaysia (where the density is still quite low). Although most Asian countries have made remarkable progress in reducing the rate of population growth, the policy regimes under which such population programmes have been enforced show wide variations. In China, there is a strict policy of mandatory limitation of the number of children per couple to one, with some exceptions made for farmers and minority groups. Indonesia's programmes were enforced with a heavy hand by the government until recently. For others, the programmes function under a

Table 3.5 Demographic indicators

Country/state	Life expectancy			Population growth		Total fertility growth	IMR	U5MR	Births attended by trained health personnel (%)	Maternal mortality (per 1,000 live births)
	total	male	female	1980–92	1992–2000					
1	2	3	4	5	6	7	8	9	10	11
Kerala	71.7	68.8	74.4	1.4	1.1	1.8	13	27	94	1.3
India	61.3	61.1	61.4	2.1	1.7	3.0	74	115	34	5.7
Sri Lanka	72.2	70.0	74.6	1.4	1.1	1.7	16	19	94	1.4
Thailand	69.5	66.8	72.2	1.8	1.3	1.8	29	32	71	2.0
Malaysia	71.2	69.0	73.5	2.6	2.2	3.4	12	13	94	0.8
Indonesia	63.5	61.8	65.3	1.8	1.4	2.5	53	75	36	6.5
China	68.9	66.9	71.1	1.4	1.0	1.8	43	47	84	1.0

Note: Data for columns 2, 3, 4 and 8, 1994; column 9, 1995; column 10, 1990–92 and column 9 from 1990. For Kerala, column 2 uses data from 1990–92 and column 11, 1990.

Source: Population growth rate from World Bank (1994); all others from UNDP (1997). Source for Kerala, GOK, *Economic Review* (1993, 1995a and 1996c); Srinivasan and Shariff (1997).

Table 3.6   Communication facilities

Country/ state	Daily newspapers (copies per 100 people)	Post office (per 100,000 people)	Main telephone lines (per 100 people)
1	2	3	4
Kerala	7 (20)	17.2	2.1
India	3	17.6	1.3
Sri Lanka	3	23.0	1.1
Thailand	7	7.3	5.9
Malaysia	12	12.4	16.6
Indonesia	n/a	5.4	1.7
China	n/a	n/a	3.4

Note: Data for column 2: 1992; column 3: *c.* 1991; column 4: 1995. Column 2: figure in brackets for Kerala indicates the number of newspapers and periodicals per 100 people.
Source: For all countries, UNDP (1997). For Kerala, CMIE (1996), GOI (1994) and GOK (1998a).

system of incentives. The appropriate indicator here is the Total Fertility Rate (TFR), indicating the average number of children per couple in the fertility age group. When a society reaches and maintains a level of two, it will reach a replacement level of population within one generation. That this has been achieved in Kerala by the end of the 1980s is a remarkable achievement. Several studies exploring the causative factors for such a demographic transition in the context of low per-capita income have pointed out the crucial role of education in general and that of women (mothers) in particular (Nair 1981; Krishnan 1976; Bhat and Rajan 1990). Other factors, such as the role of the state, have helped accelerate the process. Improved access to health care facilities, especially for pregnant mothers, have subsequently played a crucial role in ensuring the survival of newborn children. This is indicated by the percentage of births attended by trained health personnel. In this respect Kerala's record is on a par with Sri Lanka and Malaysia.

Educational capability is often captured in terms of the literacy rate or the rate of enrolment in schools. As with many other indicators, this again is only a proxy for the wider notion of education. In Table 3.6, we report indicators that are vehicles for dissemination of information, to extend the notion of education beyond schools. It goes without saying that communication plays a crucial role in facilitating information dissemination. The print media occupy a prominent place in this because of their long historical existence relative to other communications media such as radio, telephone and television. The limited statistics relating to the number of daily newspapers per 100 people place Kerala in joint second position with Thailand, with Malaysia coming out first. However, when one combines the data on the number of both newspapers and periodicals (for which data are available for Kerala), the widespread nature of the role of the print media in Kerala is clear. At least one newspaper or periodical copy is available for every five persons or every three adults in Kerala. This statistic, however, gives us no idea of the reading habits of the population. Given the high level and pace of social and political activism in Kerala, the habit of reading is quite widespread, as we shall see later in Table 3.8. This is the cumulative result of a historical process of social and political mobilization of the masses in general and the poorer sections in particular. It is perhaps for this reason that the first and second places for the largest circulation newspapers in Indian languages are two Malayalam (the language of Kerala) newspapers, *Malayala Manorama* and *Mathrubhumi*. Yet the Malayalam-speaking population in India is less than 4 per cent! Similarly, book publication is likely to be on the higher side in Kerala and more widely distributed because of the existence of a network of village libraries throughout the rural areas.

What we have attempted in this section is not only to demonstrate Kerala's achievements in poverty alleviation in a comparative setting but also to go beyond the summary measures by examining some detailed indicators. Given the very low level of per-capita income, Kerala's achievements are quite remarkable when compared to the Asian Six, some of whose per-capita incomes are many times that of Kerala. It is also important to mention that not all initial conditions were favourable to Kerala. We think that some of the positive initial conditions – such as early commercialization and the transformation of the labour force into mainly non-agricultural activities, the early foundations of improving access to education and health care to the poorer sections, and the relatively better position of women – were overshadowed by negative initial conditions. These were: the high population density of a poor agrarian economy dependent on the outside world for the supply of food grains (because of the commercial and cash crop nature of agriculture); the very low per-capita income, lower than the all-India average until the late 1970s; the high incidence of income poverty until the mid-1970s; and the very high rate of unemployment among all the Indian states. Nevertheless, the problem of poverty was taken care of in a remarkable manner during the last quarter of the twentieth century; though the foundations for such an outcome were laid a long time before, through what may now be called public action. Before we turn to consider this, a brief discussion of Kerala in relation to all-India may be in order.

Kerala and all-India

Amartya Sen and Jean Drèze, writing about economic development and social opportunity, have dealt with the problem of sharp interregional differences within India. They remarked that India should learn from within, pointing to the achievements of Kerala in expanding social opportunities to the poorer sections and thereby achieving a faster pace in human development (Drèze and Sen 1996). Here we will briefly consider the gap between Kerala and India in terms of poverty and its alleviation. Two things emerge. One is that the gap between Kerala and all-India has tended to widen over time. Second, and more importantly, the gap between the women in Kerala and all-India is wider, bringing into focus the need for a greater gender sensitivity in human development in India.

Table 3.7 presents a number of indicators relating to income-poverty, educational attainments from literacy to reading habits, and a number of basic health indicators. Wherever appropriate, these indicators are provided separately for men and women to bring the gender dimension into sharper focus. Progress in poverty alleviation in both all-India and Kerala has been much faster since the mid-1970s. Nationally, the constraint on the supply of food grains was relieved since the mid-1970s as a result of the 'Green Revolution', although its spread has been uneven. Second, the rate of growth of the Indian economy began to improve, and since the early 1980s has attained a long-term annual average growth rate of 5 per cent, which is unprecedented in Indian economic history. Consequently the constraint imposed on poverty alleviation as a result of low economic growth has been somewhat relaxed since the early 1980s. For Kerala, the picture has been the reverse. Kerala's economic growth since the mid-1970s to late 1980s has been around 2.5 per cent with a per-capita income growth of less than 1 per cent. Remittances may have partly relieved this constraint. It is only since the late 1990s that the rate of growth of Kerala's economy has started to pick up and show signs of improvement (Kannan 1998). However, it is interesting to note that it is precisely during the period of low economic growth that much of the progress in poverty alleviation has been achieved in Kerala, which points to the role that concerted public action played.

As mentioned earlier, Kerala in fact had a higher incidence of income-poverty than all India. Table 3.7 tells us that during 1973–74 Kerala's income-poverty was nearly 10 per cent higher than that of all-India. But

Table 3.7 Progress in selected aspects of poverty alleviation in Kerala and all-India

Indicator	Period		Kerala	India
Income-poor (head-count) as % of population	1973–74		59.8	54.9
	1993–94		25.4	36.0
Life expectancy at birth (years)	1951–61	male	45.3	35.7
		female	57.4	43.5
	1990–92	male	68.8	59.0
		female	74.4	59.4
Infant mortality (per 1,000 live births)	1951–60		120.0	140.0
	1993		13.0	74.0
Incidence of severe child undernourishment (%)	1975–79	boys	10.2	14.6[*]
		girls	10.4	15.3[*]
	1988–90	boys	2.4	9.0[*]
		girls	1.6	9.0[*]
Females/100 males	1961		102.1	94.1
	1991		104.0	92.7

[*] For seven Indian states only, where the survey was conducted: Kerala, Tamilnadu, Karnataka, Andhra Pradesh, Gujarat, Maharashtra and Madhya Pradesh.
Source: Compiled from GOI (1994 and 1997).

within two decades Kerala not only reduced its incidence of income-poverty by 58 per cent (compared to only 34 per cent for all-India), but it is now lower than all-India by 30 per cent. That means a faster decline in Kerala compared to all-India. A combination of income-poverty and health status measurement can bring out the ugly fact of the undernourishment of children. When we examine this fact we find that the incidence of 'severe' child undernourishment in Kerala was lower than all-India even during the mid-1970s, but it was lower only by around one-third. By the late 1980s this dimension of poverty in Kerala had been reduced to a very low percentage, thereby increasing the gap with all-India to a considerable extent. In the case of life expectancy, Kerala enjoyed an initial advantage even during the 1950s and by the 1990s its achievement was comparable to many high-income countries, whereas the Indian average is yet to catch up with many other Asian countries, especially the Asian Six reported here. In the case of infant mortality, Kerala's IMR was

Table 3.8 Poverty alleviation: educational record

Indicator		Period		Kerala	India
Literacy (% of population above 7 years of age)		1961	M	55.00	34.30
			F	38.90	12.90
		1991	M	94.50	63.90
			F	86.00	39.40
Literacy among scheduled castes (ex-untouchables)		1961	M	31.60	17.00
			F	17.40	3.30
		1991	M	85.20	49.90
			F	74.30	23.80
Literacy among children	aged 6–11	1986–87	M	97.40	64.70
			F	97.40	48.90
	aged 12–14	1986–87	M	99.50	75.30
			F	99.10	54.50
Dropout rates (%)	class 1–4	1993–94	M	−5.35	35.05
			F	−3.05	38.57
	class 1–10	1993–94	M	33.42	68.41
			F	24.51	74.74
Rural children aged 12–14 who have never been enrolled in a school (%)		1986–87	M	0.40	26.00
			F	1.80	51.00
Proportion of population aged 6 and above who have completed primary education (%)		1992–93	M	65.80	48.60
			F	60.50	28.10
Rural children attending school (%)	5–9 years	1987–88	M	86.90	52.50
			F	82.80	40.40
	10–14 years	1987–88	M	93.30	66.10
			F	91.20	41.90
Proportion of readers in the estimated adult population *(any daily)*		1989	M	53.40	23.60
			F	35.80	11.50
Proportion of readers in the estimated adult population *(any publication)*		1989	M	63.30	26.60
			F	54.20	15.40
Proportion of readers among agricultural labourers *(any publication)*		1989	M	45.90	3.10
			F	11.90	0.70

Source: Compiled from GOI (1994 and 1997).

80 per cent of that of all-India in the 1950s; during the 1990s it was less than 20 per cent. Again, the gap has widened considerably.

Let us now consider education in some detail. Kerala certainly enjoyed an initial advantage here too, but the gap has now widened. This is true not only for the literacy rate for the whole population but also for the socially depressed classes known as the Scheduled Castes, who are the socially excluded untouchable communities in the traditional social structure of India. Kerala's progress in this respect warrants special attention, as the literacy rate of this segment of the population is now considerably higher than that of the general population in India. The significance of this achievement is of great social importance to such a caste-ridden society as India's. This can be gauged from the fact that the literacy rate of women belonging to Scheduled Castes in Kerala (74 per cent) is higher than the literacy rate for men in the general population for all-India (64 per cent)! The high current rate of illiteracy could be due to the high illiteracy among adults. This means that future illiteracy can be reduced if it is ensured that children become literate now. A measure of this for younger (6–11 years) and older (12–14 years) children shows that the problem of illiteracy will be a very real one in the foreseeable future in India unless urgent steps are taken immediately. Children of school age were literate in Kerala by the second half of the 1980s, whereas in all-India 35 to 45 per cent of children were reported to be illiterate. Furthermore, school drop-out is no longer a problem in Kerala, whereas more than one-third of children drop out of primary level in all-India. Drop-out rates for the entire schooling period (classes 1 to 10) is one-third for boys in Kerala but two-thirds in all-India; only a quarter of girls drop out in Kerala, whereas in all-India this figure is three-quarters. Similar differences are to be found with regard to children in rural areas.

The ability to read and write is one thing; how much it is translated into practice warrants a different measurement. One such measurement in terms of reading habits is presented in Table 3.8. More than half the adults in Kerala are reported to read at least one newspaper whereas the figure is less than a quarter for all-India. For women the statistics are more than one-third for Kerala but around 12 per cent for all-India. If we take reading habits in general as the reading of any publication, then nearly two-thirds of men in Kerala are reported to read at least one publication. This proportion is close to the proportion of adults in the total population; this means that almost all adults have the habit of reading. Similarly for women, the proportion is 54 per cent, which suggests that more than 85 per cent of adult women have the habit of reading. The proportions for all-India are quite low at 27 and 15 per cent of the male and female population, respectively. From the point of view of poverty alleviation, measurement of reading habits should be done with respect to those who are considered income-poor. This has been presented in terms of the reading habits of agricultural labourers, who constitute the bulk of the poor in India. By the late 1980s nearly 46 per cent of male agricultural labourers in Kerala were reported as having the habit of reading; the proportion for women agricultural labourers was 12 per cent. For all-India the statistics are a mere 3 per cent and less than 1 per cent, respectively. Given Kerala's share of the total number of agricultural labourers in India, it is not difficult to see that these all-India figures represent the contribution of this share. It may not be an exaggeration to say that reading habits among the poor in India are almost non-existent, due to their illiteracy. The significance of reading as a habit, even among the poor agricultural labourers, in Kerala is indeed a measure of the social change that has taken place in the state during the last fifty years.

Let us now shift the focus to the gender dimension in poverty alleviation in Kerala and all-India. On all indicators presented in Tables 3.7 and 3.8, the gap between women in Kerala and India has widened. While women in Kerala have moved fast to close the gap with the men of Kerala, the women in India are falling behind both their men and the women in Kerala. Indeed, this puts an additional burden on poverty alleviation efforts at the all-India level. For example, the literacy rate of women in all-India (which includes Kerala) in the early 1990s was equivalent to what the women in Kerala had achieved in the early 1960s (39 per cent)! Less than 40 per cent of the women in India were literate in 1991; in Kerala only around 15 per cent of the women were illiterate in that year. Literacy among girl children and school enrolment at primary level are total in Kerala, while there is a long road ahead for girl children in India as a whole. The same is true for the incidence of severe undernourishment. The survival rate of women in Kerala is greater than that of men, as evidenced by a higher and increasing percentage of women in the total population. The reverse is the case for all-India, where the proportion of women was not only low to begin with but in decline. For every 1,000 men there were only 941 women in India in 1961 (as against 1021 in Kerala); this has declined to 927 in India while it increased to 1040 in Kerala. That sums up the position of women in Kerala and all-India.

In terms of basic human capabilities, women in Kerala have achieved levels that it would take women in the rest of India at least another couple of decades to reach. The pace of catching up will certainly be dependent on the success of poverty alleviation, because it is the wide gap between the poor and the non-poor in the rest of India that accounts for such disparities. Women in Kerala, it is now widely acknowledged, played a crucial role in its demographic transition. Despite the very low levels of income, women have enhanced life expectancy; birth and death rates have been reduced, especially the infant mortality rate; the average number of children per couple has been brought down to below replacement levels; the average age at marriage has been raised, and women have planned their families in such a way that they are now available for a longer period of time for productive economic activities. As a 1987 survey (with a sample size of 10,000 rural households) shows, morbidity rates for acute illnesses were similar for men and women (20.3 and 20.9 per cent respectively) although morbidity rates for chronic illnesses were higher for women (15.58 per cent) than men (13.75) partly due to their reproductive role ('diseases of the uterus'). It is also interesting to note that the prevalence of handicaps (of various sorts) was lower among women (1.74 per cent) than among men (2.42 per cent). It is perhaps a tribute to the capability of Kerala's women that the incidence of severe undernourishment among girls has not only been brought down to a negligible percentage but is also lower than that for boys (Kannan et al. 1991).

In terms of education, the achievements are equally, if not more, impressive. Illiteracy is no longer a problem for Kerala women, including those belonging to the Scheduled Castes. Drop-out rates for girl children in Kerala are lower than those for boys; the situation is the reverse for all-India. Girls and young women seem to desire education more than boys and young men. In 1993, 49.2 per cent of schoolchildren (classes 1 to 10) were girls, and they accounted for 50.6 per cent of all students at the high school stage (classes 8 to 10). In higher education, excluding professional courses, young women accounted for 54.2 per cent of the total students (GOK 1998a).

What is it in Kerala that has contributed to such a generalized process of fulfilling basic human capabilities and reducing poverty while not putting women in a position of distinct disadvantage, unlike in the rest of India and in many other countries?

The Process

Kerala's successful promotion of basic human capabilities, and thereby the alleviation of poverty, has a history of several decades of sustained public action that began at the turn of the twentieth century. But the impact of this long-term process began to be felt only since the mid-1970s. This fairly long time-lag can be explained by the slow rate of growth of the economy and the consequent constraints on the state to devote a higher proportion of its resources for poverty alleviation. Even today the reduction in income-poverty is far less impressive compared to the achievements in basic human capabilities such as educational attainments and health status. Yet the prime mover in the decline of poverty has been education. And that was brought about by public action in the form of the social mobilization of large sections of the population in general and, later, of the labouring poor in particular. Let us examine briefly the nature of this sustained public action.

The state of Kerala came into existence as a unified political-administrative entity only in 1956 when the reorganization of Indian states took place along linguistic lines. Prior to that and during British colonial rule, Kerala consisted of three separate entities. Two of them, Travancore in the south and Cochin in the centre, were ruled by maharajas who were under the suzerainty of the British colonial government. The northern part, Malabar, was a district in the Madras presidency of British India. It was the linguisitic and cultural unity of the three regions that made the idea of Kerala a political reality. The advent of colonialism shook the very foundations of the social, economic and cultural fabric of Kerala. Due to the diverse nature of Kerala's natural resources (tropical rainforests and marine fisheries along the long coastal belt) and the commercial nature of its agricultural crops, Kerala had experience in trading with the outside world, thus linking its deep interiors with the trading centres. But this did not disturb the social equilibrium, dominated by a rigid caste structure, until in the nineteenth century colonial capital started penetrating directly into the Kerala economy in order to exploit its natural resources and cheap labour. Such penetration accelerated from the middle of the nineteenth century in the form of expanding plantations and logging, necessitating the opening up of the interiors through the construction of roads and other infrastructural facilities. Large- and small-scale manufacturing was giving rise to an agroprocessing industry based on the coconut tree, involving such products as coconut oil and coir goods. Extension of the area under rice cultivation, in response to a growing shortage of food grains, further accelerated the commercialization of such agriculture. As a result, a class of rural proletarians emerged by the turn of the twentieth century. Although the caste structure was not dismantled, its foundations became much weaker as a result of the economic mobility and proletarianization, particularly among the intermediate castes (Kannan 1988: ch. 2). Such is the economic background for the subsequent emergence of social movements striving for social and economic emancipation of the poorer sections of society.

The social reform movements started as protests against the institutionalization of social exclusion practised by the upper-caste Hindus. Later on, these movements became the vehicles for reform of the communities from within, in which education was accorded the highest priority. The most important of all such movements was the one that emerged from a numerically significant intermediate caste, known as Ezhavas. This movement was led by Sree Narayana Guru, a religious scholar and philosopher, who combined erudition with social activism and used the former to strengthen the latter. The initial struggles for emancipation were such symbolic acts as the right to enter temples and the right of passage on public roads. The movement took an organizational form in 1905; one of its major activities was the establishment of educational institutions. The political message of the movement was one of empowerment through organization. The movement influenced not only the members of the Ezhava community but even those who were socially above them. Thus, an upper-caste but influential non-Brahmin community known as the Nayars also took to such work on a community basis, and formed an organization in 1915 with the aim of establishing educational institutions. The Christians, who were emerging as an economically strong community, had already established their own educational institutions through the work of missionaries and indigenous church organizations. Liberal doses of patronage for this were received from the colonial government out of religious affinity. Muslims also took up community work and later established an organization, similar to the other communities, to start educational institutions. But the most significant of such developments, from the point of view of poverty alleviation, in terms of material deprivation and social dignity, was the organization of the marginalized communities, some of whom were considered untouchables. One such, known as the Pulayas, a landless agricultural labouring caste, formed their own association as early as 1907 in Travancore, emphasizing the need for education of members of the community, the wearing of clothing on the torso, and self-respect; they sought to abolish all symbols that oppressed them and made them inferior.

The wearing of clotheing on the torso for women was already perceived as an issue of dignity, because it was denied to the lower castes in order to emphasize the superiority of the upper castes. Earlier the Ezhavas had rebelled against a government edict to tax their women who wore upper body clothing. They successfully fought for this right, which was later emulated by other lower castes.

A qualitatively new development took place when the community-focused social reform movements gained popularity, due both to the influence of Western liberal thinking and the socialist revolution in the Soviet Union. The need to break away from the restraints of caste was felt by the more radical elements within the social reform movements. The emerging proletarian nature of the labour force provided a good breeding ground for the growth of secular forces. Their aim was a casteless society;

they questioned the existence of God and thus the need for religions. Starting around 1917, this new movement, known as the Brotherhood Movement, fought against religion and its influence on the people. This in turn led to a rationalist movement, especially among the youth, which embraced atheism. This started around the second half of the 1920s and influenced the latter-day leaders of the radical political movement.

The radical political movement first emerged as a leftist group within the Indian National Congress. In Kerala this group quickly turned itself into a communist organization, thus breaking away from Gandhian methods and from traditions of social and national struggles for social reform and national independence. It is this movement that was more successful than any other in mobilizing the labouring poor, cutting across caste identities, and capturing the initiatives from the better-off sections of society for national independence. This radical political movement attracted the wrath of both the state and the wealthy in society. Working underground and fired by an ideology of liberation, it influenced the poor in every area of Kerala. This method of organization was critically dependent on education. Political study classes, publication of radical literature, work among the intelligentsia to influence arts and literature, and the setting up of village libraries were some of the means by which the movement sought to communicate effectively with the masses. From the early 1930s to the late 1950s, when the Communist Party was elected to govern the newly formed state of Kerala, there was a process of relentless work among the poor for organization and political conversion.

Even after the formation of the State of Kerala, the relevance of these various forms of social movement did not fade although they experienced varying degrees of decline from their original objectives with the emergence of vested interests. With regard to basic educational provision, one of the institutional legacies of this half a century of mobilization was the establishment of what are called village libraries, throughout the length and breadth of Kerala. These libraries, established in the mid-1930s, were a demonstration of the ideological convergence of all movements on the importance of education of the masses. The Gandhian social reform activists also made notable contributions, as indeed did the activists of the radical political movement. The village libraries came into existence through the initiatives of these social activists with strong local level support; the local youth was involved in their establishment and maintenance. After the formation of the State of Kerala in 1957, the libraries were recognized for their contribution to nonformal education. The government accordingly instituted a system of grants-in-aid for maintenance; libraries with the minimum prescribed facilities such as a building, books and members became eligible for such grants. Around five thousand libraries were recognized. However, the total number of village libraries today is reckoned to be in excess of fifteen thousand. Many of the large number that do not enjoy the grant-in-aid from the government nevertheless receive assistance from local governments, known as panchayats; this may take the form of a radio set, or free newspapers and magazines. It is these village libraries that were used as centres for adult literacy and post-literacy classes. They also functioned as the venue for political meetings and youth events, and as women and child-care centres. The libraries are now an established part of village life in Kerala.

The ground prepared by the social and political movements and the network of village libraries subsequently provided a space for the emergence of yet another qualitatively new kind of social activism among the educated in Kerala society: what is now known as the Kerala People's Science Movement (Kerala Sastra Sahitya Parishad or KSSP). The Movement was started by a few teachers and writers, who were also social and political activists, during the early 1960s. This Movement sought to popularize knowledge about nature, the world and the immediate society among children and rural people through classes, meetings and the publication of popular books. The movement subsequently focused on developmental issues and problems facing the people, and incorporated much of the intelligentsia into its ranks. Issues such as the quality of education, health care, environmental dimensions of development and decentralization of development were widely debated within Kerala society, thus forcing the attention of the decision-makers on these issues.

In sum, then, the potential for the poorer sections of society to acquire education as a basic human capability was achieved through a process of mobilization spanning several decades. The process of acquisition was by and large through 'out-of-school' or what may loosely be called non-formal education. It was not confined to making people literate, although that was one of its principal functions; it extended to raising awareness by focusing on social and political issues that were intimately related to the emancipation of the poor. For example, an emphasis on personal hygiene and proper dressing were as much a part of the process as learning to address the poor in non-derogatory terms. One aim, above all, was to instil in the poor the value of educating their children. Today, in consequence, a very high premium is attached to education by the poorer sections of society, who send their children to school and enable them to benefit from as much education as possible. Another key emphasis of the radical political movement was organization of the labouring poor. Thus unionization of labour was not confined to 'industrial' establishments or urban areas but extended to all labouring poor, irrespective of the organization of production, in both rural and urban areas. Thus, a large proportion of the labouring poor are part of the labour movement, as agricultural labourers, agroprocessing workers in small workshops, self-employed workers such as those working under piece rates, and workers in service-type jobs such as the loading and unloading of goods. They have over time acquired a bargaining strength that is rare in the rest of India except in the private corporate and public-sector enterprises and institutions.

The Impact

An important legacy of the drive for education was expansion of the formal education system, especially after the formation of the state. The striking feature of this expansion was the degree of accessibility accomplished: in most cases schools were established in very close physical proximity to the villages they served. According to the First Economic Census, conducted in 1977, 99.7 per cent of villages in Kerala had a primary or junior school within 2 km, 98.6 per cent had a middle school within 2 km, and 96.7 per cent had a high or higher secondary school within 5 km; comparative all-India figures are 90.1 per cent, 43.8 per cent and 20.9 per cent respectively (Kannan 1988: 20).

Another impact of education, defined in its broad sense, has been on the health status of Kerala citizens. As we have already discussed, Kerala's health transition has been made possible by the spread of education among all sections of its population. Women played a significant role in this transition. When life expectancy as well as child survival rates improved, it became feasible to limit family size. The spread of child immunization, the popularity of medical personnel attending childbirth, and better nourishment of children are factors related to the educational position of women. The remarkable progress made by women in catching up with men in literacy and schooling, along with the successful enrolment of children, are factors that have helped facilitate the improvement in the population's health status. Notwithstanding the advances made, there is genuine concern about the quality of health care services in the state as reflected in the high reported incidence of morbidity (Panikar and Soman 1985; Kannan et al. 1991).

A further impact of education is on reducing income poverty. Education and its contribution to raising the social and political consciousness of the people in general and that of the poorer sections in particular have been instrumental in the successful mobilization of the masses. This took the form of a demand for state intervention in poverty alleviation. Between the mid-1970s and the late 1980s, the growth rate of the economy was quite slow – less than 1 per cent per annum in terms of per-capita income. Nevertheless, impressive gains in poverty alleviation were made. The state played a crucial role in this process, in spite of the unfavourable conditions. The Public Distribution System in Kerala was started in the early 1960s, yet it was only in the mid-1970s that the quantity of commodities distributed could be increased. A number of direct poverty alleviation programmes were established. Prominent among these were the provision of free midday meals to primary-school children, institution of supplementary nutrition programmes for pregnant mothers and pre-school children from poorer households, the granting of an old-age pension to rural workers in a number of occupations, and implementation of national programmes of poverty alleviation such as the Integrated Rural Development Programme. The combined benefit of all these programmes worked out at around 21 per cent of the annual expenditure of rural labour households in the 1980s (Kannan 1995: 722).

In addition to these basic achievements, education played a much larger role in the evolution of Kerala's society. The growth of the print media and communication facilities, the enlargement of cultural space for an expanding segment of the population, the social and political activism of the people – all are traceable to the spread of education.

Some Lessons

What lessons are to be drawn from the Kerala experience in poverty alleviation? The most important one, in our view, is the sociopolitical context in which the process has taken place. In the Asian context in general and the Asian Six in particular, success has been achieved by the intervention of a strong state. In some countries, such as China, the state has intervened directly in all spheres relating to poverty alleviation. In the Southeast Asian countries, also, the state has taken primary responsibility for poverty alleviation. It should be noted, however, that the potential for non-state public action has been limited. In countries such as Indonesia, the heavy hand of the state has not provided much political space for the poor. In the Indian context, also, the state's role has been important. Yet the concern in India is not the absence of a political voice for the poor or the lack of opportunities for public action by non-state actors, but the frustratingly slow pace of poverty alleviation. This is due primarily to the hierarchical and oppressive social structure, which is heavily loaded against the emancipatory demands of the poorer sections. What Kerala has demonstrated is the feasibility of poverty alleviation in the context of a political democracy that does not impose any limitations on the freedom of political choice or public action of the people. The exercise of such political choice compelled the state to respond to the demands of the poorer sections that were no longer constrained by the social structure. Public action thus played a dual role in removing the fundamental social constraints and giving a political voice to the poor.

The second lesson relates to the role of economic growth in poverty alleviation. The trickle-down theory does not enjoy much empirical support in the Kerala context. Poverty alleviation was accelerated during a period of very slow economic growth. It must be said, however, that two factors were favourable: the improved supply of food grain in the national context, and the flow of remittances from abroad. Nevertheless, these factors could not have contributed to poverty alleviation without concerted public action. Kerala has proved that poverty alleviation can be achieved with or without economic growth if concerted public action is focused on the problem.

The third but no less significant lesson from the Kerala experience concerns the role of women. We have seen how women caught up with men in terms of literacy, school enrolment, and performance indicators such as retention rates. Certain historical and cultural factors may have provided an enabling environment for such a process. The matrilineal system is a case in point; although influence is likely to have been indirect since most of the families in poorer sections in Kerala did not operate according to the matrilineal principle. The impact of the early social movements during the 1911–21 period and that of the radical political movement during 1931–51 was perhaps much more crucial. The impressive gains in literacy at these times are thus particularly noteworthy. Studies so far carried out also emphasize the central role of women's education in Kerala's demographic transition, and its close relation to the process of enhanced health status. In the economic sphere, however, women have had to contend with less than their due share, particularly in terms of employment and earnings. This can be attributed partly to the continuing slow growth of the economy. Yet other powerful constraints are in play, such as segmentation and discrimination in the labour market. The need to go beyond poverty alleviation has now become imperative for Kerala if it is to meet the challenges of unemployment and further enhance the quality of life of its people.

The rest of the world has recognized Kerala's achievements in social and human development. The current concern in Kerala is to focus on the commodity-producing sectors and on the issue of unemployment, particularly among the educated. The mismatch between social development and economic growth has attracted the attention of scholars for some time (see Kannan 1990a and 1998; Thomas Isaac and Kumar 1991; and Heller 1995). This paradox – 'social development coexisting with economic backwardness' – has been a formidable challenge for Kerala. Arguably the one major positive economic impact of social development is in the sphere of international labour migration. As a result of the phenomenal growth in demand for labour in the Arabian Gulf states, there has been a steady flow of labour migrating to these countries for work. Two-thirds are in the category of semi-skilled but school-educated workers. These people would certainly not have been able to seize the opportunity to work abroad had they not received at least minimal levels of education. The remittances of these workers have helped the households in Kerala to increase their average expenditure on consumption. This in turn created a boom in construction and a steady growth in the service sector. It is the productive sectors of the economy – agriculture and industry – that have performed poorly, especially between the mid-1970s and the mid-1980s. Inadequate investment in infrastructure coupled with poor management of existing infrastructure, short-sighted strategies on the part of trade unions to prevent technological change, and the state's inability to attract investment: these are some of the major problems confronting Kerala in its quest to translate its remarkable achievements in social development into meaningful opportunities for economic advancement.[4]

Notes

1. It should be noted, however, that the extent of freedom of political choice varies from country to country.

2. However, it must be mentioned that such a density is unlikely to be felt by the visitor to Kerala because of its habitat pattern, which is one of high dispersal rather than concentration. In terms of urbanization, only Malaysia and Indonesia are distinctly more urbanized than Kerala. Both India and China are slightly more urbanized than Kerala, while Sri Lanka and Thailand are less urbanized. In the context of Kerala, urbanization, measured in strict terms, does not hold much meaning. This is due not only to the dispersed and continuous nature of its settlement pattern but also to the presence of a number of urban amenities in rural areas and the relatively low level of industrialization of urban areas. The Kerala situation is referred to by some as 'rurban', meaning neither rural nor urban (Sreekumar 1990).

3. It should be recalled that one of the three constituent indicators that make up the HDI is per-capita income. Since Kerala's per-capita income is the lowest among these countries, a relatively lower HDI score is not surprising.

4. I have dealt with these issues in terms of what I call 'development dilemmas' in Kannan (1998).

4

Social Capital and the Developmental State: Industrial Workers in Kerala

Patrick Heller

I India /
015
Z13

Strong State, Strong Society

Kerala's successes on the social development front have been tied to the effectiveness of public action, most notably in the work of Drèze and Sen (1996). Public action and, more specifically, the capacity of the state to provide public goods and deliver basic needs have in turn been explained as the direct outcome of Kerala's unique history of social mobilization (Ramachandran 1997). The relationship between state capacity and patterns of social mobilization has, however, been largely undertheorized. Why social mobilization in Kerala has underscored the emergence of a developmental state (albeit one that has been more redistributive than growth-oriented) rather than producing the proliferation of distributional coalitions and subsequent paralysis of state action highlighted in the rent-seeking literature has not been satisfactorily addressed. The analysis presented in this chapter borrows from recent contributions to the literature on social capital by arguing that under certain conditions state and society can become enmeshed in patterns of interaction that have positive-sum outcomes. Kerala's high levels of social development and successful redistributive reforms, I argue, are a direct result of repeated cycles of engagement between a programmatic labour movement and a democratic state. The resulting forms of embeddedness not only explain the success of public action but have also created the institutional forms and political processes required for negotiating the class compromises through which redistribution and growth can be reconciled.[1] These dynamics are explored through a close examination of both the organized factory sector and the unorganized (informal) sector.

By any account, Kerala's developmental successes are tied to what are clearly exceptionally high levels of social capital. Even the most casual observer of Kerala society would be quick to note the sheer density of civic organizations and the vigour of associational life. Keralites of all walks of life, it would seem, appear to have an irresistible inclination to combine, associate and organize, and to do so without the outbreaks of violent disorder that many scholars of developing societies might predict. Despite extremely high levels of social mobilization, Kerala has largely been spared the sectarian and casteist violence that has recently been on the upswing throughout most of India.

Across both the formal and the informal sectors of the economy, rates of unionization are high. The state boasts the most extensive network of cooperative societies in the country, as well as numerous NGOs. Kerala's caste self-help and social upliftment societies have a long history of active civil engagement. Its 'library movement', literary associations and film industry have earned it a reputation as a cultural centre rivalled only by Bengal. A network of private and semi-private schools sponsored by communal and caste organizations, which overlaps with an extensive public school network, has put a school in every village and provided near-universal primary school enrolment. The state's high levels of literacy and education have in turn spawned a prolific and diverse vernacular press.

The vigour and dynamism of civil society are matched only by the size and activism of the state. Kerala has the most developed social welfare system in India, including the most extensive network of fair-price shops (public food distribution) and rates of social expenditure that continue to be significantly higher than the national average.[2] Through the implementation of the land reforms of 1970, by far the most radical in the subcontinent (Herring 1983), the state transformed the agrarian social-property structure, destroying the traditional landlord class and creating a new class of small proprietors. The government-run system of primary health care units has reduced infant mortality to near First World rates. And, even by Indian standards, the state has been very active in regulating the market, restricting labour-displacing technologies in traditional industries, legislating work conditions, and hiring practices in industry as well as in agriculture, and aggressively enforcing minimum wages.

At this broad level, then, there is strong support for the assertion that state intervention and social initiatives can produce synergistic outcomes (Evans 1995). State interventions aimed at providing public goods have built directly on existing social capital resources and have in turn reinforced social capital. The expansion of public health and educational services has had a 'crowding-in' effect, as the competition between public and private delivery services has increased overall efficiency. Pressures from below, exerted by well-organized groups, and a highly developed culture of civic participation have not only created a demand-side dynamic – to which right- and left-wing governments have necessarily had to respond in a competitive electoral system – but have also increased the accountability of local officials.[3] The comparatively corruption-free and logistically successful provision of low-cost housing, school lunch programmes, subsidized food, and day care have been attributed to the active and informed participation of local groups (Franke and Chasin 1989). Clearly, democracy in Kerala works.

Viewed in this light, one might be tempted to conclude that Kerala looks a lot like the northern parts of Italy described by Putnam (1993a) in his defining study of the relationship between social capital and democracy. Regional governments in northern Italy, he argues, have been successful in providing public goods because of a long history of civic engagement and active community organization. Similarly, the claim has often been made that Kerala's successful social development can be traced back to the social structure of nineteenth-century Travancore and Cochin (the princely states that constituted the southern half of pre-Independence Kerala). Competition between the minority Christian community and the majority Hindu community, as well as between various caste groups, produced a flurry of organizing and a proliferation of community associations. These associations, drawing on the reserves of social capital that inhere in tightly knit communities, promoted educational, health and cultural activities, which became the basis for successful political movements demanding more jobs and more political representation from what was a Brahmanical state. The fact that these associations continue to play an active role in Kerala only reinforces the impression of a direct link between this tradition of civic engagement and Kerala's social development.

Taken alone, however, the pre-Independence 'invigoration' of civil society can hardly explain Kerala's rather unique developmental trajectory. While the mobilization of nineteenth-century civil society did represent the first organized challenge to the hegemony of the Brahmanical state and might explain a general receptiveness (later reinforced by parliamentary democracy) of governments in Kerala to social demand groups, this high degree of associationalism in and of itself cannot explain the structural transformations that have underscored Kerala's social development. The redistributive thrust of Kerala's development has carried with it a direct attack on traditional structures of power as well as the prerogatives of capital. It has as such entailed a fundamental realignment in the balance of class forces.

Not all forms of social mobilization promote developmentally useful forms of state intervention. Specifying the conditions under which synergy occurs requires carefully untangling the relationship between state capacity and actual patterns of demand aggregation. Geared as they are to securing narrow group interests, the politics of caste and communal groups, for example, fuel the politics of patronage and distribution. The resulting process of 'demand-overload' is precisely the phenomenon that a wide range of commentators have argued has incapacitated the Indian state (Brass 1990; Rudolph and Rudolph 1987). A vigorous civil society rooted in interests bounded by parochial loyalties is clearly at odds with the more universalistic project of the developmental state. The modes of action and domination associated with traditional forms of social control and organization do not moreover lend themselves to the instrumentalities of the bureaucratic state (Evans and Rueshemeyer 1985) and in the Indian case have been explicitly tied to the problem of 'public inertia' (Drèze and Gazdar 1997). Strong 'traditional' societies, as Migdal (1988) has argued, can produce weak states.

With large minority communities of Christians and Muslims (roughly 20 per cent of the population each) and the balance of Hindus divided into what by most accounts was once the most rigid and orthodox caste structure in India, Kerala's social structure is as diverse as any in the subcontinent. The state in Kerala has certainly not been spared the 'mischief of factions', as the proliferation of small community-based parties illustrates. But what sets Kerala aside from other Indian states (with the possible exception of West Bengal) is the particular class-based character of social mobilization that has dominated its post-Independence political life. The cacophony of fragmented societal demands has taken a back seat to demands of a more programmatic and encompassing character. And in so far as interests and social resources have been mobilized primarily, although not exclusively, along class lines, a democratically accountable state and a mobilized society have become organizationally and functionally linked in a manner conducive to the transformative projects broadly associated with development, particularly those of a redistributive character.

In arguing that class mobilization and the resulting forms of state intervention have produced a sequence of encounters – which, while anything but smooth, have in the aggregate been mutually reinforcing – two historically and analytically distinct sequences can be identified. In the first, the organized militancy of lower-class groups eroded traditional structures of domination clearing the path for state penetration. The bureaucratic–legal capacities of the state were in effect activated and extended by mobilizational pressures from below. The resulting synergy underwrote the politically and administratively daunting tasks of implementing structural reforms and building an extensive network of welfare services in an impoverished society. The legal and social protections enforced by an activist state in turn heightened labour's capacity for militancy. The most concrete and tangible effect of this synergy was redistributive development. A less visible but equally critical outcome of repeated interactions between the state and lower-class organizations in a competitive electoral democracy was the institutionalization of lower-class power.

The second sequence emerges from the contradictions of the first: redistribution and militancy precipitated a crisis of accumulation. As capital fled and labour agitations disrupted production, a stagnant economy threatened to unravel the successes of Kerala's social development. The response has been the emergence of various forms of class compromise, in which labour has significantly curtailed militancy in an explicit effort to create more favourable conditions of investment and growth. The emergence of the politics of compromise – the only viable strategy for securing future growth in a dependent, but democratic, capitalist economy – is a direct result of a cohesive and disciplined labour movement that has explicitly come to terms with the limits of militancy. An activist and embedded state has facilitated the process of class compromise both through direct mediations and by providing the institutional backdrop – the rules of the game – against which capital–labour conflicts can be negotiated.

The Developmental State and Social Mobilization

Putnam notes that in Italy dynamic 'civic communities' are associated with the predominance of horizontal solidarities, and that in 'uncivic' regions participation is stunted by the persistence of vertical dependencies. 'Citizens in these [civic] regions are engaged by public issues, not by patronage' (1993b: 36). Putnam attributes this difference to regional histories, yet his own account suggests that the ability to accumulate the type of social capital that contributes to democracy is predicated on a transformation of the social power structure, namely the dismantling of traditional patron–client relations. More than anything else, this has been the most important result of lower-class mobilization in Kerala.

Beginning in the early 1940s, the Communist Party of India (CPI) successfully welded together landless labourers, poor tenants and urban workers. The ideological agenda that drew these caste-differentiated groups together was the CPI's sustained attack on feudal institutions – landlordism, the attached labour system and the indignities of the caste system. With a strong cadre-based organization and a coherent transformative project, the Communists successfully built instruments of working-class power, most importantly unions, but also farmers' associations, student groups, village libraries, and a powerful cooperative movement. The success of the Communists, as its leaders have often noted, was in large part made possible by the existence of an already large reservoir of mobilizational resources from the social reform movements in the south (Travancore and Cochin) and a long tradition of peasant rebellions in the north (Malabar).

The electoral victory of the CPI in 1957 marked a watershed in the political empowerment of lower-caste rural and urban labourers and severely weakened the configurations of authority and domination of the traditional social order. In the following two decades, the Party split into the CPI and the CPM (Communist Party of India – Marxist), with the CPM emerging quickly as the dominant party and enjoying only a brief tenure in power (1967–69). This period of exclusion, combined with Communist Party rivalry, had the fortuitous effect of strengthening mobilizational politics. Deprived of state power, the CPM entrenched itself in civil society and strengthened its organizational capacity. The Congress, having learned from the success of the Communists' grassroots mobilization, followed suit and built its own mass organizations.[4] In contrast to theories that identify state capacity with regime durability,[5] it is important to underline the fact that Kerala's sustained strategy of redistributive and welfarist development has come amidst a turbulent history of coalition politics and frequent changes of government. A competitive environment of mass-based politics, expressed through tightly contested elections as well as organizational and protest activities, has created the sustained pressures from below that account for the success with which both left- and right-wing governments have delivered institutional reform and basic goods.

The bargaining capacity of working-class organizations has been built on the strength of iterated cycles of struggle (dating back to the democratic and nationalist struggles of the 1940s) to which the CPI and then the CPM imparted a highly disciplined and ideologically cohesive character. The political leverage of the working class thus resides in its 'associational autonomy' rather than the clientalistic exchange of material rewards for political subordination that characterizes authoritarian-corporatist regimes (Fox 1994: 153). This does not, however, simply follow from the democratic character of the state. Because both of Kerala's political formations (Congress- and Communist-dominated fronts) are in electoral terms closely balanced and actively vie for working-class support, the exclusionary tactics of incorporating the most organized segments of labour that predominate in most developing societies (including India) have been displaced by more 'encompassing' forms of political mobilization. This in turn has favoured demands for public goods (for example, demands for structural reforms, social protection legislation and universal entitlements) rather than the exclusionary and disaggregated politics of patronage.

The most notable result of this symbiosis of class mobilization and state intervention has been the dissolution of the social relations and the institutions of the pre-capitalist economic order. In agriculture, the 1970 land reforms were implemented on the strength of the coordination of legislative and administrative intervention with local-level activism. The reforms transferred land from landlords to tenants, decimating the social and political power of the traditional rural elite. The unionization of landless labourers and the subsequent passage of labour laws (including regulation of mechanization, minimum wages and a pension scheme) eroded the ties of dependency that bound lower-caste labourers to land-owners. Both these developments directly contributed to further democratizing village life. Elite control over local institutions such as agricultural cooperatives and panchayats (local government) has been replaced by fiercely competitive party- or union-based politics.

In industry, social legislation and pro-labour governments have provided the working class with an exceptionally high degree of bargaining capacity. Nowhere is this more visible than in the organization of the so-called 'unorganized' sector. While workers outside the factory sector in most developing societies enjoy few legal protections and have little capacity for collective action, the efforts of unions and state agencies in Kerala have combined, as we shall see, to penetrate effectively the unorganized or informal economy, drawing large swaths of traditionally disenfranchised workers within the purview of the law and the protection of the social-welfare state.

The institutionalization of lower-class interests in an underdeveloped sub-national economy has predictably produced contradictions that are only too familiar. Labour militancy and state intervention have adversely affected investment. High wages, state-enforced controls on mechanization, rigidities in labour deployment and high levels of social consumption have all contributed to either driving capital away or creating significant barriers to internal capital accumulation. In the decade that followed the peak of class mobilization in 1975, the state domestic product grew at an anaemic rate of 1.76 per cent (Kannan 1990a: 1952).[6] National and international investments during this period were negligible. Some traditional industries – in particular cashew processing and beedi (hand-rolled cigarettes) production – experienced capital flight.

How the state and mobilized social forces have responded to this economic crisis is the question to which I now turn, focusing specifically on the industrial sector, where the mobility of capital has exacted a particularly high price for state intervention and labour militancy. Rejecting the view that high levels of lower-class mobilization and the associated redistributive bias of the state have created insurmountable contradictions

– a view informed by a static, zero-sum understanding of the relationship between economic interests and political institutions – I argue, following Bates (1989), that institutions evolve dynamically in response to conflict. That class mobilization in Kerala led to struggles that produced a stalemate in the 1970s is not in dispute. But in so far as these conflicts were of a clearly defined class character, and as such instrumentally aggregated (unlike, for example, ethnic or religious conflicts), they lent themselves to the intermediation of a bureaucratic-legal state. Moreover, precisely because the working class was well organized and highly solidaristic, it had the capacity to act strategically – that is, to overcome economism and recognize the dependency of future wages on current investment. Over the past decade or so, the organized working class has undergone a fundamental political reorientation. Having exhausted redistributive strategies of development, the CPM and its unions, as we shall see, have embraced the politics of class compromise. And the logic of that compromise, much as Przeworksi (1985) has described it within the context of developed capitalist economies, entails an explicit bargain in which workers contain their militancy, and employers agree to reinvest. The role of the state in securing and guaranteeing the terms of class cooperation has been critical. To explore the evolution of these synergistic relationships between the state and labour – from securing redistributive reforms to underwriting compromise – I examine first the organized factory sector and then turn to the unorganized (informal) sector.

Militancy and Compromise in the Factory (Organized) Sector

India's industrial-relations system is characterized by a seemingly paradoxical combination of 'state-dominated' and 'involuted' forms of pluralism (Rudolph and Rudolph 1987). On the one hand, a state bent on securing rapid industrial development and maintaining industrial peace from above fashioned legislation that heavily favours 'state controlled compulsory procedures rather than open-ended bargaining among interested parties' (Rudolph and Rudolph 1987: 270). The result is that 'State policy has created a legal and procedural environment that encourages unions to depend for recognition and benefits on government and management more than on their membership and the capacity to represent its interests' (273). On the other hand, trade-union laws that grant equal legal status to any registered union (for which only seven members are required) has fuelled multi-unionism (there were eleven national federations at the last count) and has given strategic power to opportunistic union 'bosses' acting more as brokers – strategically placed between their membership, management and the state – than as organizers. Pervasive government interference coupled with the involution of labour has in effect undermined associational autonomy and favoured the politics of clientalism and cooptation over the politics of class. In the absence of more encompassing forms of association, collective action has been driven by the politics of exclusion.

In contrast to the fragmented character of the national labour movement, the labour movement in Kerala is more broad-based and organiztionally coherent. Its historical formation was largely the work of the Communist Party, which organized unions primarily as instruments of class struggle, giving 'political' unionism the upper hand over trade unionism. Struggles were defined in general, encompassing terms, linking workers in urban and rural sectors in a unified effort to secure political power. And, precisely because the terms of conflict were class-based, the labour movement in Kerala did not become dependent on the bureaucratic and pluralistic framework of Indian industrial relations. Conflicts between labour and management became the object of open struggles and hard bargaining rather than patronage. At the same time, because the state found itself confronted with organized demands that could not be coopted or channelled into the legalism of compulsory adjudication (the CPM-affiliated Centre of Indian Trade Unions or CITU stubbornly rejected binding third-party intervention), intervention took the form of 'facilitating joint consultation and joint regulation', the pillars of collective bargaining (Nair 1994).

The pronounced class character of unionism and a stronger tradition of collective bargaining have checked the spread of opportunistic deal-making and cast labour–management relations in the mould of 'regulated conflict'. Unlike the forms of state corporatism that often characterize the relationship of the state to organized labour in developing countries, unions in Kerala, born of political mobilization, have maintained organizational autonomy. While the Indian state has obfuscated class conflicts (Rudolph and Rudolph 1987), the state in Kerala has given them institutional expression.

This is most significantly reflected in the critical role that Kerala's unique Industrial Relations Committees (IRCs) play in mediating industrial conflicts. These tripartite committees are essentially consultative bodies that have few statutory powers, yet have been instrumental in forging the terms of industry-wide labour–management agreements. Appointed by the government, the committees are constituted of leaders of all the concerned labour federations, representatives from employer associations and officials from the Labour Department. IRCs presently cover nineteen industries, ranging from the capital-intensive petrochemicals industry to more traditional and labour-intensive industries such as coir and cashew production. The actual role and importance of IRCs varies widely across industries. In some the IRC essentially functions as a forum of last resort, whereas in others it formulates, negotiates and oversees industry-wide agreements on wages, work conditions and benefits. In most cases, IRCs were instituted following periods of intense labour–management conflict and were an explicit acknowledgement on the part of state officials of the futility of imposing agreements from above in a climate of highly antagonistic class relations. The overall effect was to give institutional emphasis to voluntarily negotiated settlements over the compulsory adjudication of the Indian industrial-relations system (Nair 1994).

Through the late 1970s high levels of labour militancy and state intervention adversely affected productivity growth and investment. As industrial growth and employment stagnated, it became increasingly clear that militancy was exacting too high a price. When the CPM came to power in 1981, it abandoned its past strategy of using the 'state as an instrument of mass struggle'. The subsequent CPM ministries (1987–91 and 1996–the present) have aggressively courted private capital, restrained the Pary's powerful labour federation (the CITU) and called upon the working class to develop a new 'work culture', the Party's euphemism for labour discipline. Organized labour had come to terms with the inherent limits of redistribution in a sub-national state and recognized the need to compromise with capital. A CITU leader, R. Raghavan Pillai, succinctly identified the dilemma: 'Without increasing investment and production there can be no prosperity. We don't want the redistribution of poverty'.[7]

These compromises, as they have emerged over the past decade, rest on two explicit pillars: the first is labour's strategic 'quiescence', to use Cameron's (1984) term; the second is the self-conscious embrace of increased productivity as the positive-sum basis for coordinating profits and wages.

The quiescence of labour – or, more accurately, its strategic withholding of militancy – is reflected directly in the decline of strike activity as well as in the increase in negotiated long-term agreements. As Table 4.1 shows, on all the key measures of militancy – number of strikes, workers involved and man-days lost – there has been a notable decline since the 1970s. If one moreover excludes the years of the Emergency (1975–76) – during which industrial actions were severely restricted – the yearly average of man-days lost in the 1970s was actually much higher at 1.7 million, making the figure of the 1990s (0.9 million) all the more significant. This decline, it should be emphasized, has taken place against the backdrop of ever higher levels of unionization.[8] The comparative picture is also telling. While throughout the 1970s Kerala had the distinction of ranking only behind West Bengal in total number of man-days lost (M.S. Kumar 1989), the three-year average of 1990–92 places it ninth out of fourteen major states.[9]

Table 4.1   Labour militancy in Kerala

	Strikes	Workers involved	Man-days lost
1971–1980	309	136,386	1,332,562
1980–1990	133	78,845	1,180,325
1990–1996	44	56,738	908,231

Note: Figures represent annual averages.
Source: GOK, Labour Department. *Administration Report of Labour Department* (annual).

Across the board, labour officials, union leaders and industrialists report declining militancy. In a survey of businessmen and representatives of industry associations conducted by the State Planning Board, the vast majority reported a significant improvement in the industrial-relations climate (GOK 1991: 51). S.C.S Menon, the most prominent independent trade-union leader in Kerala and a 42-year veteran of the movement, notes that labour–management relations have been routinized to the point of making the Labour Department's conciliation functions redundant.[10] Because labour has politically and institutionally secured the right and the power to bargain with capital, militancy has lost much of its strategic saliency. As the president of CITU, T.N. Ravindranath, a long-time advocate of the class-struggle line, put it, the 'principle that wages and bonuses have to be negotiated is widely accepted. The phase of militancy is over.'[11] Significantly, the last two governments have gone to great pains to advertise Kerala's 'peaceful' labour front.

The decline in militancy is closely tied to the increasingly common practice of negotiating long term labour–management agreements, which now as a matter of Labour Department policy include bonus schemes linked to productivity. This represents an important departure from past practices. Historically, bonuses have been the most explosive object of industrial conflict in Kerala.[12] In the dominant Marxist anti-capitalist discourse of the trade unions, profits were equated with exploitation, and bonuses became the means through which workers could secure their 'rightful' share of surplus.[13]

To a great extent, the emergence of class compromise has been the work of the CPM. As a highly organized, coherent and class-based political force, the CPM enjoys the strategic capacity to recognize the trade-offs between militancy and growth. A programmatic party has created a programmatic labour movement. Class-based unionism alone, however, does not suffice to explain why workers have forgone militancy and accepted compromise. Even where class cooperation opens up the possibility of a positive-sum game, the coordination of interests must have a sound material and institutional basis if compliance is to be secured.

Organized class struggle produced concrete redistributive results. The outcome of organized class compromise is less certain. Under the conditions of a private property economy, there are no guarantees that future interests will be met (Przeworski 1985: 140). Within the boundaries set by the logic of accumulation, it is however possible to reduce the degree of 'uncertainty' involved in the trade-off between wages and profits. The politically dominant position of labour provides some guarantees. The strength of unions and the extent of protective legislation have secured a high degree of social and political control over the distribution of surplus, thus minimizing the risks involved in making concessions to capital. A levelled playing field reduces the chances of unilateral and opportunistic behaviour, increasing the chances of cooperation. But it does not establish the rules of the game.

This is where the significance of institutional developments comes into play. As it has evolved under the impetus of working-class mobilization, the industrial-relations system in Kerala has facilitated the kind of hard bargaining and the coordination of interests that reduce the uncertainty and hazards of inter-class transactions. When workers are highly organized, represented by competitive unions with strong ties to political parties, their interests are clearly articulated. While the terms and the balance of forces are necessarily antagonistic, they nonetheless lend themselves to instrumental coordination. Such coordination is not, however, given by some larger economic necessity. It must be concretely shaped and managed. It must be institutionally and politically embedded.

The dilemma, as it evolved historically, was to accommodate the pressures and demands that came with class mobilization. Creating the conditions for labour–capital cooperation thus meant giving institutional expression to the class power of labour, creating a playing field on which the threat of militancy, rather than actual militancy, would define labour's bargaining position. The combination of a militant, class-based movement and democratic institutions did just that, though not without setbacks.

As the industrial-relations system matured, moreover, it defined the procedures and norms by which compromises could be developed and ultimately secured. Thus, as the respective positions of labour and capital have become increasingly institutionalized, formal bargaining practices have evolved and become more acceptable to both parties through iteration and the demonstration effect of success. These institutions cannot as such be explained in the functionalist language of 'new institutional economics' but must be seen as the product of concrete historical struggles, from which a particular configuration of social forces has been congealed. The consolidation of an industrial-relations regime based on 'regulated conflict' between aggregated interests has reduced the degree of uncertainty and increased the scope for cooperation. 'In the past', remarked the manager of OEN Industries, Kerala's most successful electronics manufacturer, 'labour would demand impossible bonuses. Management would offer nothing. A strike or lockout would follow. Now negotiations are over a 1 or 2% increase. The total bonus package is well defined and always in the 15–16% range. All these norms have removed items of conflict.'[14]

The state-mediated coordination of interests between labour and capital here closely resembles corporatist arrangements, with an important qualification. In Latin American cases 'corporatist patterns of interest representation … are frequently the consequence of political structures consciously imposed by political elites on civil society' (Stepan 1978: 47). The process in Kerala has been negotiated: it begins with the mobilization of workers and finds expression through, and not outside of, democratic institutions. The state's role in mediating conflicts between capital and labour was not initiated from above, but rather emerged in response to the political imperatives of managing class struggles in a parliamentary setting. This 'democratic' or 'left' variant of corporatism bears an important similarity to European social democracy. The growth strategy undergirding class compromise specifically seeks to build on the comparative advantages in labour productivity and social organization that reside in the democratic welfare state – that is, advanced human capital resources and a highly developed institutional capacity for fostering cooperative labour–management relations.[15]

Organizing the Unorganized Sector

The organized factory sector of the Indian economy is dominated by state and monopoly capital. The material base for coordinating interests is actually quite large. Large-scale economic units, regularized and permanent conditions of work, and a relatively small number of organized actors have facilitated state intervention. Providing a framework for collective action in the unorganized sector (as the informal sector is called in India) has proved far more elusive. Nowhere are the developmental failures of the Indian state in fact more manifest than in the resiliency of this sector of the economy.

Out of a total of 285 million main workers enumerated in India in the 1991 census, only 9.3 per cent were in enterprises classified as organized (all public-sector enterprises and all non-agricultural private enterprises with ten or more workers). Even as a percentage of the non-agricultural workforce, the organized sector accounted for only 28.2 per cent of total employment (the figures for Kerala are roughly the same).[16] In sum, almost three-quarters of the non-agricultural workers in India are either service workers employed on a casual or semi-permanent basis, manufacturing workers employed in small workshops or unregistered factories (sweatshops), or self-employed.

While somewhat arbitrary, the organized/unorganized dichotomy does capture the fundamental distinction of the dualistic character of labour markets in the developing world. The organized sector is characterized by the contractual relations of a class-based social organization of production, closely linked with the development of the modern state. Workers in this sector enjoy legal protections and institutional conditions that are favourable to collective action (which may be of a more or less autonomous character). The organization of production in the unorganized sector, however, is rooted in a configuration of social relations largely beyond the reach of the bureaucratic state and modern political institutions. With large reserves of cheap and untapped labour, workers have little or no capacity for pursuing their collective interests.

Labour relations in the unorganized sector in India are extremely heterogeneous. At one extreme can be found the persistence of extra-economic forms of coercion, as in cases of bonded or attached labour. Even where labour is formally 'free' and has taken the wage form, the inherently asymmetrical social and political relations that condition transactions belie the formally 'contractual' character of exchanges. The spread of the wage form notwithstanding, exchange relations remain fundamentally conditioned by a wide range of acute social vulnerabilities. Working conditions and patterns of recruitment are segmented along caste, gender and regional lines (Mies 1982; Harriss et al. 1990; Singh 1991; Breman 1993). And because of the sheer oversupply of unskilled casual labour, dependent clientalistic patterns prevail, with workers relying on jobbers, recruiters, gang bosses and other intermediaries, often kinsmen, caste mates or co-villagers, for access to labour markets. As Breman notes, 'the immobilizing effect caused by horizontal division is increased by the pressure emanating from the need to invest in vertical dependency relationships' (Breman 1993: 210).

The powerlessness of workers in this sector is matched only by the powerlessness of the state. Rare legislated efforts to improve work conditions or fix minimum wages have been implemented indifferently at best. Out of 1,500,674 establishments covered under the rules framed by the states under the Minimum Wages Act (1948), only 87,103 actually submitted returns as required by law (GOI 1984: 84). The inability of the state to curb exploitative labour practices is nowhere more visible than in the area of child labour. Despite legislated prohibitions, the number of working children in India is estimated at anywhere between 13 and 44 million.[17] The capacity of the Indian economic bureaucracy tightly to control product markets (the infamous licence-permit raj) stands in sharp contrast to its near complete failure to penetrate the labour relations of the unorganized sector, a fact captured quite appropriately in the official usage of the term 'unorganized'.[18] The failure of the state to bridge the gap between the organized and unorganized sectors, and the implications for economic and social development, are now widely recognized.[19] The availability of large reserves of cheap labour is a disincentive to techno-logical innovation. Depressed wages limit the scope for stimulating growth through effective demand. Finally, by reinforcing traditional economic and social inequalities the unorganized sector has stymied the develop-ment of human resources, and hence productivity.

In Kerala the unorganized sector has become something of a mis-nomer. A large segment of workers outside the public sector and outside the registered factory sector are in fact unionized. Over half the state's two million agricultural labourers belong to the CPM-affiliated KSKTU (Kerala State Karshaka Thozhilali Union), the single largest union in the state. Large segments of workers in Kerala's traditional industries, cashew and coir, and its two largest casual labour markets, construction and headload work, have been unionized.[20] In the beedi (traditional cigarettes) industry – the archetypal labour-squeezing, putting-out industry – unions have organized the largest and most successful producer cooperative in the state, with a membership of over 32,000 (Thomas Isaac, Franke and Raghavan 1998). Even mahouts (elephant handlers) have a union. The organizational success of unions in this sector is a direct outgrowth of the broad-based character of Kerala's labour movement. As early as the 1940s, the organizing strategies and demands of a small, but militant core of coir factory workers were quickly extended to coir workers in the rural household sector, other non-factory occupations and agricultural work-ers. Even before Independence, agricultural labourers and other rural workers were demanding the same benefits granted to industrial workers, including security of employment, fixed work days and the right to bargain collectively (Kannan 1992: 9).

Responding to these pressures from below, the state in Kerala has actively intervened in the unorganized sector. Through a series of direct regulatory and institutional reforms, as well as broader welfare measures, the state transformed traditional labour markets and underwrote labour's organizing efforts. The state actively supported unions in building and financing labour cooperatives for toddy tappers, beedi workers, coir-processing workers, cashew-processing workers and handloom weavers (Kannan 1992: 12). Minimum wage committees were appointed first for the coir and cashew industries and then gradually extended to forty-five other industries, including the 'handling and care of elephants' (GOK 1990a). Enforcement remains uneven, but labour-market interventions coupled with the provision of universal welfare entitlements have, piece-meal, created a social wage. Other measures, such as the regulation of mechanization in the coir industry and the prohibition of cottage out-sourcing in the cashew industry, have effectively leveraged labour's bargaining position. Government wage data conclusively show that the income differential between workers in unorganized occupations and the modern factory sector has declined noticeably, particularly since the mid-1970s (Kannan 1990b). Wage gains in one sector are, moreover, quickly trans-mitted to other sectors (Krishnan 1991b), suggesting that increased bar-gaining capacity and solidaristic wage policies have eroded the asymmetries of traditional labour-market boundaries. Finally, social policies have curbed the most egregious labour practices. Universal primary education has practically removed children from the workforce.[21]

Unionization and state intervention have thus fundamentally trans-formed the traditional character of labour relations. Protective social legis-lation and horizontal mobilization have supplanted patron–client and despotic relations of employment with more formal and contractual ones. By its very nature, however, this sector does not readily lend itself to the coordination of conflicting interests. The terms of employment are often semi-permanent or casual, production is decentralized, market fluctuations are pronounced and profit margins narrow. In these conditions of both material and institutional instability, managing and accommodating the demands of a mobilized labour force is necessarily difficult. The economic consequences of labour militancy have in fact been dramatic. Between 1970–71 and 1990–91, growth in the manufacturing sector of the unorgan-ized economy (that is, unregistered factories) averaged a sluggish annual rate of 1.6 per cent, and a number of footloose industries (Oommen 1979) fled to neighbouring states. The militancy of headload workers (unloading and loading of goods) and construction workers is often cited as the most important deterrent to investment in the factory sector (Sankaranarayanan and Bhai 1994). As an editorial entitled '[T]empting the Investor' recently noted, 'the State's labour problem is confined to the unorganized sector (primarily headload workers) and cannot be solved unless their demands – security of tenure, wages, welfare schemes and so on – are met.'[22]

The response of the state has been twofold. The first has been to initiate targeted welfare programmes to provide these casual workers with some degree of security. Since 1987, the state legislature has, with bipartisan support, enacted welfare schemes in all the major unorganized sectors. The second has been to draw on the model of the IRCs in initiating tripartite negotiations and designing new industrial and labour policies.

Coir production, which employs roughly half a million workers in the treatment, spinning and weaving of coconut fibre, is a case in point. Unions have historically opposed mechanization and supported price controls on the supply of coconut husk from which the coir fibre is extracted. In the face of increasing competition from Tamil Nadu and Sri Lanka in the 1980s, the unions, the coir manufacturers and the state agreed in 1990 to an ambitious restructuring plan involving mechanization, price deregulation, extension of the cooperative sector and job re-training. The plan's principle architect has described it as a 'social consensus project'.[23] The accord rests on an explicit compromise: in exchange for their support of phased mechanization the unions have been guaranteed a degree of institutional control (through the cooperative sector) over the modernization process.

The most dramatic example of cooperation between the state and unions in formalizing labour relations and containing militancy comes from the headload sector. More commonly known as 'coolies', headload workers have historically been amongst the most degraded, socially and economically, of all occupational groups.[24] Although physically demanding, the work is unskilled and semi-permanent. These conditions favoured the development of spot markets in labour, with few barriers to entry, although hiring patterns were often on communal or caste lines.

Headload workers first organized in urban markets as part of the larger mobilization of labourers in the 1950s. Local unions successfully established a 'complex system of work sharing, compartmentalization of the labour market, specification of tasks and elaborate wage schedules' (Vijayasankar 1986: 23). The localized character of unions coupled with the absence of a legally sanctioned bargaining framework, however, produced particularly disruptive forms of militancy. Because of fierce inter-union rivalries, coupled with the fact that headload workers in Kerala have a long history of serving as the musclemen (*goondas*, as they are known in India) for political parties, agitations were often violent (often pitting CPM workers against merchants with ties to communal organizations) and extortionate practices not uncommon. Strike actions paralysed large markets, closed down factories and had a disruptive ripple effect on the entire economy. The payoff for headload workers was, however, handsome. Since 1964 real wages have climbed steadily (Vijayasankar 1986). In the mid-1980s, urban headload workers commanded wages that were 75 per cent higher than those of factory workers (Kannan 1992: 17).[25]

Recognizing, as one government official put it, that 'the lack of govern-mental legislative regulation of employment conditions and wage levels was leading to a state of anarchy in the headload labour market all over the state' (Vijayasankar 1986: 120), a CPM-led government acted by legis-lating the Headload Workers Act (1980) and a companion Act, the Kerala Headload Workers (Regulation of Employment and Welfare) Scheme (1983). The scheme is particularly significant because it represents by far the most ambitious effort of its kind in India. Through state intervention and a tripartite corporatist formula, the scheme aims to institutionalize contractual relations of employment in a casual labour market.[26]

The Scheme regulates conditions of work (work hours, carrying loads), strengthens the arbitration role of the Labour Department, establishes a broad range of welfare measures, and, most importantly, creates self-governing local tripartite committees charged with registering, pooling and compensating workers. Constituted in major markets and composed of equal numbers of Labour Department officials, union representatives and merchants, the committees negotiate wages and bonuses for two-year periods and allocate work to union-based labour pools. The imple-mentation of the schemes did at first elicit resistance from some unions. While the pooling system has largely been patterned after the segmented labour markets carved out by the unions, there have been fears that this institutionalization will erode the unions' capacity to enforce entry barriers. Some local union bosses also opposed the formalization of transaction costs because it effectively eliminated their brokerage fees. As one Labour Department official put it, 'With this regulatory system, there is less room for unscrupulous practices.' But the committee system has been aggressively pushed by the labour federations, in particular the CITU.[27] Welfare Board officers readily credit the CITU with having successfully mobilized worker support for the scheme.

In a relatively short period of time the headload sector has progressed from a classic case of an informal, unorganized spot market in labour, embedded in patron–client networks, to an open, competitive but con-flictual and disorganized exchange between local power groups, to a formalized and bureaucratized exchange relation governed by tripartite corporatist institutions. In the absence of institutional and legal moor-ings, and rooted as it was in local conditions, militancy originally took a particularly disruptive form. With labour enjoying strategic control over the labour process and capital having no exit option, the returns on militancy were high. Under these conditions of unbounded conflict, the logic of collective action exacted high social and economic costs. This ultimately necessitated the intervention of the state, which through legis-lative and administrative reforms secured an institutional basis for formal contractual relations. State action was facilitated by the support of the CPM, which was eager to bring rogue local unions into line.

Formalization and bureaucratization have allowed for the institutionalization of labour gains while reducing externalities. Transaction costs have been reduced. Payoffs to intermediaries, downtime resulting from disputes, and the costs of negotiation have been replaced by a relatively streamlined administrative system. Because the scheme is entirely self-financing (all administrative costs are covered by levies) the state exchequer is spared further strain. And the forced savings and deferred wages of the welfare fund guarantee long-term welfare benefits generally reserved for the organized sector.

State intervention has thus helped secure collective goods that were beyond the logic of the previous system of labour relations. But the rationalization of the headload sector does not simply follow from the penetration of a modern bureaucratic state. It was made possible by mobilization from below. The pooling system through which workloads are allocated is thus little more than an administrative revamping of the market barriers the unions had secured.

Conclusion

The 'synergy' of state and class mobilization in Kerala has produced two forms of social capital. The first underwrote the provision of redistributive goods; the second facilitated class coordination. Mobilization along class lines and democratic institutions triggered a 'virtuous cycle' of collective action. Under the leadership of a Communist Party that was committed to building a broad-based coalition of lower-class groups, urban workers and the rural poor agitated, built associations and won elections. The instrumental and universalistic character of the movements' demands invited effective state intervention. The mobilizational resources of lower-class groups combined with the legal and bureaucratic capacity of the state successfully to transform the institutions and property relations of a traditional, vertically organized social structure. With this came the 'deepening' of democratic structures (O'Donnell 1993), as the levelling of social forces (in particular the demise of traditional rural elites) saw representation and engagement replace patronage and dependency. The degree to which state–society interactions promoted the expansion of 'public legality' and associationalism is most dramatically illustrated by the successful mobilization of the unorganized sector. The most visible product of this synergy between a society mobilized along class lines and a democratically accountable state has been the efficient and comprehensive provision of social services and the development of human capital resources.

The 'embedded autonomy' (Evans 1995) of the state, however conducive to social development and redistributive reforms, was by its very nature antithetical to the forces of the market in a dependent economy. Financial capital is mobile; social capital is not. The labour movement was faced with the vexing dilemma that too much collective action in an economy governed by private investment is a negative-sum game.

The decline of militancy and the emergence of class compromises, however, suggest that the labour movement has come to terms with the limits of militancy. In the face of severe economic crises social actors in a poorly institutionalized democracy will resort to disaggregated strategies and seek to 'privatize' the state, making the formulation and pursuit of long-term collective goals all the more difficult (O'Donnell 1993). In India, the increasing fragmentation of the polity, the much discussed 'deinstitutionalization' of the Congress Party and the resurgence of electoral alliances rooted in parochial loyalties, appears to be a case in point. In Kerala, the disciplined and programmatic character of the Party, rooted as it is in the solidaristic politics of class, has allowed for a more strategic and aggregated response to the challenge of reconciling redistribution with growth. In the factory sector, organized labour has embraced increased productivity as the basis for a positive-sum coordination of class interests. In the unorganized sector, the organizational capacity of unions has been combined with bureaucratic intervention to formalize conditions of work in an effort to stabilize labour relations and provide a more secure investment climate.

The rules of the game that facilitated such strategic actions are a product of the state's relationship to organized social forces. State actions gave institutional expression to the interests of organized labour, facilitating what Cohen and Rogers call an 'artful democratic politics of secondary associations' in which 'public powers are used to encourage less factionalizing forms of secondary associations' (1992: 395). Specifically, this is reflected in the extent to which the industrial-relations system in Kerala favours collective bargaining between organized interest groups and tripartite mediations over the 'involuted pluralism' and compulsory adjudication of the national labour scene. But how has the interaction of the state with organized working-class interests specifically contributed to increasing the likelihood of positive-sum forms of class cooperation?

First, this interaction has created well-defined interlocutors with whom the state can formulate and negotiate policy initiatives. Second, in its welfare capacity the state has created the material basis for class compromise by providing basic public goods and social protection to the most vulnerable sections of society. Third, a wide range of state institutions – pension funds, welfare boards, labour courts, IRCs, minimum-wage committees and so on – have created both the distributional mechanisms and the formally defined and legally enforced procedures through which conflicting interests can be mediated. The cycle of iterated negotiations between these groups has made the interdependence of interests more transparent, and outcomes less uncertain. Overall, this has increased the possibilities for class cooperation. Whether or not this will secure future economic growth remains an open question, particularly in light of Kerala's dependence on both the national and the world economy. Nonetheless, what is certain is that the synergy between working-class mobilization and state capacity has directly contributed to building the political and institutional foundations most likely to 'manage' effectively the contradictions of democratic capitalist development.

Notes

1. For a full elaboration of this argument, see Heller (1999).
2. In 1992–93, per-capita expenditures on health and education in Kerala were 39 per cent and 44 per cent higher than the average for all states (GOK 1998b: 59).
3. Jeffrey notes that as early as the 1950s 'Education was a commodity that governments could take credit for distributing – or be blamed for withholding' (1992: 55).
4. The power of Communist unions in the rural sector is virtually unchallenged. In the industrial sector, the CPM-affiliated communist labour federation, the Centre of Indian Trade Unions (CITU), is the largest (415,000) and most disciplined in the state. The Congress-affiliated Indian National Trade Union Conference (INTUC) is smaller and more loosely structured. Nonetheless, it is present in most large factories, and, as one Party leader noted, 'because of the influence of the CITU, only in Kerala is the INTUC a 'front organization for the Congress' (Interview, A.C. Jose, 7 July 1992, Ernaukulam).
5. The classic statement of this theory if of course Huntington's (1968). Kohli (1987) has given this argument new life and a new twist by arguing that the success of the CPM's attack on poverty in West Bengal is a function of regime characteristics – its organizational coherence and its long tenure in power (since 1977).
6. For a comprehensive discussion, see *EPW* (1990a and 1990b).
7. Interview, 3 April 1992, Trivandrum.
8. Between 1975–76 and 1991, the number of registered unions increased from 4,491 to 7,998 (GOK, Labour Department Administration Reports).
9. Calculated from CMIE, Basic Statistics, vol. 2 (1993: Table 8.10).
10. Interview, 12 November 1992, Ernakulam.
11. Interview, 22 November 1992, Ernakulam.
12. In 1962–63 out of 141 work stoppages, 121 were precipitated by the bonus issue (Nair 1973: 85).
13. As one industrialist put it, 'unions didn't understand that there is a profit–wages nexus. Profits were seen as the concern of management.'
14. Interview, 19 November 1992, Ernakulam.
15. It is too early to tell if class compromise will successfully underwrite sustained accumulation. A poorly developed industrial base, the geographical concentration of national capital in historical growth centres, and lingering perceptions of Kerala

as a bastion of labour militancy present formidable barriers. There are, however, some positive indications. In his analysis of total factor productivity in Kerala's registered factory sector between 1976 and 1987, Arun (1992) found a growth rate of 7.11 per cent that was significantly higher than the national figure of 3.9 per cent. And after a two-decade long drought of private investments, the five years 1993–1997 saw the gap between Kerala and the national levels of per-capita investment close dramatically (CMIE 1997).

16. Calculated from CMIE (1993: Tables 9.5 and 9.6).

17. The lower figure is from the 1981 census; the higher from a Labour Ministry study that included children paid in kind as well as in cash (Weiner 1991: 21).

18. Breman actually makes the claim that the informal sector has persisted *because* of state intervention. 'Under government surveillance, unfree labour and capitalist production relations are quite compatible one with the other' (Breman 1993: 189).

19. Drawing on CSO National Accounts Statistics, Abhijit Sen (1991) has calculated that income per worker in India in 1984–85 (in 1970 prices) in the unorganized sector was Rs. 1,324, compared to Rs. 6,300 in the organized (private) sector. The gap, moreover, has been steadily increasing with unorganized wages falling from 26.6 per cent of organized wages in 1960–61 to 21.0 per cent in 1984–85 (1991: Table 3). A detailed survey of sixteen occupations in Bombay, Deshpande found that factory workers earned Rs. 477 per month compared to Rs. 280 for small-sector workers and Rs. 181 for casual (unorganized) workers (1983: 26).

20. There are no reliable official data on levels of unionization in this sector (only unions in the organized sector submit official returns). There is general agreement that Kerala is the only state in India where a sizeable section of workers in this sector have been unionized (Singh 1991; Kannan 1992). Figures obtained from the CITU for the district of Trivandrum do, however, provide a rough measure. Although nominally an industrial trade-union federation, over 80 per cent of registered members were in the unorganized sector. Out of a total of 63,031 members, almost two-thirds were headload, construction or coir workers.

21. The retention rate in primary schools – the percentage of children having entered primary school who complete the fifth grade – is 82 per cent in Kerala as against 26 per cent for India (Weiner 1991: 174).

22. *Indian Express* (Cochin Edition), 22 September 1992.

23. Interview with Thomas Isaac, Chairman of the Task Force on the Coir Industry, 10 November 1992, Trivandrum.

24. The use of the term 'headload worker', *chumattu thozhilali*, is itself an explicit rejection of the low social status associated with the term 'coolie'.

25. While wages in the rural sector are not as high, they are nonetheless closely linked to urban rates (Krishnan 1991b).

26. The scheme directly addresses the principal demand of workers in the unorganized sector. In the words of one Party official: 'As rightly characterized by the headload workers movement a worker in the informal sector is a "Nathan Illatha Thozhilali" i.e. a worker without a master or a citizen disowned by the society. This movement had declared its primary objective to be to discover or identify a master for the headload worker' (K. Vijayachandran, interview, 6 July 1992, Ernakulam).

27. In interviews a number of CITU officials candidly acknowledged that the scheme was a means to tame its affiliated local unions, which had become 'unruly' and 'irresponsible'.

5

Kerala's Development Achievements and their Replicability

V.K. Ramachandran

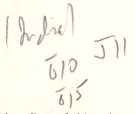

The question that the editor of this volume has asked me to address in this chapter is: Is it possible to replicate the development achievements of Kerala in other states? I shall attempt to address this question by first describing the specific development achievements of Kerala that socially concerned people should seek to replicate. Second, I shall attempt to reformulate the question I was asked to address. Third, I shall describe the socioeconomic and political movements and transformations with which Kerala's major development achievements are associated. Finally, I shall discuss the relevance of these changes to the larger Indian situation.[1]

Development Achievements of Kerala

Health and demographic change

There has been a progressive transformation of health and demographic conditions in Kerala that is uncharacteristic of so-called less-developed societies. In this regard the state is far ahead of India (see Table 5.1). Kerala has been described as a unique case among developing states, a society where the 'health and demographic transitions have been achieved within a single generation' – that is, after the formation of Kerala State (Krishnan 1991a: 1). Fertility and birth rates have declined; the infant mortality rate, the mortality rate among children below the age of five years, and the death rate have all declined; life expectancy at birth has risen; and the ratio of men to women in the population is characteristic of a society where there is no systematic bias against the survival of girls and women. Following Krishnan (1991a), four indicators are taken here

Table 5.1 Selected demographic indicators, India and Kerala, 1994

	Total		Rural		Urban	
	India	Kerala	India	Kerala	India	Kerala
Female age at effective marriage (years)	19.4	22.3	19.1	22.3	20.7	22.3
Crude birth rate (per 1,000 pop.)	28.7	17.4	30.5	17.3	23.1	18.0
Change in average birth rate, 1987–89 to 1992–94 (%)	–8.0	–15.7	–7.3	–15.1	–11.4	–16.5
General fertility rate (live births per 1,000 women, 15–49 years)	118.3	60.2	128.6	59.9	89.7	61.2
Change in fertility rate, 1987–89 to 1992–94 (%)	–9.7	–17.3	n/a	n/a	n/a	n/a
Live births in institution or attended by qualified medical personnel (as % of live births)	50.0	98.1	43.6	97.9	88.5	98.8
Crude death rate (per 1,000 pop.)	9.3	6.1	10.1	5.9	6.7	6.4
Infant mortality rate (per 1,000 live births)	74.0	16.0	80.0	16.0	52.0	14.0
Estimated child death rate, age group 0–4 years	23.9	3.4	26.1	3.2	15.7	4.1

Source: Sample Registration System (1997).

as representing the outcomes of the health and demographic transitions in Kerala: life expectancy at birth, the infant mortality rate, and the birth and death rates.[2]

One of the most important indicators of Kerala's health achievements is high life expectancy at birth (Table 5.2). Life expectancy at birth in Kerala is higher than the levels achieved by those developing countries with 'high human development', as classified in the *Human Development Report 1998* (UNDP 1998: 148). A man in Kerala can expect to live to the age of 69, or ten years longer than the average Indian man; a woman in Kerala can expect to live to the age of 74, or fifteen years longer than the average Indian woman.

The birth rate in Kerala is also much lower than the birth rate for all of India (see Table 5.3). It has been so for the whole period covered by our data (although the difference was marginal in the 1940s); the gap

Table 5.2 Life expectancy at birth, Kerala and India (years)

	Period	Males		Females	
		Kerala	India	Kerala	India
1	1951–61	44.3	35.5	45.3	35.7
2	1961–71	54.1	43.2	57.4	43.5
3	1971–81	60.6	49.8	62.6	49.3
4	1971–75	60.5	49.7	63.0	48.3
5	1976–80	63.5	51.7	67.4	51.8
6	1981–85	65.2	54.5	71.5	54.9
7	1986–88	67.5	56.0	73.0	56.5
8	1990–92	68.8	59.0	74.4	59.4

Sources: Rows 1–3: Census of India, cited in Zachariah et al. (1992: ch. 3, Table 3); rows 4–7: Sample Registration System, cited in ibid.; row 8: Drèze and Sen (1995: Statistical Appendix, based on Sample Registration System data).

between the Kerala figure and the all-India figure was greater at the end-point in the time-series (1994) than at any time in the past. The decline in the birth rate and the general fertility rate in Kerala continued to be steeper than in India as a whole in the most recent period for which we have data, 1987–89 to 1992–94 (Table 5.1). Kerala's low birth rate is associated with comparatively high rates of birth control. Low fertility rates in Kerala are also associated with a higher age at effective marriage among women in Kerala than elsewhere. The all-India average, which was 19.4 years in 1981, was lower than the Kerala average, 22.3 years (Table 5.1).[3] The average age of a woman at the time of the birth of her first child is also higher in Kerala than in any other state (National Family Health Survey 1995a and 1995b; Kannan et al. 1991: 87).

Improved child health and higher levels of education, particularly female education, are among the most important reasons for Kerala's low and declining birth rate and the general acceptance of a small family norm.[4] Caldwell and Caldwell (1985) conclude that parental education has a greater influence than income on fertility.

The death rate in Kerala has declined steadily, and more rapidly than the Indian average (Table 5.4). So has the infant mortality rate (Table 5.5). The infant mortality rate in Kerala in 1994, 16 per 1,000 in rural areas and 14 per 1,000 in urban areas, placed Kerala higher than the average for developing countries with 'high human development', among

Table 5.3 Birth rates, Kerala and India (per 1,000 pop.)

Period	Kerala	India
1951–60	38.9	41.7
1970	31.6	36.8
1974	26.5	34.5
1977–79	25.7	33.1
1981–83	25.6	33.8
1983–85	23.7	33.6
1985–87	21.5	32.6
1987–89	20.7	31.5
1989–91	19.4	30.1
1990–92	18.5	29.5
1994	17.4	28.7

Sources: Krishnan (1976: Table 1); CMIE (1991: Table 2.11); Sample Registration Bulletin (January 1994: Table 11); Sample Registration System (1997).

which the average rate of infant mortality was 29 per 1,000 in 1996 (UNDP 1998: 156). The decline in the infant mortality rate in Kerala has been associated with important improvements in pre-natal and post-natal health care and higher levels of institutional child birth. Survey data from the Zachariah et al. (1992) study showed that for groups of people among whom there was immunization, hospitalization and ante-natal and post-natal care, infant mortality rates of 6 to 7 per 1,000 were achieved in Kerala.

The proportion of infants and children who were vaccinated was much higher in Kerala than in India; immunization coverage improved substantially in the 1980s, and all the data point to a notable improvement in this respect in the last years of the 1980s.[5] A noteworthy feature of studies of immunization of children in Kerala was that incomes were not the major determinant of immunization.

Certain features of female empowerment in Kerala are vital to its achievements in respect of child health and health conditions in general; their importance really cannot be overemphasized.[6] Female literacy and girls' schooling are, of course, critical factors in Kerala's performance in this sphere. Other factors relating to female empowerment, and relevant to Kerala's better performance in child and general health than elsewhere, that have been discussed in the literature include: a higher average age at marriage, higher rates of female employment in the organized

Table 5.4   Death rates, Kerala and India (per 1,000)

Period	Kerala	India
1951–60	16.0	23.0
1961–70	11.0	18.0
1971–75	8.6	15.5
1976–80	7.3	13.9
1981–83	6.6	12.1
1983–85	6.5	12.1
1985–87	6.2	11.3
1987–89	6.2	10.7
1989–91	6.0	9.9
1990–92	6.1	9.8
1994	6.1	9.3

Sources: Nag (1983: Table 1); Zachariah et. al. (1992: ch. 3, Table 2); Sample Registration Bulletin (January 1994: Table 11); Sample Registration System (1997).

Table 5.5   Infant mortality rates, Kerala and India (per 1,000 live births)

	Kerala	India		Kerala	India
1951–60	120	140	1982	30	105
1961–70	66	114	1983	33	105
1971	58	129	1984	29	104
1972	63	139	1985	31	97
1973	58	134	1986	27	96
1974	54	126	1987	28	95
1975	54	140	1988	28	94
1976	56	129	1989	22	91
1977	47	130	1990	17	80
1978	42	127	1991	16	80
1979	43	120	1992	17	79
1980	40	114	1994	16	74
1981	37	110			

Sources: 1951–60 to 1961–70: computed from Census of India volumes in Bhattacharjee and Shastri (1976), cited in Nag (1983: Table 4); 1971 to 1990: Sample Registration System, various issues, cited in Zachariah et al. (1992: ch. 3, Table 1); 1991 and 1992: Sample Registration Bulletin (January 1994: Table 8); Sample Registration System (1997).

sector, higher levels of health awareness and information among women, and of maternal utilization of the health system, and the decision-making role of women in Kerala households. Of great importance also are social and cultural attitudes towards female survival: primary-data-based studies in Kerala emphasize the absence of parental discrimination in providing health care to boys and girls.[7]

Food distribution

Child nutrition in Kerala is substantially better than in the rest of India, as results from the National Family Health Survey show (see Table 5.6). The results from surveys conducted in seven states, including Kerala, by the National Nutrition Bureau in the 1970s and late 1980s show that Kerala progressed in respect of nutrition over this period and that nutritional outcomes in Kerala were superior to the outcomes in all seven states together (Ramachandran 1997).[8]

The public food-distribution system in Kerala, the best among India's states, gives basic nutritional support to the people of the state. There is a two-tier system of public distribution of essential commodities. About 90 per cent of the population of the state hold ration cards (which entitle households to buy subsidized rice, wheat, sugar, cooking oil and kerosene); the average amount of foodgrain bought from ration shops by an individual in Kerala was 69.6 kg in 1991 (Kannan 1993). By way of comparison, the annual per-capita offtake from the public food-distribution system in Uttar Pradesh and Bihar in 1993–94 was 4.3 kg and 5.6 kg, respectively (Swaminathan 1999).

Table 5.6   Children under 4 years classified as severely malnourished, India and Kerala, 1992–93

Region	Children below 3 standard-deviation level (%)				
	Weight for age		Height for age	
	boys	girls	boys	girls
India	20.2	21.0	28.4	29.4
Kerala	5.4	6.9	1.0	1.5

Source: National Family Health Survey (1995a and 1995b).

Literacy and education

A cardinal feature of culture and society in Kerala and of Kerala's political and economic development is the high proportion of literate and educated persons in the population. Literacy – and, in particular, female literacy – is an essential (and is often regarded as *the* essential) facilitator of Kerala's achievements in the spheres of health and demographic change. Literacy is a foundational feature of Kerala's political culture, crucial in the creation of public opinion and essential to the individual and political rights that are so conspicuous a feature of social and political life in Kerala.

With regard to the proportions of persons in the population who are literate, Kerala and the rest of India are in different leagues (see Table 5.7). National Sample Survey data from the 42nd Round (1986–87) on age-specific literacy show very high rates of literacy in the younger age groups, over 97 per cent each among males and females in each age group between 6 years and 24 years, in rural areas and urban areas. In every age group below 34, even the *rural female* literacy rate in Kerala is higher than the *urban male* literacy rate in India as a whole (Table 5.8).[9] As can be expected, the number of years of schooling of people in Kerala was higher than in the rest of the country (Table 5.9). According to data from the Census of India 1991, child labour was lower in Kerala than in any other state (see Table 5.10).[10]

Owing to the prevalent levels of literacy, the dissemination of information by means of the written word goes much deeper in Kerala than elsewhere in India; this has important implications for the quality and depth of public opinion, and of participatory democracy in the state.[11]

Table 5.7 Literate persons in the population aged 7 years and above, India and Kerala, 1997 (%)

| | Urban | | Rural | | Combined | |
	male	female	male	female	male	female
India	88	72	68	43	73	50
Kerala	96	90	96	90	96	90

Source: National Sample Survey, 53rd round, January to December 1997.

Table 5.8 Literate persons in the population, India and Kerala, 1986–87 (%)

Age group	Urban				Rural			
	male		female		male		female	
	India	Kerala	India	Kerala	India	Kerala	India	Kerala
6–11	64.7	97.4	48.9	97.4	81.5	97.0	77.3	97.9
12–14	75.3	99.5	54.5	99.1	89.5	98.6	81.7	99.7
15–24	69.3	98.4	45.3	97.2	88.6	99.1	76.0	97.2
25–34	60.6	96.1	32.5	91.3	86.2	98.8	66.4	95.2
35–44	54.7	92.1	24.9	80.9	81.2	97.8	57.6	86.5
45–59	46.0	86.7	18.7	69.3	76.0	92.5	47.8	78.5
60+	38.5	81.0	14.9	53.1	71.2	90.5	33.9	70.2
All	52.4	84.1	31.6	79.6	74.0	88.7	59.0	84.8

Source: National Sample Survey (1993).

Table 5.9 Median years of schooling, India and Kerala, 1992–93

Age group	Urban				Rural			
	male		female		male		female	
	India	Kerala	India	Kerala	India	Kerala	India	Kerala
6–9	1.8	2.2	1.8	2.4	1.2	2.2	0.0	2.3
10–14	5.7	6.1	5.5	6.5	4.5	6.3	2.7	6.3
15–19	9.4	9.4	9.1	9.7	7.8	9.4	0.0	9.5
20–24	10.1	9.4	8.6	9.8	7.9	9.4	0.0	9.4
25–29	10.0	9.4	7.8	9.4	5.9	9.1	0.0	8.8
30–34	10.1	9.3	7.1	9.0	5.0	8.4	0.0	7.4
35–39	10.0	8.3	5.9	8.3	4.6	7.4	0.0	5.6
40–44	10.0	8.9	5.1	7.1	4.1	7.4	0.0	5.4
45–49	9.4	8.1	4.2	5.3	3.4	5.9	0.0	4.5
50+	7.0	5.8	0.0	3.9	0.0	4.5	0.0	2.6
Total	7.7	7.7	5.0	7.2	3.6	6.7	0.0	6.1

Source: National Family Health Survey (1995 a and b).

Table 5.10 Working children as a proportion of all children, different states, union territories and India, 1991 (%)

	All children	Boys	Girls
Kerala	**0.48**	**0.54**	**0.42**
Andaman and Nicobar Islands	1.09	1.65	0.50
Delhi	1.24	2.05	0.33
Goa	1.65	1.75	1.54
Haryana	2.07	3.00	0.98
Himachal Pradesh	2.48	2.17	2.80
Punjab	2.82	4.90	0.47
Manipur	3.04	2.65	3.44
Uttar Pradesh	3.09	4.62	1.33
Bihar	3.37	4.68	1.89
West Bengal	3.47	5.07	1.80
Mizoram	3.66	3.52	3.80
Gujarat	3.75	4.74	2.68
Orissa	4.22	5.61	2.80
Maharashtra	4.32	4.14	4.52
India	**4.33**	**5.18**	**3.40**
Assam	4.33	6.25	2.33
Tamil Nadu	4.37	4.43	4.30
Nagaland	5.17	4.75	5.62
Madhya Pradesh	5.96	6.62	5.25
Meghalaya	6.56	7.61	5.49
Karnataka	7.38	8.24	6.51
Dadra and Nagar Haveli	8.01	7.35	8.70
Andhra Pradesh	9.23	9.10	9.37

Source: Census of India 1991.

Can Kerala's Achievements be Replicated?

The case of Kerala has attracted wide attention because, first, its achievements in respect of basic educational, health and demographic achievements are far ahead of the rest of India. Second, it is noteworthy that the improvement in the well-being of people in Kerala occurred despite low incomes. When we speak of replicating Kerala's development experience, the reference is clearly to the first feature of Kerala's economy; there could be no wish to reproduce the combination of relatively high levels of 'human development' and low incomes, high unemployment and low industrial production and agricultural productivity. The question: Can Kerala's health, demographic and educational conditions be replicated? is not very interesting either – after all, there are many societies that have achieved these levels and better.

The question that I shall attempt to answer in this chapter is, I believe, a more interesting one: At present levels of income, can public action ensure that the people of all states of India are provided with educational, health and demographic achievements similar to those attained at present by the people of Kerala? My answer is yes, provided certain necessary social transformations occur. The next two sections deal with the means by which change was brought about in Kerala and with development issues in India.

Socioeconomic and Political Contexts

The achievements of the people of Kerala are the result of major social, economic and political transformations. These changes have roots in Kerala's history, but they were also, in an important sense, achievements of public action in post-1957 Kerala. They were possible because there was mass literacy, because agrarian relations were transformed, because there were important changes in the conditions of unfreedom of the people of the oppressed castes, because of enlightened social attitudes towards girls' and women's survival and education, and because of the public policy interventions of governments in Kerala. All of these conditions are replicable.

This section will deal with certain key features of change: land reform, movements against caste oppression, education, the role of the left in Kerala, women's agency and the role of governments (for a more comprehensive historical review, see Ramachandran 1997).

Land reform

The progressive transformation of agrarian relations is intrinsically important, since such transformation undermines pre-capitalist relations of unfreedom in the countryside. It is important instrumentally as well: societies dominated by pre-capitalist landlordism suppress the forces of production in rural society, and they have little stake in improving the conditions of health and education of the masses of their people. In a recent study published by the Inter-American Development Bank, a group of scholars present the results of a comparative study of two sets of countries. They took one group of small and resource-rich countries that were distinctly less developed in the middle of the last century but that are at the top of the table today (the Nordic countries: Denmark, Norway, Sweden and Finland) and compared them with four medium-sized Latin American countries (Colombia, Ecuador, Chile and Uruguay). 'It is no surprise', a reviewer of this research writes, 'that two points emerge strongly that are just what also emerge from East Asian comparisons: the role of early agrarian reform … and the role of education'.[12] The significance of education and changes in archaic agrarian relations are lessons from Kerala's experience as well.

A foundational feature of Kerala's development experience, and of the state's social and economic progress, is the transformation of agrarian relations. The transformation brought about by the people of Kerala after independence was more radical than in any other state of India. The history of this change is a history of public action – which took the form of mass struggle and of legislative action – against some of the most complex, exploitative and oppressive rural social formations in the country.[13]

Landlordism dominated social and economic arrangements in villages throughout Kerala; there were also important differences between regions in agrarian relations and land tenures, associated, *inter alia*, with differences in administration, administrative policy and the nature of government, and in the development of the productive forces (which includes differences in farming practices, irrigation, land use and land colonization and the development of agricultural entrepreneurship). Land reform, or passing and implementing new laws to alter or abolish old land tenures and to create new ones was crucial to the transformation of agrarian relations in Kerala. The first Communist government represented a turning point in that transformation; a few days after it took office in 1957, the legislative process for land reform began.

Land reform in Kerala had three major components.[14] The first involved that burdensome, complex and rampant affliction of Kerala agriculture, tenancy. Tenancy legislation had four main features. First, it sought to provide security of tenure to tenants. It is noteworthy that action on this front began less than a week after the Namboodiripad government came into power. By an ordinance of 11 April 1957 (the government was formed on 5 April), evictions were prohibited and land holdings restored to tenants who were evicted after the formation of the state of Kerala. Second, arrears of rent were cancelled. Third, the rights of *janmi* landlords and intermediaries on tenanted land were taken over by the government. Where land rights were vested in the government, all rent payments were stopped. Fourthly, tenancy legislation sought to give land to the tiller.

The second main component of land reform involved homestead land (*kudikidappu*) occupied by the rural poor. Occupants of such land were to be given ownership rights. Government subsidized half the purchase price, and the rest was due in instalments. There were subsidiary provisions in respect of *kudikidappu* regarding, first, security of tenure; second, making occupancy rights heritable; third, discharging arrears of rent; and, fourth, rent control.

The third component of land reform concerned the imposition of limits on land ownership and the distribution of land identified as surplus to the landless. The land ceiling in Kerala, which was imposed on household land-holdings, varied with the size of household; it did not exceed 25 standard acres.

Put very briefly, the implementation of the first two sets of land reforms (concerned with tenancy and homestead land) was relatively successful; the implementation of reforms relating to the identification of land above the ceiling and its redistribution was not. Using official data, Radhakrishnan reported that the first set of reforms resulted in the transfer of 1,970,000 acres to 1,270,000 households; the second set of reforms resulted in the transfer of 20,000 acres of homestead land to 270,000 households; and the third led to the transfer of 50,000 acres to 90,000 households (Radhakrishnan 1989: 185).

Two important studies provide village-level information on the implementation of land reform. Of Kodakkad in north Malabar, Radhakrishnan writes that the 'land system now is strikingly different from … the pre-reforms period,' and that 'the land system is no longer characterized by the extreme concentration of land in a single group'. He continues that the old forms of class–caste correspondence in land ownership in the village no longer exist (Radhakrishnan 1989: 229). In Nadur, a village in central Kerala, 'the land reform redistributed substantial amounts of land from the biggest owners to small holders and the landless'. Land reform 'reduced both land and income inequality', and the 'land reform undermined the material basis of caste and class inequality' (Franke 1996: 148).[15]

The Kerala Agricultural Workers' Act came into effect on 2 October 1975. It has been described as a trade-union act for agricultural workers, and is the only one of its kind in the country. Legislation for unemployment insurance for agricultural workers was enacted in 1980–81 and agricultural labour pensions were started in 1982. Franke and Chasin calculated that, at 1986 prices, the pension was enough to buy rice for an adult for about ten days in a month (Franke and Chasin 1992).

The gains of land reform should not, of course, be exaggerated. The scope of land reforms in any single region is circumscribed by the class character of the Indian state and the government in power in New Delhi.

Land reform in Kerala did not transfer agrarian power to agricultural labourers and poor peasants, and it did not end capitalist landlordism.[16] It did not lead to the establishment of production cooperatives or collectives or to other post-capitalist forms of agrarian production organization (or, for that matter, to the creation of a panchayat system as in West Bengal).[17] Land reform in Kerala was not followed by substantial increases in crop production, as was the case in West Bengal; nor were there substantial increases in rural employment.

Despite these limitations, the achievements of land reform in Kerala are far from negligible. Land reform abolished statutory landlordism and ended the *janmi* system. It reduced the concentration of ownership of land holdings. It broke the back of Namboodiri landlordism and weakened Nayar landlordism. It protected tenants, and ended systems of rack-renting and those illegal exactions from the poor that characterized the old system. It provided house sites to tens of thousands of families. Further, agricultural workers' wage struggles and the achievements of the people in gaining agricultural and house-site land contributed to raising rural daily wage rates in Kerala significantly,[18] and to the introduction of social security schemes for agricultural labourers.[19]

Social reform movements

In Kerala, as elsewhere in India, the caste system was an enemy of social progress. The traditional caste system in Kerala had special features, as did traditional systems of marriage, inheritance and succession.[20]

Some of the worst forms of untouchability in the country were practised in Kerala, and the persecution of people of the oppressed castes took savage forms. The rules of the caste system also included complex rules on distance pollution ('unapproachability') and included, against some castes, rules of 'unseeability'. The people of the 'slave castes' (for instance, the Pulayar, Parayar and Cherumar castes) and the people of the aboriginal tribes of Kerala, as well as those born into the Ezhava (or Thiyya in north Kerala) caste did not have access to public places, temples, bathing tanks, public paths and roads and educational institutions. The employment of people born into these castes in occupations outside their traditional caste callings was also prohibited. Persons of oppressed castes were not permitted to wear clean clothes, or cloth other than coarse cloth, nor any clothes at all above the waist; they were not permitted to keep milch cattle or use the services of oil presses, to use metal pots and pans, or to carry umbrellas or wear slippers on their feet. They were not permitted to take Sanskrit given names, and there were rules that governed the words that could be used in conversation with persons of status-superior castes: for example, the use of the first-person singular was not permitted (it had to be 'this slave' or 'this inferior'); a person of an oppressed caste could not refer to 'my money' but to 'copper'.[21]

There were caste-based movements among many castes in Kerala. Among the most well known of these were the reform movements among the people of the Ezhava caste and the Pulaya caste and among Nayars and Namboodiris. The Nadars of south Travancore – particularly in Kanniyakumari and Tirunelveli – were also organized into a caste-based movement; the centre of activity and organization of the Nadar caste organization was in Tamil Nadu. Something of the heterogeneity of the caste-based reform movements is apparent even from this list, which consists of oppressed castes as well as oppressor castes. Caste movements were active in the movement for social reform and for changes in social practices, particularly the practice of untouchability; they also made efforts to reform internal caste rules and to alter, by means of state intervention through legislation, inheritance laws and rules of family organization.

The Ezhava social reform movement of the late nineteenth and early twentieth centuries was one of the most important caste-based social reform movements of the modern period in India.[22] It was, one scholar writes, 'the most radical aspect of the social awakening that accompanied the rise of capitalism [in Travancore] and was the most sweeping mass movement that Travancore had known' (Thomas Isaac 1985). The movement's early leaders – persons such as Sree Narayana Guru, Kumaran Asan, Dr Palpu – and the chief caste organization of the Ezhava people, the Sree Narayana Dharma Paripalana Yogam or SNDP Yogam, have been described as the first organizers and inspirers of the mass democratic movement of cultivating peasants and the landless in Kerala (Namboodiri-pad 1984: 99). Although the Ezhava social reform movement became widespread, and was active in Malabar and Cochin, its origins were in Travancore, as was its real organizational strength.

An outstanding, perhaps even unique, feature of the Malayalam renaissance of the nineteenth and early twentieth centuries was that people from a caste that was considered outcaste and whose members were considered untouchable by caste Hindus – that is, people of the Ezhava caste – played a distinguished part in the renaissance.[23] Kumaran Asan, educated in Calcutta, was the first secretary of the SNDP Yogam, and was the first lyrical poet in modern Malayalam.

Political and ideological trends within the Ezhava social reform movement and the relationship between this movement on the one hand and the workers' movement on the other was discussed in a few contributions to the scholarly literature.[24] In the 1930s and 1940s, social and economic differentiation within the caste led to a clear demarcation of conservative and radical trends in the social reform movement (Thomas Isaac and Tharakan 1986). With the economic advance of an Ezhava elite, the conservative section of the Ezhava leadership turned against the national movement, the movement against princely rule and the coir workers' movement in Travancore.[25] Another section moved to secular, radical positions (turning, for instance, the old Narayana Guru precept of 'One Caste, One Religion, One God for Man' to 'No Caste, No Religion, No God for Man') and identified with and participated in the agricultural workers' and coir workers' movements, with the movement against autocracy, and, later, with the left movement (see Thomas Isaac 1985; Thomas Isaac and Tharakan 1986). The turning point, according to Thomas Isaac's (1985) analysis, was the general strike of workers in the Alleppey area in 1938, when the pro-government positions of the conservative leadership isolated it, and undermined its hold on working Ezhava people. In later years, peasants and agricultural labourers as well as coir workers of the Ezhava caste joined the Communist Party and mass organizations led by the Communists in large numbers.

Educational change

The historical processes by which Kerala established itself as a frontrunner in education are complex; nevertheless, their main features can fairly simply be enumerated. Kerala got ahead because

1. the link between mass education and mass schooling was recognized early in Kerala;
2. social movements recognized the value of education and worked to overcome the three great obstacles to mass education in India, those created by class, caste and gender discrimination; and
3. efforts to build schools were supported by the state, which also made the investments necessary for mass schooling.

In the early nineteenth century, school education was an important component of the activity of Christian (particularly Protestant) missionaries in Kerala. Their schools served as exemplars: they focused on the poor and the children of the oppressed castes; they encouraged the education of girls; and, in addition to the religious aspects of education, they introduced courses of secular instruction.

Missionaries also influenced the state in Travancore. In 1817, the young ruler of the state, Rani Laxmi Parvathi Bai, issued the justly famous Royal Rescript that said that 'The state should defray the entire cost of the education of its people in order that there might be no backwardness in the spread of enlightenment among them, that by diffusion of education they might become better subjects and public servants and that the reputation of the state might be enhanced thereby.' The Rescript was remarkable because it declared universal education, paid for by the state, to be an objective of state policy. It was also remarkable for the fact that it was issued as early as 1817, in a princely state (no comparable statement was made, in the nineteenth century or the twentieth, by any government in British India, since universal education was never British policy), and by a young – 15 years old at the time – female ruler.

Nevertheless, for all the progress that was made in terms of educational policy during that period, there was no mass literacy at the end of the nineteenth century. Even in Travancore – where Christian missionaries were most active and where the nineteenth-century state was most interventionist – less than a quarter of all males and less than 5 per cent of all females were literate. Although official policy in Travancore and Cochin created what Richard Franke calls an 'official environment of support for education', it required female education, organized movements of people of the oppressed castes and, later, the left movement to establish comprehensive schooling and mass literacy.

To take the caste question first. As has been discussed, some of the worst forms of untouchability and distance pollution were practised in Kerala, and one of the most important reasons for Travancore pulling decisively ahead of Malabar in respect of literacy in the 1920s was the spread of education among people of the Ezhava caste, the upper tier of Kerala's (roughly speaking) two-tier system of untouchability. The change in literacy levels on a social scale came in the 1930s, with higher levels of education among people of the Ezhava caste, and the change occurred when the Ezhava social reform movement became a large-scale mass movement, more than four decades after Sree Narayana Guru began his public mission. In the 1920s and 1930s, there was a rapid expansion in enrolment, in educational investment and in affirmative action – in the form of scholarships, fee concessions and unrestricted access to primary schools – which consolidated the basis of mass education.

The emphasis on education in the social movements of the oppressed castes is remarkable. At the first meeting of the Sree Narayana Dharma Paripalana Yogam, the main organization of the Ezhava community, its leader Dr Palpu declared: 'We are the largest Hindu community in Kerala. ... Without education no community has attained permanent civilized prosperity. In our community there must be no man or woman without primary education.' The most striking feature of the early history of the Ezhava social reform movement is the commitment to gain access to primary education for all boys and girls, and to higher education as well. The great leader of the Pulaya masses, Ayyankali of Travancore (1863–

Table 5.11   Expenditure on education as a percentage of development and non-development expenditure (Revenue Account), all states and Kerala

Year	Kerala	All states
1959/60	37.0	19.6
1960/61	35.1	19.5
1962/63	32.1	19.9
1964/65	33.8	20.2
1965/66	35.4	19.7
1966/67	36.0	19.1
1971/72	36.4	21.9
1981/82	32.2	21.4
1990/91	27.8	18.4
1991/92	25.3	17.4
1992/93	26.9	17.4

Note: Figures for 1960/61 and 1991/92 are based on revised budget estimates; figures for 1992/93 are based on budget estimates; all other figures are based on final accounts.
Source: *Reserve Bank of India Bulletin*, successive issues, cited in Ramachandran (1997).

1941), also placed education, including schooling for girls, at the centre of his programme of social liberation.

Female literacy leads to mass literacy; Robin Jeffrey, in his work on Kerala, refers to the old wisdom that 'literate men have literate sons; literate women have literate children'. Jeffrey illustrates his argument on the role of female literacy in achieving mass literacy in Kerala by using the example of Baroda as a control; Baroda was another princely state with similar levels of male literacy at the beginning of the century, and where the princely government declared a policy of mass primary education. It nevertheless lags far behind Kerala in respect of literacy in the contemporary period. Kerala got ahead because Kerala's culture and sociopolitical movements in the state fostered female literacy.

For all the favourable conditions, however, *mass* literacy in Kerala as a whole is recent. When the State of Kerala was formed in 1956, the main priorities of its first government were land reform, food security, education and health. Land reform empowers the rural poor and helps facilitate their access to education. The extension of mass literacy to the rural poor, and particularly the rural poor in Malabar, took place after 1956. This was also the period when literacy spread decisively to backward districts in the state. The gap between Malabar and Cochin and

Table 5.12 Non-plan government expenditure on education in fourteen states, 1986–87 (Rs. per capita)

	Primary	Secondary	Higher
Kerala	83.0	48.0	27.0
Andhra Pradesh	39.0	26.0	21.0
Bihar	43.0	13.0	12.0
Gujarat	61.0	38.0	15.0
Haryana	38.0	42.0	17.0
Karnataka	54.0	23.0	20.0
Madhya Pradesh	43.0	27.0	10.0
Maharashtra	58.0	49.0	18.0
Orissa	33.0	29.0	11.0
Punjab	44.0	62.0	21.0
Rajasthan	42.0	28.0	11.0
Tamil Nadu	51.0	29.0	21.0
Uttar Pradesh	33.0	23.0	7.0
West Bengal	34.0	43.0	14.0
Fourteen states	45.0	31.0	15.0

Source: Report of the Ninth Finance Commission, December 1989, cited in Government of West Bengal (1992), pp. 17–19.

Travancore in respect of literacy widened during the period of British rule in Malabar, and mass schooling in Malabar was established after the formation of Kerala.

The proportion of total government expenditure spent on education in Kerala is much higher than the corresponding proportion spent by all states (see Table 5.11), and it is of note that the proportion of total expenditure spent on education by the states of Travancore and Cochin exceeded 15 per cent in the 1920s (see Ramachandran 1997). Most primary-school children go to state-run or state-supported schools. In the late 1980s, Kerala's non-plan expenditure per capita on primary education was the highest among fourteen states (see Table 5.12).

One of the first strike actions of agricultural labourers in Kerala (some suggest that it was *the* first) was organized by Ayyankali in 1914.[26] Ayyankali attempted to gain admission for a Pulaya girl to a government school in Ooroottambalam village in Neyyatinkara taluk near Thiruvanantha-puram. The people of the upper castes of the area began a campaign of violence against the Pulayas for this act, and, after violent clashes, burnt the school down. Ayyankali organized a strike of agricultural labourers, and work stopped in the fields of the upper castes. The government intervened, and, after a magistrate's inquiry, the strike ended in success for the workers. In retrospect, this stirring and deeply significant histori-cal event encapsulated the diverse components of Kerala's struggle for mass education, involving as it did elements of class struggle, the strug-gle against caste and gender discrimination, and the recognition of the people's right to education by the state.

The role of the left

The Communist Party, and the organizations of workers, peasants, agri-cultural labourers, students, teachers, youth and women under its leader-ship, have been the major organizers and leaders of mass political move-ments in Kerala since the end of the 1930s, and have been the major agents of the politicization of the mass of Kerala's people. Kerala is one part of India where the Communist Party assimilated the most progres-sive features of diverse local sociopolitical movements and gave them a new philosophical and political direction. These different movements in Kerala included the freedom movement, the radical and anti-caste sections of the social reform movement, the movement against landlordism, the movement against autocracy and monarchy, the movement for the lin-guistic reorganization of the region and for the establishment of a unified Kerala, and, of course, the modern movement of workers, peasants and radical intellectuals.[27] Communists were among the early organizers of mass political organizations of women in the state.[28] Communists played a leading part in the literary movement and in the cultural movement (including the theatre movement) in Kerala. Schoolteachers were key activists and mass organizers of the national movement and the Commu-nist Party; they were the first organizers of the *granthashala* (library) movement and the movement for literacy in Malabar. In the 1970s and 1980s, Communists were the main activists in the popular science move-ment led by the Kerala Shastra Sahitya Parishad, and in the Total Literacy Campaign of 1989 to 1991.

The modern state of Kerala was formed in 1956, and elections were held to the first Legislative Assembly in 1957. Of all the political forces in the state, only the Communists had a coherent vision for Kerala's future; they knew what they were going to do and how they would go about it. In June 1956, the Communist Party in Kerala met in Thrissur to discuss a policy framework for Party activity in Kerala, and the docu-ment that emerged from the meeting, 'Communist Proposal for Building a Democratic and Prosperous Kerala', provided the basis for the Communist election manifesto of 1957, and, indeed for future public policy in the state.[29] The first government of Kerala was a Communist government, and the major features of its agenda and of later Communist-led governments in the state were, among other things, land reform, health, education and strengthening the system of public distribution of food and other essential commodities. There is little doubt that the movement for decentralized government initiated by the Communist-led government that came to power in 1996 (and discussed elsewhere in this volume) is the most significant movement in rural development in India in the last few years. It has been noted in the scholarly literature that, brief though the periods of Communist rule in the state have been, each was decisive in consolidating the basic agenda for Kerala's transformation.[30]

Land reform and the public distribution system are recognized as unmistakably Communist projects; Communist governments also worked on policies that helped bridge the gap between regions, they drafted early legislation on local self-government, and the administration of 1987–1991 provided administrative and institutional support to the Total Literacy Campaign. Kerala's electorate has kept the Communists on a tight leash (Thomas Isaac and Mohana Kumar 1991); at the same time, the left has made many parts of its agenda part of the broad social consensus in the state. Put another way, even when the left loses the elections, it does not mean that the electorate rejects the socioeconomic programme of the left *in toto*; it is not, for instance, a vote against the literacy programme, or for agrarian counter-reform, or against the system of public distribution of foodgrain (see Herring 1992).

Radical individuals in Travancore began to make an impact on intellectual life in Kerala from the early part of the century; the Communist movement, however, began in Malabar. There is a stimulating scholarly literature and memoirs by leading participants, and novels as well, on the left movement in Malabar in the 1930s and 1940s, which deals with the events of the time and with the people who lived and died in its cause.[31] The number and quality of the extraordinary mass organizers and leaders for which the Communist movement in Malabar is famous – of whom E.M.S. Namboodiripad, A.K. Gopalan and P. Krishna Pillai are the best known – were remarkable. Selfless, enlightened and acutely sensitive to injustice, the Communist organizers of Malabar faced extraordinary repression by the ruling classes in order to achieve a better future for the people of Kerala and of India. E.M.S. Namboodiripad himself is the most eminent social theorist Kerala has had. No person has played as important a part in the sociopolitical and cultural life of a region of India for as long a period in the twentieth century as he did in Kerala.

Women's agency

Two issues regarding the place and role of women in Kerala's development achievements are worth emphasizing. First, Kerala's women have made outstanding gains in the fields of education and health and are more equal participants with men in education and health achievements than in any other part of India. Kerala is the only state where mass literacy has been achieved, among women as well as among men. Literacy among adolescent girls was almost universal in 1986–87. Women's literacy is supported by society and the state, and there has never been any organized opposition to female literacy and education in Kerala. At 74 years, female life expectancy at birth in Kerala is fifteen years higher than the Indian average, and almost six years above the corresponding figure for men in Kerala. Girls and women have access to the health care system in Kerala, and primary-data-based surveys show that, in general, the rates of immunization of girls are as high as those of boys. As a result of progressive social attitudes in Kerala towards the survival of girls and towards female survival in general, the proportion of females in the population was 1,040 per 1,000 males in 1991; the all-India average was 927.

Second, Kerala's experience is a dramatic example of the role of women's agency in advancing the social and economic development of a society. Female literacy and education are crucial determinants of child survival, general health and hygiene. These, in turn, determine progress in other demographic and health indicators: the expectancy of life at birth, the birth and death rates, the infant mortality rate and general morbidity. Kerala's achievements in the sphere of health would have been impossible without female literacy, and without an enlightened social attitude towards the survival of girl children and women. Female literacy ensures next-generation literacy; literate mothers generally have literate children. Women in Kerala have been, historically, important participants in the trade-union movement (and particularly in the coir and cashew industries and in the plantations), in the peasant and agricultural labour movements and the movement for land reform, and in the movement for food.[32]

State governments

It remains to review certain features of action by state governments in Kerala. The areas of state government intervention in Kerala that have been most significant for the people have been land reform, health and education, and the public distribution system. The state has also introduced a series of measures that are intended to provide protective social security to persons outside the 'organized' sector, who are not usually covered by such schemes. Government policies have also attempted to reduce disparities in major development achievements between the north and the south. Government action in these spheres has been in response to political action by political parties and mass organizations of the people.[33] Government action on land reform, for instance, began a few days after the first government of Kerala took office.

Education, as discussed earlier, was an early concern. There is also no doubt that government policy after the formation of Kerala has played a key role in raising health standards and in demographic change.[34] Throughout the post-independence period, health expenditure as a proportion of total expenditure has been higher in Kerala than in any other state. Although the economic history of health care in Kerala is yet to be written, the data indicate high levels of expenditure in the princely states of Travancore and Cochin (particularly the former) on health and education (although a greater proportion was spent on education than on health) from the 1920s (see Ramachandran 1997; Jeffrey 1992: 188ff.). In terms of hospitals and dispensaries, the health infrastructure in Kerala is far better developed than in India as a whole: in 1989, there were 106 hospitals and dispensaries per 1,000 sq km in Kerala against 12 in India, and 254 hospital and dispensary beds in Kerala per 100,000 persons against 77 in India (CMIE 1991). While per-capita expenditure on health was only marginally higher in Kerala than in other states in the late 1980s (Krishnan 1991a), an important feature of health expenditure in Kerala has been the emphasis on mother and child care and immunization as well as on curative medicine (Krishnan 1991a; Kabir and Krishnan 1991; Panikar 1979).[35]

The two-tier public distribution system was established and strengthened in the 1970s and the 1980s; early attempts to establish an extensive public food-distribution system of a permanent nature in the state began with the 1957 ministry (see above, p. 93). As with land reform, the establishment of ration shops and other state-run stores to sell food and some basic articles of consumption to the people has been described as a 'Communist project' (Herring 1992).

A highlight of Kerala's development experience is that public action after 1957 helped close the gap in important respects between Malabar and the southern districts of Kerala. The disparities in health and education facilities in Travancore and Malabar have been usefully discussed in Kabir and Krishnan (1991). In respect of literacy, it is clear that the literacy gap between Malabar and the princely states widened substantially during the period that Malabar was part of British India, and it narrowed only after mass schooling was established in Malabar after 1957. The reduction of differences between the north and south in respect of literacy, medical facilities, infant mortality, immunization, and fertility and death rates, and in infrastructural and general cultural development, is a standing example of the achievement of people and governments in *recent* decades.[36]

Kerala's Relevance to India

This section addresses directly the question raised above: At present levels of income, can public action ensure that the people of all states of India are provided with educational, health and demographic achievements similar to those attained at present by the people of Kerala?

Any society that is still weighing the benefits of universal school education or debating its feasibility is, in an important sense, a pre-modern one. Universal school education, need it be repeated, is of immense intrinsic and instrumental importance and governments should not be given the luxury of debating whether or not to provide schools for all and ensure that all children are in school. Universal school education must be seen as a social priority – whatever the financial costs. In the Indian context, these costs are not very great, in fact. A recent analysis has estimated that the additional costs required to provide school facilities for all children in the age group 6 to 11 years amounts to about 2.85 per cent of national income for five years (for detailed state-wide figures, see Swaminathan and Rawal 1999; Ramachandran, Rawal and Swaminathan 1997).[37]

The public food-distribution system in Kerala provides about 70 kg of foodgrain a year to those who use it. Although this amounts to only about 50 per cent of their requirements, it provides them with essential nutritional support. Extending that allotment to about 600 million people in India would require an allocation of about 42 million tonnes. This constitutes about 23 per cent of India's total foodgrain production of about 180 million tonnes. In a country of endemic malnutrition, surely this must be considered a feasible target for allocation through a public food-distribution system.[38]

Kerala's health gains are distinguished by the fact that they were achieved at relatively low public cost (see Krishnan 1991a). Krishnan points out that per-capita health expenditure was only marginally higher than in other states; in 1990–91, Rajasthan, Punjab and Tamil Nadu actually spent more per capita than did Kerala on medical, public health, family welfare and water supply and sanitation expenditures (Seeta Prabhu and Chatterjee 1993).

If per-capita public expenditures in Kerala and elsewhere are not so different, what explains the difference in health outcomes between them? First, Kerala has been consistent in its health expenditures, and health policy has been a continuing concern of governments. Second, Kerala was the only state of India where the socioeconomic arrangements were in place to absorb international advances in the last three decades in epidemiology and public health. The ratio of medical establishments to population is substantially higher in Kerala than in the rest of India. In an era of mass literacy, and where social and political consciousness are high, people demand better health facilities, use the health system more, and use it better. Joan Mencher illustrates vividly the impact of education and political consciousness on the demand for better health in Kerala:

> In Kerala, if a Primary Health Centre were unmanned for a few days, there would be a massive demonstration at the nearest collectorate led by local left-ists, who would demand to be given what they knew they were entitled to.... [T]he availability of doctors at a primary health facility, and public knowledge that something will be done at any time of the day or night if it is an emergency, has gone a long way to lowering child death. (Mencher 1980: 1781–2; see the discussion in Caldwell 1986, and also Antia 1994)

Third, public investment in health and general health consciousness has also served to increase private health expenditure in Kerala (see data in Krishnan 1991a).

A major obstacle to implementing programmes that improve the quality of people's lives in India is, of course, the policies of structural adjustment and stabilization that the government of India and all major political forces other than the left are now bent on implementing. Indeed, developments in this sphere at the national level pose a threat to the very sustainability of the development achievements of Kerala.

The need to press the political demand for expanding public action, and public investment, in the spheres of education and health is particularly acute during periods of so-called structural adjustment. Recent studies (see, for example, Kakwani et al. 1990) associate adjustment directly with declining public resources allocated to education: education's share of the public budget and GDP increased in all country groups *except* intensely adjusting countries after 1980 (see Noss 1991). Gross primary enrolment rates increased in all country groups from 1970 through 1985 except among intensely adjusting countries; the rate of growth of primary enrolments declined in intensely adjusting countries after 1980. Another set of measures associated with structural adjustment packages aims at cost-recovery, by introducing or increasing 'user fees', reducing student subsidies, and increasing 'community participation in school construction and maintenance' (see, for instance, Noss 1991). Another recent study shows that in countries that have undertaken World Bank-supported adjustment programmes, there was a slowdown in the increase in average female combined first- and second-level gross school enrolment rates in a number of adjusting countries (Ross 1995). The record is similar on the health front; the collapse of health entitlements in the former Soviet Union and ex-socialist countries of Eastern Europe provide the most conspicuous contemporary international example (for a review, see Ramachandran and Swaminathan 1996).

As the foregoing shows, at present levels of aggregate income in India, the major development outcomes of Kerala can be reproduced. However, the Kerala experience shows the rest of India that, if the living standards of the people are to be transformed radically and on a sustainable basis, public action cannot be confined to the issue of public expenditure: the prerequisites of change are social transformation by means of land reform and struggle against the worst forms of caste and gender discrimination.

Where does the rest of India stand in these respects? Land reform, other than in states ruled by the left, has not even been on the agenda of state governments. Indeed, part of the programme of structural adjustment is to roll back land reform legislation. This is a requirement with which at least two state governments are hastening to comply: witness the recent legislation in Karnataka and Maharashtra undermining the land-ceiling component of the land reform package. Another lesson of Kerala for the rest of India is that social progress requires that movements for social liberation integrate the class struggle, the struggle against caste oppression and the struggle against gender oppression. In the present Indian context, radical change also requires that policies of stabilization and structural adjustment, and the anti-poor 'austerity' that is inherent in them, be held back.

It is clear that social change on this scale and in this direction requires *political* action; political change, in turn, comes about through the practice of political parties. There is only one force in Indian politics – the left – whose basic agenda includes land reform, the struggle against caste and gender discrimination, and the struggle against programmes of stabilization and structural adjustment. I believe that the ascendancy of the left in Indian politics – and, with it, an integrated movement against agrarian backwardness and against caste and gender discrimination – is a necessary condition for replication on a national scale of the positive achievements of the people of Kerala.

Notes

Acknowledgements are due to T.M. Thomas Isaac, Jesim Pais, R. Ramakumar and Madhura Swaminathan.

1. Sections 1 and 3 of this chapter draw on Ramachandran (1997), which attempts a more detailed account of Kerala's development achievements and their history, and which has a more extended bibliography.

2. While the evidence is of progressive change in the pattern of morbidity and of improved facilities to deal with illness, medical evidence also indicates that much remains to be done to control the incidence of water-borne and air-borne infections in Kerala (for a discussion, see Ramachandran 1997).

3. For district-level primary data from three districts, see Zachariah et al. (1992).

4. Caldwell (1986), Kannan et al. (1991), Zachariah and Patel (1982), Raj (1994).

5. The main sources of data on immunization in Kerala in recent years are the National Sample Survey (1991), from the 42nd Round, conducted in 1986–87; a survey of immunization in 1989 that was part of a national review of the Universal Immunization Programme (cited in Krishnan 1991a); the survey of Zachariah et al. (1992); and the National Family Health Survey of 1992–93 (1995a and 1995b). The first and last sources have comparative data for individual states and for India.

6. Caldwell (1986), Sen (1993), Caldwell and Caldwell (1985), Krishnan (1991a), Nag (1983 and 1989), Raman Kutty (1987), Soman et al. (1990), Panikar (1979), Mari Bhat and Irudaya Rajan (1990), Raman Kutty et al. (1993), Kannan et al. (1991) are some of the contributors to the literature on women's agency and health in Kerala.

7. Raman Kutty (1987), and Soman et al. (1990).

8. Important new nutritional data on the calorie intake per person per day in India's seventeen most populous states have recently been released by the National Sample Survey (NSS) Organization. The most salient feature of the new data is the deeply disturbing finding that, at the all-India level, average calorie intake declined steadily in rural and urban areas between 1972–73 and 1993–94. There were, however, exceptions to the overall trend of decline in calorie intake. There were only two states in which the calorie intake per person increased between 1972–73 and 1993–94 in rural and urban areas: Kerala and West Bengal (see Swaminathan and Ramachandran 1999).

9. These data are confirmed by data from the National Family Health Survey (1995a and 1995b).

10. Although public provisioning in Kerala has been more effective than elsewhere, and better distributed between the sexes and between social groups and regions, traditional patterns of inequality have not been entirely eliminated. There are at least three distinct pockets of deprivation in contemporary Kerala, three social groups that are substantially behind the rest of the population in terms of education and other development achievements. These are the traditional coastal fishing communities, the people of the scheduled tribes of Kerala's highlands, and the underclass of Tamil migrant workers in the state. Although it may be said that, in numerical terms, these three groups are relatively small (the scheduled tribe population in Kerala, for instance, represents about 1 per cent of the total population), the persistence of acute deprivation among these three groups is, nevertheless, an important cause for social concern, and calls for greater attention from state authorities and political movements.

11. For descriptions of the spread of information through newspapers, see Ramachandran (1997), Jeffrey (1992, 1987a and 1987b), and Aiyappan (1965: 95–6).

12. Thorp (1993).

13. The earliest attempt to account for pre-capitalist agrarian relations in Kerala

theoretically was by E.M.S. Namboodiripad in the 1930s and 1940s; he described feudalism in Kerala as being characterized by *janmi–savarna*–chieftain (landlord–upper-caste–chieftain) domination of agrarian society (see Namboodiripad 1994 for discussion).

14. There is an extensive scholarly literature on this subject, from which this summary derives. Raj and Tharakan (1983) and Radhakrishnan (1989) have the best analytical summaries. The latter is a very useful full-length study of land reform, with before-and-after data that include data from a village study. See also Namboodiripad (1985), Raj (1992), Herring (1983), Saradamoni (1981), Franke and Chasin (1992), Franke (1996). On the Communists and agricultural labour after 1957, see Kannan (1988) and George (1980).

15. See the accounts in Radhakrishnan (1989: ch. 6), and Franke (1996: ch. 7).

16. In an interview in 1992, E.M.S. Namboodiripad characterized landlordism in contemporary Kerala in the following way. In his opinion, although 'the old type of *janmi* ceased to exist', there is still 'landlordism of another type' – that is, of landlords 'who get their lands cultivated through wage labour and those who live on usury and are also the dominant section in rural trade' (interview, April 1992).

17. The programmes of group farming that were introduced in the late 1980s during the 1987–91 United Front government were very interesting experiments, and indicate areas of possible public action in the future, but they did not survive or spread.

18. Total agricultural wage earnings are, of course, another matter, since earnings depend also on the number of days of employment.

19. On social security schemes for agricultural labourers, see Gulati (1993).

20. See the references to the literature on castes, caste practices and caste hierarchy in Kerala in Ramachandran (1997).

21. For references to literature on the conditions of life of people of the oppressed castes and of slavery and the literature on social hierarchy in Kerala, see Ramachandran (1997).

22. In Kerala's caste hierarchy, the Ezhava caste was the upper tier of the two levels of untouchability. Considered outcaste and untouchable by caste Hindus, Ezhavas were also considered ritually superior to the Pulaya and other slave castes. On the movement led by Narayana Guru and on social change among the Ezhava people in the late nineteenth and early twentieth centuries, see Chandramohan (1981 and 1987).

23. Author interview with P. Govinda Pillai in April 1992. See also Pillai (1994), in which he discusses a contrast between Kerala and Bengal in this regard.

24. On this phase, see Thomas Isaac and Tharakan (1986), and Thomas Isaac (1985).

25. See the references cited in Ramachandran (1997).

26. See Saradamoni (1980), and George (1990).

27. See Namboodiripad (1984): 207.

28. See Meera Velayudhan's (1992) interview with Kalikutty Asatty, a proletarian and social and political activist who went from the SNDP Yogam to the Communist Party and worked in the trade-union and women's movements.

29. See Namboodiripad (1994), and Nossiter (1988): 121–2.

30. Thomas Isaac and Mohana Kumar (1991). See also Namboodiripad (1984), and, for an assessment of Kerala's development that highlights the role of the left and of public policy in the modern period, Franke and Chasin (1992).

31. For references to this literature, see Ramachandran (1997).

32. For a summary of the range of activities of the left women's movement in Kerala, see AIDWA (1994: 44–86). While the extraordinary historic gains of women in Kerala cannot be underestimated, there are still important spheres in which women's equality has not been achieved, and in which discrimination persists. Representatives and supporters of the women's movement in Kerala express the opinion that sociopolitical and economic advance among women in recent years is not commensurate with the historic achievements of women in the spheres of education and health. Work participation rates among women are low, rates of unemployment are very high, and gender differentials in the labour market persist across caste, income and education categories. A substantial section of the women's labour force is concentrated in traditional occupations – coir-work, cashew-processing, bamboo-work, for example – that are now stagnant or in decline. The representation of women is very low in elected bodies – parliament, the legislative assembly and local bodies – and in trade-union executives, even in trade unions in occupations where most workers are women. The women's movement in Kerala has drawn attention to dowry-related deaths in Kerala and to sexual harassment and other crimes against women. On these issues, see the references in Ramachandran (1997).

33. 'The demands of class organizations were not confined to issues of land and wages alone ... they were also concerned with the social provisioning of many basic needs as well as with a variety of social and cultural issues. Left-led governments in Kerala set new paradigms of radical redistributive state policies. Class organizations succeeded in implementing land reform, improving the level of wages and conditions of work and strengthening a radical sense of self-respect and awareness among the people' (Thomas Isaac 1994: 58).

34. See Krishnan (1991a), and Zachariah (1994). Zachariah writes that 'much of Kerala's success in moderating fertility and mortality in such a short span ... was due to the policies which successive governments in Kerala followed since independence' (1994: 94).

35. Health expenditure has risen steadily from the early 1960s, and Krishnan's estimates indicate that an important feature of the health system in Kerala is the rise in private medical expenditure since the mid-1970s (see 1991a: Table 30). Remittances from emigrant Malayalees are likely to have played a key role in this development, and in the general expansion of health expenditures (Krishnan 1991a: 33ff.).

36. On the relative backwardness of Malabar in respect of medical facilities, see Kabir and Krishnan (1991a) and Jeffrey (1992: 25ff.). On changes in health achievements in Malabar, see Kabir and Krishnan (1991); see also Caldwell (1986).

37. See also the People's Report on Basic Education (PROBE 1999). PROBE cites a statement by Manmohan Singh, former union finance minister, on this issue: 'I sincerely believe that money can be found if representatives of the public, that is, Members of Parliament and Members of State Legislatures, give sufficient importance to this quest for universalizing access to education' (PROBE 1999: 135).

38. On this question, see Swaminathan (1999). For an analysis of how to extend the public distribution system, including proposals for the dispersal of agricultural production, see Gulati and Krishnan (1975).

6

The New Popular Politics of Development: Kerala's Experience

Olle Törnquist

India, in common with many other developing countries, faces a number of dilemmas. This chapter focuses on three of them, and looks to the politics of development of Kerala for possible solutions. The first dilemma is how to cope with the problems generated by the attempts of such leaders as Jawaharlal Nehru to free the country from the deleterious effects of colonialism by means of central planning and a powerful nation-state structure. How can more democracy and more popular participation be promoted under present conditions?

The second dilemma is what to do about the fact that the majority of Indians are being marginalized still further as national economic policy is adjusted to an expansive global capitalism. The demands for structural adjustment are not as severe as in crisis-stricken East Asia, but the tendencies are the same. How, then, will it be possible to sustain and to renew India's classical ideal of combining sustainable economic growth with socioeconomic equalization?

The third dilemma is how to ensure that ordinary people can influence emerging questions of this sort when the established parties and mass organizations that are comparatively progressive are (a) characterized by the earlier struggle against colonialism and 'feudal' landlords, (b) undermined by boss-rule, commercialism and populism, and (c) threatened by leaders exploiting religious and national chauvinism. How, under such circumstances, can new questions and ways of mobilizing be placed on the agenda without undermining the real progress that, despite everything, has been achieved?

The most popular answer nowadays to these questions, both in India and elsewhere, is that the solution lies in more civil society, and in less but 'better' politics. Achieving this is thought to require, on the one hand, privatization, deregulation and decentralization, and, on the other, a strengthening of the 'core' functions of the state, together with greater support for free media and voluntary organizations.[1] The two questions we shall discuss here is whether these prescriptions are appropriate, and whether there is any alternative. Ideally, this would mean studying a so-called critical case – a case where the problems in question are present; where attempts have been made to apply the prescriptions mentioned; where there are signs that these prescriptions have not always worked; and where efforts have been undertaken to develop alternatives. But such ideal objects of study do not, of course, exist in reality.

Nevertheless, the densely populated state of Kerala has uncommonly much to offer. With its strong civil society, its land reform, its extensive educational system, and its high level of social welfare, Kerala and its 30 million inhabitants certainly diverge from the rest of India. To be sure, lessons drawn from 'the land of coconuts' cannot be applied without some modifications to other states in the union. Yet, many of India's problems are found in Kerala, too. Moreover, some of the popular prescriptions have already been tested in that state, and under relatively advantageous conditions. So if such methods lead to problems in Kerala, it follows that the results are likely to be still worse elsewhere. Furthermore, by studying the new alternatives that have started to emerge, we may be able to move from criticism to constructive insight.[2] So let us look more closely at what it is that makes Kerala so interesting.

The Significance of Kerala

To begin with, Kerala is not just uncommonly beautiful; it also has one of the Third World's strongest civil societies. The fragmentary nature of its civil society of course bears discussion – the fact, for example, that almost watertight boundaries often separate the different arenas and associations. (We shall take up this question later on.) Yet public debate is lively, the free media are multiple, and the majority of citizens are literate and voluntarily participate in a multitude of wide-ranging organizations – socioreligious associations, educational bodies, development organizations, environmental groups, women's organizations. This is nothing new. This strong civil society has its roots in popularly based demands that began in the latter half of the nineteenth century in the two British-dominated principalities of Travancore and Cochin, in the south of what today is Kerala. The demands were for greater equality in religious and social life, for the right of all to seek public employment, for fairer economic legislation, and for state support for the improvement of health care and education – in other words, a sort of embryo bourgeois revolution, though one which was inhibited by colonialism.

In addition, there are the political parties, the trade unions and the cooperatives (which many scholars would claim are part of the political and economic spheres rather than the civil sphere). This organizational life is nothing new either; it is the result of a bifurcated process of politicization during the first half of the twentieth century. On the one hand, the civic organizations were rooted in the socioreligious and often caste-related associations of civil society. On the other hand, the political and economic groups were affected by increasingly important class interests as well – for example, among landowners, tenants and agricultural labourers. While civil society was strongest in the south of what today is Kerala (in the comparatively autonomous and enlightened princely states), the strongest class-based organizations emerged in the more feudal north – in Malabar, which was governed by the British as a district of the Madras province.

Second, Kerala also has – alongside these strong popular organizations – state agencies and organs of considerable prominence. The historical pattern has been that political groups, civic associations and economic interest organizations have demanded state regulations and programmes (within the business and health sectors, for example), as well as state support for such institutions as private schools and credit cooperatives. (And following democracy's breakthrough, of course, political parties have competed to represent voters in the parliament and government of the state.) However, restructuring of the export-led, raw-materials-based economy has not featured among the results. And now the economy is in crisis. Nevertheless, popular organizations and the state in Kerala have established India's most extensive programmes for education, health care and the distribution of inexpensive basic goods. Furthermore, radical parties and interest organizations have pushed through India's most consistent land reform. In consequence, Kerala has stood out for several decades as a benign exception which showed, many thought, that it was possible to pursue a humane path to development without needing first to prioritize a rapid and socially brutal economic growth. Apart from the weak economic performance, one could speak of a sort of Scandinavia of the Third World.

Third, these achievements have contributed – unaccompanied as they are by economic modernization – to the emergence of new problems. To begin with, social and economic benefits have seldom been tied to economic growth (in the form, for example, of alliances between trade unions and modernization-oriented entrepreneurs). The economy still appears to bear a colonial stamp. The production of raw materials for export predominates, but is less profitable than it was. Agriculture of the 'usual' kind is stagnating. Industry remains small and weak; the only branch that is growing is the commercial and service sector, which of course includes the import of consumer goods. In addition, demands from below for measures from above have helped to produce unwieldy, expensive, centralized and badly coordinated state organs. The bosses and employees of these organs, moreover, have developed their own special interests. The different groupings in civil society, finally, have left their stamp on the parties and on political life in general, as have a range of trade unions and cooperatives.

In this way, then, Kerala has developed a system of politically organized special interests. This system has provided subventions to various groups, but it has also weakened common efforts at economic development. In short, the successful work of distributing the pie to as many persons as possible has been done in such a way, and with such specific interests in the foreground, that it has become difficult to make the pie grow at the same time.

Since the mid-1970s at least, much production has tended to stagnate, both in industry and in agriculture. Since 1996, moreover, the price of the only product that is really expanding – rubber – has fallen by half. The unemployment statistics, furthermore, have risen, and are now usually estimated at a fifth of the educated labour force, while paradoxically the state has seen an influx of manual labourers from the neighbouring states to take up sundry jobs that the youth of Kerala shun. Moreover, the state authorities are receiving too little in the way of taxes to defray the costs of the far-reaching welfare system, which is accordingly in disrepair. This problem is exacerbated by the fact that the state authorities are subordinate to New Delhi on tax questions. In addition, Kerala benefits only to a limited extent from all the monies repatriated by migrant workers who hail from the state. Finally, the state's ability to protect and reform exposed sectors has diminished on account of the more liberal economic policy pursued by India in recent years.

Were one inclined to put the point harshly, one could say that, while public consumption is being reduced – as is the ability to make strategic productive investments and to improve quality within the public sector – the comparatively high level of private consumption (including the ever growing private sector in health care and education) is being maintained by the labours of young Keralites who toil under miserable conditions in the Gulf states and elsewhere in India, and who send home a portion of what they earn (young Keralites, that is, whose parents struggled for decent conditions in Kerala). These monies are reckoned to account for between 10 and 30 per cent of Kerala's gross annual product. But, just as former tenants have turned petty bourgeois and seldom work together with others to produce more on the lands they obtained through the land reform, the incomes earned by migrants are individual in nature, and are often spent unproductively.

Fourth, there have also been very impressive efforts since the late 1980s to come to terms with many of these problems – efforts building on renewed popular initiatives stemming in part from civil society, and in part from political groupings and state agencies at both central and local levels.

It is on these attempts that I shall concentrate in the remainder of this chapter. What is the purpose of these campaigns? Does the work on them indicate that activists have found a way to handle the many problems on which we have touched, and with which India in general and Kerala in particular are confronted? What do their experiences tell us about the widely accepted prescriptions to promote more civil society and less but 'better' politics?

The analysis that follows takes up two different issues: the first generation of campaigns, which took place under the government of the left–centre front between 1987 and 1991; and the impressive attempts beginning around 1994 to undertake renewed efforts. The first period is covered in my research with P.K. Michael Tharakan.[3] The study of the second period is not yet concluded. Here I must rely on my interview materials, on running press coverage, on certain key documents, and on my own and others' preliminary observations.[4]

Impressive Campaigns without Sufficient Social and Political Base

The most important driving force in the work of reform was (and is) the Kerala Sastra Sahitya Parishat (KSSP), the 'People's Science Movement' of Kerala, winner of the 1996 alternative Nobel prize. The KSSP began as a rather narrow educational organization aimed at spreading rational thinking and scientific methods to 'the people'. In the 1970s, however, the association was broadened and changed. Tens of thousands of activists opposed, in the name of environmentalism and alternative development, a large power plant in Silent Valley in northern Kerala. The work was carried forward by students, youths, retired administrators and scientific experts. The KSSP is not just a typical progressive and urban-based middle-class organization; it also builds on the unusually strong educational ideals of the peasant and labour movements in Kerala. During the struggle for national liberation, for instance, three movements were formed: the political movement, the trade-union movement, and the library movement. Moreover, Kerala still contains no large cities in which modern social life is concentrated. In the lowland countryside, as well as a good way up into the mountains, semi-urbanized areas lie close up against one another; these have their own middle-class groups and organic intellectuals.

Like many other development-oriented non-governmental organizations (NGOs) in India and elsewhere, the KSSP worked along two parallel tracks: first to scrutinize public development policies and sketch out alternatives – for example, within health care and education; second to carry out pilot projects to show how people themselves could change their situation – for example, by installing cheap stoves which reduce inside smoke and require less fuel. Like other radical NGOs, finally, the KSSP took the view that an alternative path of development presupposes far-reaching social and economic change. In contrast to most like-minded groups in India, however, the KSSP did not turn against the previous generation of progressive political and trade-union organizations. Rather, the KSSP reasoned that alternative development work and traditional political commitment both can and should enrich each other.

Many KSSP members were accordingly active in political parties which typically, though not always, formed part of Kerala's left–centre front. This front is dominated by the largest reformist (and, in practice, social-democratic) communist party – the Communist Part of India–Marxist or CPM. At the same time, however, it is often the case that other parties within the front – including breakaways from the Congress Party – wield an influence out of proportion to their numbers. Their voters, after all, are strategically important in the hard fight to win majority elections in single-member districts.

Within the CPM, the ideas of the KSSP enjoyed the least support among those who called for a revitalized policy of centralized and state-led modernization; this group included many trade unionists connected with industry and parts of the public sector. Others, however, were more favourably disposed, if for no other reason than that certain Party leaders bore a grudge against the 'trade-union fraction'. This does not mean, however, that the two sides of the Party took distinct views of development policy. In and around the Party there are many patterns of conflict, which only partly coincide with each other.[5] On the specific question of development, I have distinguished instead between 'state-modernizers' and 'popular-developmentalists'. These tendencies are found in many different groups – both within and outside the CPM.

Since the left won the first state elections in Kerala in 1957, it has on and off – sometimes divided, sometimes united – been able to wield governmental power. After many years in opposition, the left–centre front in 1987 again succeeded in winning an election and forming a government.

This was mainly the result, it would seem, of widespread dissatisfaction with rule by the right–centre front under the leadership of the Congress Party. In fact, after the work of land reform had been completed during the 1970s, the left had been unable to renew itself. The reform-oriented groups within it, moreover, were in a clear minority. Yet, after lengthy discussions, these groups were able to initiate three innovative campaigns. In these, they were supported not so much by the dominant party, the CPM, as by parts of the government, as well as by a series of volunteer organizations (with the KSSP as the leading force).

The first campaign: mass literacy drive

It may seem strange that the primary efforts of the most literate state in India were focused on eliciting the engagement of the comparatively small proportion of the population (*c.* 20 per cent) who could not read or write. The reason was threefold. First, human (rather than just economic) development requires that all are able to take part; second, it was politically important to try to emancipate the many poor groups which had hitherto relied chiefly on religious patronage; and third, a massive literacy drive, coupled with various follow-up activities, was an excellent way to mobilize the efforts of all those who had previously been attracted by the KSSP.

The pilot campaign was carried out in the district of Ernakulam (including the small but internationally known city of Cochin). Enthusiasm was at a high level. Unlike most Indian NGOs, the KSSP did not focus its efforts (any longer) on a project of its own, but rather on a broad and massive collaboration among a large number of volunteer organizations and interested parts of the central and local administration. In this case, both the literacy commission in New Delhi and the district administration under the leadership of a previous chair of the KSSP were engaged. A great many activists and volunteers were mobilized. To start with, 50,000 volunteers carried out an investigation of all 600,000 households in the district, whereafter 18,000 largely volunteer instructors made contact with those persons who could not read or write. The initial results were impressive. After just a single year, in February 1990 Prime Minister V.P. Singh could proclaim Ernakulam as the one completely literate district in India. The KSSP garnered appreciable international recognition (which by rights ought to have extended to the local administration). The popular-developmentalist forces in Kerala had by then got the wind in their sails. The campaign in Ernakulam was used as the model for a larger campaign in the state as a whole. It was applauded by the literacy agencies in New Delhi. Furthermore, it inspired a multitude of groups in India as a whole.

Yet there were also significant problems. The campaign soon began to run out of steam. For one thing, the organizations had not prepared – though they should have known better – any proper programme to follow up the campaign. For another, political parties and groups did not show themselves to be especially interested in engaging a large number of new sympathizers from the very poorest groups. Finally, it proved even harder than anticipated to get cooperation between campaign-oriented volunteers and permanent public administrators to function well.

The second campaign: group farming

Notwithstanding Kerala's most consistent land reform, production had not notably increased. A particular worry was the production of rice. The large number of small landowners seldom joined in collaborative efforts. Sometimes, in fact, they worked at cross purposes to each other, as was seen in the transition from rice cultivation to coconut production, which made the irrigation of the remaining rice fields more difficult. In addition, centrally directed agencies that controlled vital components within agriculture also found it difficult to cooperate at the local level: some, for example, were responsible for irrigation pumps; others for the electricity required to run them. Furthermore, conflicts arose between small landowners and agricultural labourers. And finally, the countryside was being affected in great measure by the incomes of mobile migrant workers. In many cases, landowners and their families preferred to concentrate less on agriculture than on other activities which were more profitable in the short term, including land speculation on the outskirts of the many towns and urban areas. For a substantial portion of the rural population – including supporters of the left parties – property and speculation seemed to have become more important than work and production.

Earlier attempts at collective solutions had failed miserably. Nor could the left in Kerala follow the example of their comrades in West Bengal. In West Bengal, the formation of separate organizations for agricultural labourers had been prevented; in Kerala, such organizations already existed. In West Bengal, tenants and small farmers had not been furnished with more land, but rather with political protection; in Kerala, by contrast, the land had already been redistributed. In West Bengal, the policy had been tied to the decentralization of administration and development efforts on the one hand, and continued central political control on the other; in Kerala, the odd combine of Indira Gandhi's Congress Party and the rather small pro-Moscow Communist Party of India (CPI) that was in power when the land reform was implemented never dared to undertake decentralization. (They would, in that case, have lost power to that section of the left led by the CPI, which was much stronger on the local level.) All of the factions then turned their efforts to conquering and keeping the power that had been concentrated in the central organs of the state government.

Yet something still had to be done in Kerala. The strategy that emerged was to promote volunteer cooperation among cultivators – or 'group farming'. First, an unusually dynamic minister of agriculture saw to it that the operations of his ministry were delegated to its local units, and that most of the support it disbursed went to the cooperating farmers. Second, certain experts sought, together with local interest and volunteer organizations, to mobilize popular support and participation. The campaign won broad support, including within the left–centre front and the government. It also produced results in the form of higher rice production and reduced tension between landowners and agricultural labourers. Soon, however, a series of new problems came to the fore. The active collaboration of the agriculture ministry was important, but its delegation of tasks to local units of the ministry conserved the old top-down approach, and this did not resolve the lack of cooperation between different centrally directed agencies at the local level. The rise in production, moreover, was at least as much due to subsidies and a heavier use of pesticides as to cooperation among farmers. Landowners often seemed more interested in obtaining external support than in cooperating with one another. And, just as in the case of the literacy campaign, political parties and groups were not very interested in truly committing themselves to development work and to this way of to winning over new sympathizers.

The third campaign: resource-mapping

In order to remedy the problems arising in connection with the lack of follow-up in the literacy campaign, as well as in connection with the inadequate grassroots work in support of cooperative cultivation, a third campaign was launched – 'resource-mapping'. Anyone who has visited the central office of a local government in Scandinavia, for instance, knows that all development work carried out there is based on a far-reaching mapping of local resources and the manner in which these are used. This is lacking, wholly or in part, in India and in Kerala. This deficiency could quickly be remedied with the help of modern methods of measurement, including the use of satellites. Yet the purpose of the campaign in Kerala was not just to create maps; it was also to ensure that people would be able to use them! The mapping of resources, it was hoped, would promote local consciousness of existing resources, and discussion about how these could be put to better use. Some able and committed geographers, accordingly, sketched out a programme whereby they themselves would attend to the advanced aspects of the mapping, while volunteer groups would gather a large portion of the information. Thereafter, they would be able to discuss different development initiatives together with local politicians, experts and interested parties.

The resource-mapping programme got under way too late, however, to benefit from the enthusiasm that had been built up during the literacy drive. Thus, aside from the activists of the KSSP, it was for the most part devoted youth that took part. Once again, neither local administrators nor political groups showed any great interest. It now became clear, moreover, that successful local alternative development required that local governments (panchayats) already possessed some resources as well as a measure of decision-making power.

The lack of any significant measure of local self-rule proved, in fact, to be a fundamental obstacle to *all* of the new popular initiatives. The real problem, however, was that decentralization in turn required that parties and politicians make the 'right' political decision. With a few exceptions – like the communist patriarch E.M.S. Namboodiripad – there was no great interest in such circles for measures of this kind (any more than there is among bureaucrats in the present centralized administration). It was only the rhetoric that interested them.

Furthermore, activists who had engaged in alternative work outside the formal political system were without direct opportunities of their own for affecting the political process. Nor was it the simplest thing in the world to mobilize broad popular support for radical political and administrative changes. Results could not be expected to last over the long term. As mentioned earlier, moreover, decentralization was not coupled – as it had been in West Bengal – to the implementation of land reform. Without massive development efforts, therefore, broad material interests in favour of decentralization and alternative projects were lacking. It had been far different in the case of earlier reforms, such as the redistribution of land, when the advantages for the individual were plain for all to see. Accordingly, no far-reaching social movement – one able to live on, irrespective of which parties formed the government – emerged. The campaigns stood and fell, rather, with the commitment of devoted activists (associated first and foremost with the KSSP) and certain favourably disposed politicians and administrators. When, consequently, the left–centre government lost the state elections in 1991 (which were held in connection with the national elections, in which many citizens expressed their sympathy for the murdered Rajiv Gandhi by voting for his party), it was not merely the case that the government had to resign; the campaigns in large measure collapsed as well.

New Development Efforts on a Firmer Basis

Many committed activists refused to give up, however. Instead they licked their wounds, assessed their experiences, and sought out new paths. As we have seen, earlier experiences indicated that a true decentralization of resources and decision-making to district and local governments was the key to success; they also indicated, however, that established politicians were unlikely to carry out such measures on their own. Therefore activists themselves had to find a forceful way to exert pressure for their cause.

This time their efforts were facilitated, paradoxically enough, by the fact that the central government in New Delhi also sought to effect a certain degree of decentralization, albeit for wholly different reasons (namely, to promote its new liberal economic policies, and to reach out directly to districts and local governments in states where it did not control the state government). Activists in Kerala were able to mobilize broad support (including leading moderate academics and other person-alities) for their criticism of the conservative state government, which had not even carried out the kind of decentralization championed in New Delhi. And politicians from the centre–left opposition were not, of course, slow to join in. On the contrary, activists enticed them into making one binding promise after another regarding the decentralization they would implement when they were returned to power.

At the same time, of course, the new conservative state government obstructed the literacy, group farming and resource-mapping campaigns. It was a tough time, and many sympathizers fell by the wayside. Yet many others struggled on as best they could. This was particularly true of resource-mapping, where work continued on a series of pilot projects. Important knowledge was gained in regard both to resources and to the various ways that local development programmes could be initiated.

In 1994 the activists succeeded, moreover, in staging a counter-offensive – by mobilizing all the knowledge, skills and drive at the command of the many academic and organic intellectuals in Kerala who sought alternative, but less dogmatic, roads to development. A large-scale 'Kerala Studies Conference' was organized, with some 1,500 participants and 500 papers. (The contrast could not have been greater with the 'Tamil Studies Conference', a propagandistic spectacle arranged scarcely six months later by the Chief Minister of Tamil Nadu, Ms Jayalalitha.) The skilful manner in which the proceedings in Kerala were carried out – on the basis of local resources and the volunteer efforts of academics, political activists and trade unionists – prompted the small group of international participants to ponder, in mute admiration, their own diffi-culties in getting even small workshops to function properly.[6]

The movement was not able to follow up this conference with as many regional seminars as had been planned. Furthermore, concrete local development programmes were still conspicuous by their absence when the left–centre front formulated its strategy for the local elections of 1995, and the state elections of 1996. Nevertheless discontent with conservative rule was massive: the left–centre front made gains at all levels and formed the new state government.

This time the reformers had a much better starting point. The politicians had pledged to institute decentralization, and the activists them-selves had amassed a great deal of theoretical and practical knowledge about how alternative development could be furthered from below. Accordingly, before the forces of hesitancy were able to put obstacles in the way, leading reformists within the left–centre front were able to present complete and comprehensive plans – which they did rapidly and with great tactical skill – for what could and should be done under the aegis of the Kerala State Planning Board. The road was now open for renewed efforts at alternative development on the local level (except for where industrial and fiscal matters were decided at state level).

What were the major ideas behind the new efforts? To begin with, the reformists emphasized that both the district and, especially, the local governments (panchayats) held the authority to decide only the details, and lacked any resources of their own to speak of. Indeed, this had been the case ever since the founding of the state. Changing the activities and expenditure distribution of the state would take time. Nevertheless, a start could be made with the investment budget. Following the victory of the left–centre front in 1996, the reformists duly pushed through a decision that district and local governments would receive as much as between 35 and 40 per cent of the investment budget (compared to the previous negligible amounts) through the State Planning Board.

Second, the reformists claimed that almost all planning up to that point had been done from above. Alongside the 'district collectors' (chief district administrators), different departments and agencies had each been responsible for their own little sub-units, even on the lowest levels. Activities had been neither coordinated nor formulated on the basis of local needs and opportunities. It was time to turn this arrangement up-side down. Goals and operations must be formulated and coordinated locally. A certain degree of central and regional coordination was neces-sary, the reformists conceded, though this should be accomplished through the State Planning Board and in broadest possible cooperation with all interested parties. It was hoped that the new effort would be less party-dominated and party-political.

A critical argument among reformists was that most of the popular movements – the political and trade-union movements especially – had hitherto mainly demanded state and local measures, and furthermore had done their utmost to ensure that such measures would favour their own members and sympathizers. This, the reformists claimed, had helped to cause conflict between different special interests, and to create expectations that the state would take care of everything. Thus the participation of citizens themselves had been set aside, and development efforts to the benefit of all had been neglected. The goal now was rather to promote cooperation and complementary volunteer efforts on the basis of the broadest possible discussion within each district and locality of what needed to be done. Broad committees of cooperation and voluntary action were formed on a range of levels. This was not, of course, a kind of apolitical developmentalism. On the contrary, it was a conscious political project on the part of reformist left–centre forces to ensure that *all* local governments and citizens would enjoy equal opportunities to participate in the new efforts to be undertaken. It was a matter of striving to implement the best possible policies for and with the popular majority, rather than for and with the members and clients of each distinct group.

The reformists worked with public agencies, established popular organizations, and new volunteer associations (of the KSSP type). Experiences from the earlier campaigns showed the necessity of working via institutionalized and legitimate organs (like the local governments) if all volunteer forces were to be capable of working together and cooperating on projects that would be tenable over the long term. Voluntary commitment presupposed political initiative and legitimacy. At the same time, the wish was to continue to attract new blood (outside of the established organizations), in the form of committed experts and youth. At the lowest level, activists sought to create neighbourhood fora capable of unifying the splintered fragments of civil society. All documents and decisions, furthermore, were to be made public. Activists hoped, of course, that in the end these grand efforts to introduce and practise deepened democracy would result not merely in improved economic and social development, but also in the renewal of the established trade-union and political movements, and of the state and local governments as well. The parties, for example, would no longer appoint those who could help 'their own', but those able to develop entire localities and districts.

Finally, the new efforts were in the first instance social and extra-parliamentary. The most important thing, the argument went, was not growth at any price, but rather the engagement of ordinary people, so that they would be able to influence development themselves. And, according to the activists, it was almost as important that it should not be the experts and politicians who discuss how the laws and directives for

decentralization ought to be carried out, but rather the citizens themselves who, by pursuing projects of their own, should discover what they
can accomplish, and thereby develop the commitment to bring about
true decentralization.

How was all this to be accomplished? A six-step plan had already
been formulated in outline before the new left–centre government took
power in the middle of 1996. First, the necessary information materials
would be collected, and a large number of persons trained (about 600 at
the central level), whose task it would then be to train roughly 15,000
others at the regional level; these latter would then be charged with
training some 100,000 persons at the very local level. The idea was that
a similar educational process would then be undertaken at each subsequent step in the campaign.

Between mid-August and October, all of the roughly 1,000 local
governments in Kerala wishing to take control over their portion of the
investment budget conducted – with the help of the above-mentioned
trainees – general meetings in basic localities. All citizens were entitled to
take part in these meetings, and to have their say about which problems
were the most serious, and which development projects the most urgent.
Some 10 per cent of the entire population, approximately 3 million people,
a fifth of whom were women, were estimated to have taken part. Reports
and follow-up were then introduced at subsequent meetings.

Between October and the end of 1996, the general goals of each local
government were combined with a comprehensive analysis of its history
and resources. These reports were put together by working groups that
had been appointed at the general meetings. The reports were then approved at development seminars – in which local elected politicians and
local administrators took part – and then sent via the districts to the
State Planning Board. This was one of the high points of the campaign.
The quality of the reports was high – equal, in several cases, to that of
a Master's thesis.

From the New Year to March of 1997 – when the economic circumstances became clearer – a good 10,000 working groups formulated concrete projects on a range of levels. From March to June, the groups
reviewed what specific resources could be mobilized, and drew up local
plans. During the remainder of the fiscal year, finally, these local government plans were integrated at block (sub-district) and district levels. During
the first year, over 2.7 billion rupees[7] were distributed in the form of
projects that had been drawn up by the central state authorities but that
would be implemented by local authorities, and as much as 7.5 billion
rupees in the form of grants to local projects. The mobilization of supplementary local funds and voluntary labour was also encouraged. The

general directives included an instruction that at most 30 per cent be invested in roads and the like, that a somewhat higher proportion be invested in the social sector, and that priority otherwise be given to measures that promote production. All this was to be done, furthermore, completely transparently and without expanding the public sector.

Thereafter, it was hoped, it would be possible to go ahead and realize the plans. However, the working groups had not functioned sufficiently well. An additional phase – of expert examination and correction – was required. The work was therefore delayed; in October 1997 it seemed that an impasse had been reached. Several politicians were hesitant. Many publicly employed administrators and experts on the central state level had not been deployed to the local bodies and were dragging their feet. It was only after political intervention (from, among others, E.M.S. Namboodiripad), and after the mobilization of tens of thousands of volunteer experts, that the projects began to be implemented.

New Lessons

It is still rather early to start evaluating the second campaign as a whole. It is undoubtedly unique and bold, and has drawn widespread attention, including internationally. Judging from the reports of colleagues, the local press and local contacts (including both the prime mover of the campaign and his critics), it appears to have gone well. Of the thousand local governments, the campaign leadership is highly satisfied with the results in about 15 per cent, dissatisfied with the results in 20 per cent, and moderately impressed with the results in the rest. The goal now is to work to classify a majority of the local governments as highly successful. Several problems are manifest and criticism is building up among political groups as well as ordinary people on the panchayat level. Yet the fact that many politicians are expressing unease signals that the campaign and the decentralization that they did not take seriously are now becoming real and part of mainstream politics. The criticism from below is mainly a sign that people are getting engaged, are able to look into previously non-transparent practices, and are capable of standing up against the abuse of resources and corruption, which used to be hidden and took place higher in the system where commoners could not fight it. With these relative reported achievements in mind, we can begin the work of drawing lessons from the difficulties encountered and the experiences gained.

To begin with, the campaign has not tackled all the problems. Kerala's lack of industrial development, its negative balance of trade, and the difficulties faced by its many migrant workers are just some of the issues which must be addressed by other means. On the other hand, activists have never claimed that alternative local development is the cure for all ills. And the fact remains that only some 35 per cent of the investment budget is available for these purposes. Significantly, with a few exceptions, clear connections are still not being made between the various local projects and larger-scale central economic investments, or between the situation of migrant workers and the best possible use of these workers' savings. The campaign's leaders are aware of such problems, however; the issue is rather the obstacles they face. One possibility is to build further on the cooperative sector, which seems appropriate in view of the fact that the public sector cannot be expanded. In which case, the cooperatives would have to be reformed and liberated from political and economic special interests. In fact, activists are hoping that legislative revisions will lay the basis for this.

Those critics are right who aver that the campaign does not put the class struggle foremost, and that it scarcely amounts to a deathblow to capitalism. But that, of course, is not the point. As under colonialism, a good proportion of the problems facing Kerala today derive from the fact that dynamic economic development of virtually any sort – the capitalist kind included – is inhibited. At an earlier stage, the left sought to solve this dilemma through such methods as land reform – methods which would make it possible for the beneficiaries themselves to increase production. The reformers of today wish only to reconnect to this development-furthering strain within the progressive movement, and to find new ways by which the mass of the people themselves – as opposed to just the well-to-do – can be stimulated to invest and to increase production.

The most serious problem in this respect is that it remains unclear exactly what the new obstacles to development are – now that the large landowners and tenancy system of old have been disarmed. This is the case because contemporary exploitation, subordination and capital accumulation are very complex issues, and many of the clear old class lines have disappeared. It is also the case that many supporters of the left–centre front are themselves involved in patron–client relations within trade unions, or are party to speculation in land, or are involved in the unproductive use of – for example – cultivable soil and migrant workers' incomes.

Alongside this overarching and somewhat abstract criticism, however, it may be instructive to focus on three of the very concrete problems encountered by activists, and to ask what these indicate.

First, certain critics charge the campaign with partiality to the left–centre front in general, and to the CPM in particular. The argument is that the leaders and key activists of the campaign come from the front (especially from the CPM), and that state resources are used to benefit the front's (especially the CPM's) supporters. Most indications suggest, however, that this is a political half-truth. Indeed, the campaign is obviously political, though it is not (at the time of writing) narrowly party-political; nor does it restrict benefits to certain groups. It is political inasmuch as its activists cooperate with political and trade-union organizations, and inasmuch as they use volunteer organizations and state resources on behalf of local development policies which are not exclusive in nature, but which are instead generally beneficial. It is undeniable that most of the leaders and key activists of the campaign sympathize with the left–centre in general and the CPM in particular, but this, in view of their expertise and experience and the fact that this party has the largest number of grassroots members and sympathizers, is as inescapable as the fact that campaigns for the benefit of business would be dominated by businessmen and their experts. Nor, clearly, do the campaign's leaders and activists have qualms about strengthening their own parties.

The primary logic of the campaign is that the parties will promote local development for people in general, and not just for their own supporters. There are of course cases where local politicians, administrators and related contractors take advantage of devolved funds and distribute benefits to their own clients. This is in breach of the rules stipulated for the campaign and the instructions on how funds shall be used. In response, new checks and balances are being introduced. Furthermore, there are regulations about full transparency. Local groups, associations, beneficiaries and the public attending regular general meetings at ward level are begining to keep track of abuses and fight them. Particular care has been taken to ensure that all of the interested parties in political life are present within the coordinating organs at different levels. And, as far as I know, there are few signs that local governments with a left–centre majority have received special treatment – notwithstanding the fact that some voices within the left–centre front are still wary of handing over money and power to panchayats where the left does not predominate. For the fact is that local governments in which the Congress Party predominates – some 40 per cent of the total – and in which its members exert themselves most, enjoy particularly good opportunities for obtaining substantial resources. The campaign leadership is anxious to demonstrate its impartiality.

It is fair to say, however, that those parties in the left–centre front whose members are not substantially involved in broad development work have tended to wield less influence than they would otherwise have done – if, that is, they had been able in the usual fashion to exploit their swing vote in elections, and on this basis to demand privileged representation on the full range of boards and committees. The same applies to certain ministers, whose top-down departments have been weakened, and to members of the state parliament, who no longer have access to funds of their own for the benefit of their home districts. On the other hand, those groupings and leaders within the dominant party (the CPM) who have supported the campaign appear to have strengthened their positions. In fact, attempts have been made, within both the State Planning Board and the Party leadership, to ensure that the campaign stands above the various internal disputes. Indeed, the Party as a whole is now committed to such an extent that it seems to have reached the point of no return. Recently, however, in late February and early March 1999, the campaign suffered a serious setback when the minor left-front parties, spearheaded by the CPI (Communist Party of India), managed to reduce the influence of committed expert-volunteers at all levels in favour of politicians and administrators, even though many of the latter have not yet been transferred to the local levels and have not been in any case too enthusiastic about decentralization and planning from below.

What is more, it is clear from the course of the campaign that results are not automatically best either in localities governed by the left–centre, or in areas wherein civil society and the market have long been strong (see below, Chapter 12). Popular and democratic development work is not something that can be called forth by political command; nor is it something which emerges of its own accord just because private activities are widespread and associational life is strong. Indeed, all of the private and tentative reports and observations of which I am aware, as well as my recent interviews in several panchayats,[8] indicate that the campaign has hitherto encountered its greatest problems in southern Kerala, where civil society and the market have long been strongest. Nor can the successes in the central and northern parts of Kerala be ascribed solely to the fact that the left has long had its greatest strength in those regions. For another important difference between the north and the south is the fact that social life in general is much more commercialized and privatized in the south. Nevertheless, there are important exceptions in the south where the campaign is doing extremely well; likewise it does not always succeed in the centre and north. The key question seems rather to be the presence, on the one hand, of enthusiastic local politicians, and, on the other, of genuine popular organizations which are focused on political development work, which are not narrowly party-political, and which do not just demand state and local government measures but also facilitate citizens' own actions. KSSP activists often play an important role here.

A second critical problem is that the campaign has been accused of trying to replace representative democracy, in the form of elections to posts on various levels, with red organs of popular power. To be sure, many activists have long been so frustrated with the established political system – wherein parties favour just their own supporters – that they prefer direct democracy, consensus decisions and popular participation to constitutionally regulated forms of decision-making. At the same time, however, it is important to note that the KSSP has changed over the years from a typical NGO – a private and apolitical association – into an organization engaged in politically oriented development work in co-operation with state agencies, local governments and elected politicians. Indeed, one fundamental difference between the KSSP's work during the first campaigns up to 1991 and its work thereafter was its later commitment to decentralization and to long-term collaboration with local governments. In addition, activists have become increasingly anxious to ensure that elected politicians (and state and local government employees) are represented in all new development organs.

Obviously there are conflicts. An important objective of both previous and present campaigns, after all, has been to engage larger numbers of people, young and old, in local development work, with an eye to re-vitalizing the political system. It is clearly a moot point, moreover, whether a prioritized part of the campaign ought to have been the training of elected local government politicians – including the many inexperienced (but politically less constrained) women who have come into their positions thanks to the new national quotas (which require that one-third of elected politicians be women). Now, however, this stands high on the agenda of the campaign leadership. It remains a mystery to me that donors such as Scandinavian aid organs and joint associations of local governments have not grasped this opportunity to do some good.[9]

A third concrete problem lies in the difficulties the campaign has encountered when working with established administrators and technical experts. The fact is, as indicated earlier, that the entire campaign risked being deadlocked (after only a year) when the projects that had been worked out could not be implemented, due to difficulties encountered by activists working with the experts whose go-ahead was needed. This is at least as great a problem as that presented by the state politicians who are unhappy about losing influence as a result of decentralization.

The conflicts with administrators and experts are just the tip of the iceberg. For while the development campaign is moving on at a breakneck pace, it is taking a much longer time to develop the full legal basis for political and administrative decentralization to local and district governments. The same applies to the training and relocation of all important administrators. The so-called Sen Committee, which was charged with drawing up guidelines, rapidly saw the need for some relatively radical principles. After that, however, much of its more detailed work came to a standstill. Several politicians (including some from the left–centre front) and many administrators themselves did their part to complicate and obstruct the process. The work – which has been characterized by concession and compromise – is moving forward slowly. In late February 1999, finally, amendments were made to the Panchayat Raj Act. Yet it remains to be seen when and how the actual regulations will be worked out and implemented, together with the deployment of sufficient administrative personnel.

This consequence is due, first, to the special interests mentioned earlier, as well as to the fact that activists cannot easily fight such interests, deeply rooted as the latter are even among members and supporters of the left–centre front. Second, however, disputes over principle also enter the picture, as in the debate over the influence that elected representatives ought to wield in comparison with rule-bound administrators. On the one side are those who say that all administrators on the local level (including the 'district collectors') should be subordinate to elected representatives on that level. On the other side are those who say that the 'delicate balance' between politicians and administrators must not be upset, especially since the latter are required to follow various rules, and moreover, in their own view, are the only ones who are capable of holding the country on a steady course in the face of all the doings of 'corrupt and power-hungry politicians'. Third, then, is the currently more serious dispute over what influence volunteers should have in the triangular relation with politicians and administrators – in terms initially of the deployment of administrative personnel, but in the long run of popular participation also.

The answer given by campaign leaders themselves is that they have consciously refrained from getting closely involved in these political, administrative and legal conflicts, and have instead concentrated on getting real development efforts under way. It had been clear already during the struggle for land reform that it was futile to await legislation and new rules before starting to implement changes. Besides which, it was hard to organize mass movements around formal issues. What produced results was when activists mobilized people to start implementing the land reform before the formalities were altogether ready. In the same way, campaign leaders explain, the need of the moment is to heighten expectations and to begin concrete projects which really will help people, so that demands for decentralization and for new rules and principles will have a broad and powerful movement behind them.

There is a great deal going for this argument. If it is taken too far, however, unproductive tensions will arise between the popular power championed by activists and the constitutionalism defended by administrators and some politicians; tensions which in turn will complicate the institutionalization of local popular self-rule. Just as those people who expect to benefit from the policies pursued by the elite must do more than simply place demands on it, and are required to participate in governing the society themselves, so development work and expectations from below can only make possible but not create and implement the necessary pro-decentralization rules. It remains to be seen if efficient regulations regarding decentralization and deployment of personnel will be implemented; also if the forms of popular participation that have been practised can be institutionalized, so that when the campaign is weakened (through reduced involvement of expert-volunteers) the field is not opened up to local bossism, including at the hands of some leftist politicians.

Conclusion

The new development efforts in Kerala undoubtedly represent an impressive democratic and socially dynamic attempt at remedying many of the central problems found in India and the Third World: the need for greater democracy and popular participation; the need to combine economic growth and socioeconomic equalization (without harming the environment); and the need to counter antiquated boss-rule and to place new forms of mobilizing on the agenda, without undermining earlier achievements. Indeed, the state of Kerala is so special – in its well-educated citizenry, its uncommonly lively civil society, and its strong political and trade-union organizations – that its campaigns and policies may be difficult to replicate in other contexts without significant modification. At the same time, however, Kerala really is a 'critical case'. As indicated earlier, some of today's popular prescriptions have already been tested in that state, and under relatively advantageous conditions. It follows that if such methods lead to problems in Kerala, results elsewhere are likely to be negative too. And by studying the new alternatives that the Malayalees have started developing, we can take the step from criticism to constructive insight.

According to the fashionable prescriptions of the day, the problems of the Third World can be cured with more civil society and less but 'better' politics. This state of affairs, in turn, is to be achieved through privatization, deregulation and decentralization; through a strengthening of the core functions of the state; and through greater support for free media and voluntary organizations. Experiences in Kerala indicate that much of this is misleading. The lack of local self-rule was certainly a fundamental obstacle encountered in the first development campaigns. Above and beyond calling for privatization and deregulation, however, the prescriptions in vogue have little to say about how to cope with powerful interests such as those associated with the existing order in Kerala. For many years and in many cases, not even politicians of the left–centre went against the current. Furthermore, activists who had committed themselves to development efforts through civil society lacked the means on their own (outside the established political system) to clip the wings of powerful groups. And, in any case, after the land reform the very privatization, deregulation and commercialization recommended by today's fashionable theoreticians counteracted rather than promoted interest in joint productive efforts, and promoted rather than counteracted fragmentation in civil society and special interests in politics.

The key to renewed development efforts in the mid-1990s lay rather in political pressures for devolution of resources and self-government. Moreover, in order to coordinate efforts on the part of both the state and local citizens' groups, activists integrated their development projects with local government operations. Furthermore, they also initiated and coordinated the projects from above, via the State Planning Board.

Alongside the impressive results achieved, new problems also point to the importance of popular and political – but not narrowly *party*-political – mobilization. On the one hand, development work goes least well where privatization and commercialization – and the resulting fragmentation of civil society – are strongest. On the other hand, traditional leftist rule is not enough either – in a situation where organizations are antiquated and voters no longer so production-oriented.

It would seem difficult to revitalize the political system without also investing in the training of local politicians and administrators. In addition, more coordination is needed on the state and political level between local development projects and development projects of a more overarching kind. Finally, the legal basis for political and administrative decentralization is lagging behind. The results are not good when far-reaching expectations are raised, and local development projects undertaken, while the devising of political and administrative rules is left to the old elite. And now that politicians and administrators realize that decentralization and popular participation are really taking place, they are doing their utmost to avoid losing out. The bottom line, then, is the importance of institutionalizing the popular participation that has been practised, and thereby to set a pace for the introduction of useful checks and balances as well as cooperation between politicians, administrators and volunteers. Hence, the fate of the new KSSP campaign, launched in mid-1999, to engage all volunteers (including the now disempowered technical experts) in upholding the spirit of the campaign and helping people on the grassroots level to keep a watchful eye on politicians and administrators may well be crucial.

In sum, cooperation between citizens furnishes no guarantee of progress in a civil society which is strong but fragmented by commercialism and privatization. In many respects, it is *more* politics that is needed, not less. It is needed in order to facilitate the democratic coordination of various development efforts – state, local-government and civic.

Notes

This chapter was originally written in Swedish. It is here translated into English by Peter Mayers. A Norwegian version was published in an anthology on India by Cappelen Akademika. The Swedish version was published in *Socialistik Debatt* 2(99).

1. For an authoritative, current and 'global' pronouncement on this question, see World Bank (1997).

2. This presentation is based chiefly on my own studies (which began in the early 1980s) of Kerala's development efforts in a comparative perspective. See Törnquist (1989, 1991a, 1991b, 1995 and 1996) and note 4. The theoretical and operational framework is found in Törnquist (1998a and 1999). For a broader introduction, see Ramachandran (1997), Franke and Chasin (1989), George (1993 and 1998), Thomas Isaac et al. (1997), Tharamangalam (1998a), and Törnquist (1998b).

3. See Törnquist (1995).

4. See Thomas Isaac and Tharakan (1995), Thomas Isaac and Harilal (1997), Törnquist (1996), Franke and Chasin (1997), Bandyopadhyay (1997), Chekkutty (1997), and Thomas Isaac (1998). The press coverage includes, first and foremost, that in *Frontline* as well as that provided by the Kerala editions of *Hindu* and *Indian Express* (I am grateful for Sabu Philip's help here), as well as that furnished by relevant local articles and papers. I am grateful for discussions with Thomas Isaac between 17 and 27 September 1998. Finally, in addition to the tentative results from field studies in Kerala in 1996, I also include some results from a recent field trip, including visits and interviews (on the current people's planning campaign) in some fifteen panchayats in February 1999 (I am particularly grateful for Rajmohan's assistance here).

5. Rammohan's (1998) attempt to analyse conflicts within the CPI–M by using my results (among other materials) – but without taking the several different conflict patterns into account – is therefore misleading.

6. The abstracts of all the papers are gathered in four volumes published by the organizers. For a fruitful attempt at a summary, see Thomas Isaac and Tharakan (1995). (Where Ms Jayalalitha's propaganda spectacle is concerned, I base my description on Ingrid Widlund's forthcoming doctoral thesis, to be submitted at Uppsala University, on political discourse in Tamil Nadu.)

7. One US dollar corresponds roughly to 40 rupees – although locally, of course, the rupee's purchasing power is greater.

8. See note 4.

9. At the time of writing, it appears that only the Swiss have opened their eyes to this opportunity.

7

Normal Kerala within Abnormal India: Reflections on Gender and Sustainability

William M. Alexander

The people of India within the earth and the people of Kerala within India are the universe for this study. In this discourse we are bound together by an abiding interest in our sustainability within the biosphere of the earth. The availability of hard data focuses our attention on the twentieth century. Hopes for human sustainability and information about the positive role of gender lead our imagination into the twenty-first century.

We describe the development experience of Kerala to indicate a normal process of improvement and change, particularly improvement in well-being. We are not reporting sponsored development experiences, efforts of outside agents to improve the well-being of the people of Kerala. We report here improvements in well-being created by the citizens of Kerala for themselves.

Looking from the outside into India, we see a culture and society strikingly different from Western experience. For the sake of an analysis intended to enlighten 'insiders' and 'outsiders' alike, two major differences shared by India and Kerala need emphasis – a lack of earth resources and a lack of individualistic motivation (of which more below). From the Western perspective, we see these shortages as the cause of (or at least in close proximity to) three abnormalities: female suppression, low well-being and high fertility. While sharing the two major shortages of India, Kerala (nearly invisible to Western observers within gigantic India) is not experiencing the three Indian abnormalities. In Kerala we find gender equity, high well-being and low fertility – all normal human behaviours within the comfort zone of Western observers. As a means to address rapidly the essentials of our analysis within the world-view of Western audiences, simplifying labels are applied – Kerala as 'normal' and India as 'abnormal'.

Development scholars have noted the high well-being and low fertility of Kerala, but Kerala cannot be made to fit Western development theory – economic growth first and well-being later. The big foundations and other money-driven institutions which support assistance and research about development (such as the World Bank, the IMF and USAID) find Kerala an embarrassment, an aberration or a mystery that needs to be explained away. Their enormous aid programmes expended in other Indian states have failed to create the levels of well-being achieved in Kerala without such aid. Should Western development theory be challenged or is a Kerala caveat sufficient?

Scientific American has called Kerala 'A Mystery Inside a Riddle Inside an Enigma' (Wallich 1995). In the community of Western scholars, India is the enigma and Kerala the mystery. Two important elements of the Indian enigma contrasted to the West are defined here – a lack of resources and a lack of individualism. Within these parameters, we shall reduce the mystery of Kerala to a riddle – a riddle with a solution. We shall compare the abnormalities of India – female suppression, low well-being and high fertility – with the normality of Kerala. A first step in riddle solving is defining *what*, and the next step is asking *why*. Replicability (of the Kerala experience) is a *how* question.

The development experience of normal Kerala has been an enlightened self-help movement focusing directly on a common human object, well-being. Indians both in Kerala and beyond Kerala are engaged in centuries-old efforts to maintain or increase the class standing of their family groups to acquire social and economic power. As we consider background differences between Kerala and India below, we will identify different family striving methods: application of the gender equity of Kerala and the patriarchy of India – the former empowering females and the latter suppressing female contributions to well-being.

Looking into the experience of normal Kerala from the beginning of the twentieth century, we notice a magnificent struggle of humans against the tyranny of Hindu caste. The battles within religious, economic and political institutions to destroy caste in Kerala provided high drama and created the base for an enduring egalitarian democracy. These struggles were understood as the oppressed overcoming their oppressors, increasing the well-being of all. Within each institutional faction – religious, economic and political – appropriate credit may be given. Much credit is due for the courage and patience of the oppressed majority. And after the fact, it is possible to credit the former oppressors with the wisdom to concede. Kerala well-being increases, which today mark the observed differences between India and Kerala, began during these early struggles. Striking differences among the well-being measures showed up in the second half of the century.

Amid the sound and fury of those struggles, the well-being successes of Kerala may be viewed as the fortunate (perhaps accidental) result of these factional fights ending in an egalitarian compromise. Why did the oppressors concede? And why haven't new oppressors come to power? Such questions lead us to seek something even more basic in the differences between abnormal India and normal Kerala. We shall look at family structural differences – gender equity versus patriarchy – differences working in favour of Kerala which may have mediated the favourable outcomes of the twentieth-century struggles.

Resource-short India

Shortage of resources is one of the first conditions of economic well-being that sets India apart in this analysis from much of the rest of the world. The low living standards and low consumption of the ordinary Indian citizen is the best-known difference between India and Western experience. Scholars have applied the word 'imperialism' to describe the behaviour of Western powers seeking more earth resources for their populations – at first military and then economic. Japan is an especially clear case: a profound shift from military expansion before World War II to economic after. Japan and many Western nations are short of earth resources within their boundaries but have a relative plenty of resources available to them extracted from less developed nations.

Even without increasing their control over resources outside of India, improved technologies have increased the total amounts of earth resources available within India. Growing population numbers have balanced the technological improvements, holding the per-capita amounts available to a low constant. This relative shortage of natural resources has limited the beneficial effect of economic growth formulas applied within India. Pressure on the limited earth resources in India has led to exploitation beyond the regenerative capacity of the several ecosystems, a phenomenon the West is beginning to experience.

Inasmuch as per-capita income figures measure the consumption of resources, the low living standard and low consumption are equally low or lower in Kerala than in all India (Thomas Isaac 1997). This equality of resource consumption allows us to set income aside as we make comparisons between India and Kerala. In this study, income is one of the *all-else-equal* factors. The equal force of income within Kerala and India allows us to avoid an application of the assumption of most development studies that higher incomes are a necessary condition of higher well-being and lower fertility.

Lack of Individualism

The second condition, which sets India apart from much of the rest of the world, is the absence of the Western doctrine of individualism – the belief that all actions are determined by or take place for the benefit of the individual. That is, in many circumstances the individual interests of mature adolescents and adults may take precedence over responsibilities to families. The individualism of economic theory holds that each citizen should be allowed freedom in the exercise of his business pursuits and any financial rewards are his alone. The nearest equivalent in the Indian experience to this powerful Western doctrine might be labelled *familialism*.

The familialism of India is solidly rooted in family; that is, persons related by blood and marriage as parents, brothers and sisters, aunts and uncles, and cousins – a lineage system of many generations. The family in India is a group much larger and much stronger than the filial bonding known in the families of the West. In India family interests take precedence over the interests (desires and choices) of each family member. Only those individual initiatives which are dedicated to and clearly benefit the entire family group are encouraged.

Individualism may be overemphasized in the explanations of human behaviour outside of India. On the other hand, it is difficult to overemphasize the importance of familialism as a determinant of behaviour in India. This generalization holds in both our normal sample (gender-equity families) and our abnormal sample (patriarchical families) in the following analysis. The individualism of the West seems to need a doctrinal statement, while familialism is so inherent throughout the culture of India that no such assertions are needed.

Well-being

Humans sometimes assist and often manage the survival of other life forms as necessary to their own well-being, seeking for themselves more than survival. Humans seek well-being within a process in which nature has a role that we call sustainability. Measured aspects of desired well-being are long life expectancies, low infant-mortality rates, high educational attainments, and low total fertility rates. These desired measures are found together and are often used to explain each other in a circular fashion. In the specific questions addressed here, the natural unity of these well-being measures is maintained as an object and purpose of successful human behaviour.

Well-being is often described as a qualitative characteristic of a society – happiness and contentment. A qualitative description of well-being has been documented with an appropriate emphasis on love and aesthetics (Ger 1997). Well-being also has several positive measures with material connections, such as long life, low infant mortality, high literacy, and stable democratic institutions – measures which shall be featured here. We also know what well-being is not. Well-being resides in societies – is not welfare defined in dollars as income per capita. And well-being is not the charity of the wealthy, public or private (Dodds 1997). Robin Jeffrey (1992) provides us with a descriptive chapter on the well-being of Kerala.

One of the desired outcomes of high well-being, low fertility, provides a central linkage in this account. The low fertility of zero population growth may be located in any society where the total fertility rate has declined to two or less – that is, an average of two children or fewer in the lifetime of each female in a given society. Inasmuch as small families are a necessary condition for human sustainability, measurements of the societal well-being necessary for the achievement of zero population growth can be applied as a materially defined sustainability benchmark.

Efficiency: Throughput and Knowledge

A material characteristic is integral to well-being, a modicum of matter and energy called throughput – that is, ecosystem services taken by humans. Throughput is a flow of matter and energy which humans withdraw from the earth's biosphere each day for their use. Important parts of the throughput taken by humans are other life forms along with sunlight, air, water and minerals. All such matter and energy taken from the biosphere for human use are eventually returned in a degraded condition where they may be regenerated and reordered in the several ecosystems of the biosphere. Throughput passes through the digestive tract of human civilization, often in a single day, usually within a year, while some regeneration takes centuries, even millennia (Daly 1996b).

Much, possibly most, human activity is the mixing of throughput with human knowledge to create the desired end, well-being. Many human artefacts and tools are huge repositories of knowledge. For example, keeping warm using little throughput in a cold climate is possible but requires a large input of knowledge. On the other hand, it is possible to keep warm using large amounts of throughput with little knowledge. The relative amounts of throughput and knowledge mixed to create well-being usually depend on which is easily available and which is in short supply.

Sustainability for humans requires a limited amount of throughput taken from the finite ecosystem services of the earth's biosphere. In simple arithmetic, the number of humans times human-taking per-capita equals an amount of throughput that cannot be exceeded on a finite earth. Either human numbers or per-capita consumption may be maximized. If we wish to maximize human numbers, we may note that the application of more knowledge can increase well-being without increasing throughput. Searching for a value for the increase of human numbers, we may be reminded by an important pronatalist: more humans may create more knowledge (Simon 1996).

Zero population growth is most easily understood as a part of or as flowing from a condition of sufficient but limited throughput. For life forms other than humans, stabilized throughput for a particular species causes zero population growth. For humans the cause-and-effect relationships go both ways, are interactive. That is, similar to other life forms, limited throughput could force zero population growth on humans, but, unlike other life forms, human choice for zero population growth may lead humans to a sustainable throughput plateau. The human choice for zero population growth is mediated by the qualitative characteristic of a society, well-being. Well-being finds material measures in several desired results: low infant mortality, long life, high education and low fertility. In human behaviour, high well-being measures correlate with total fertility rates of two or less (Alexander 1994).

As a positively defined qualitative characteristic of a society, well-being may be employed as a basic object and purpose of such society in an efficiency measure. Thus measured, efficiency is well-being divided by throughput per capita. In this formula, well-being would be set at one for any society which has a fertility rate of two children or fewer. High well-being efficiency is thus the product of a society's low per-capita throughput. Such efficiencies are guided by the skilled application of knowledge.

Improved technologies were introduced into India continually during the twentieth century. By 1935 these improvements were evident in reduced death rates. The steady decline of death rates after 1935 suggests that a human survival plateau had been passed. In Kerala the constant of gender equity appears to have acted synergistically with the new technologies. That is, the death rate decline in Kerala accelerated past the Indian decline. This synergism is particularly evident during the fifty years following 1935. Indian death rates declined from 31 per 1,000 to 12.6, while Kerala death rates declined from 29 per 1,000 to 6.6. This synergy has been even more dramatic in lowering infant mortality rates. Between 1915 and 1990 infant mortality rates dropped from 278 per 1,000 in India to 80. During the same period, these rates dropped in Kerala from 242 per 1,000 to 17 (Ramachandran 1997). In Kerala with gender equity, the decline of infant mortality was four times faster than in all India.

Table 7.1 Death rates by sex and age group in eleven villages in Ludhiana district of Punjab (per 1,000)

Age group	Male death rate	Female death rate	Male/female deaths ratio
0–14	19.2	28.8	0.667
15–44	1.9	5.2	0.363
45+	30.7	31.9	0.962
All ages	14.6	19.1	0.764

Note: Death rates between 1 July and 31 December 1959, according to the Khanna Study.
Source: Visaria (1961).

Table 7.2 Death rates by sex and age group in the rural areas of Punjab, Himachal Pradesh, and Delhi (per 1,000)

Age group	Male death rate	Female death rate	Male/female deaths ratio
0–14	18.50	23.36	0.791
15–44	1.54	3.30	0.467
45+	22.61	17.94	1.261
All ages	12.39	14.15	0.876

Note: Death rates between July 1958 and July 1959, according to the fourteenth round of the Indian National Sample Survey.
Source: Visaria (1961).

Female Death Rates

Why are female deaths abnormally high in India? The basic data have long been known. The report of the 1961 Indian census displays the findings of the Khanna Study carried out by a group of Harvard scientists, and places it within the larger context of the National Sample Survey conducted by the Indian government.

In industrialized countries the male/female deaths ratio in the right-hand columns of Tables 7.1 and 7.2 would be one or more in every age category. Comparison of these two tables shows that the abnormal death rates of females, or fatal daughter syndrome, was more intense in the Khanna Study area than in the larger inclusive area of the National Sample Survey.

Hard Data

As we proceed into real-life considerations, we must look at the comparative measures defining well-being. The high well-being measures found in Kerala will appear to all concerned observers as normal, while we may see the low well-being measures of India as abnormal. Additional data for the other Indian states and comparison nations may be found in the source.

In the event that our minds are set to see economic growth as a necessary condition for fertility declines, we need to refocus our vision. Find the significant economic growth measured in India in Table 7.3 and note that the economic growth of Kerala is close to zero. In order to gain wider perspective, note also how economic growth plays out in the three states and four nations offered for comparison. Next note the consistency of the well-being measures displayed – infant mortality, life expectancy and literacy. Kerala is not just the most desirable on each measure; critical well-being measures such as infant mortality are dramatically different between India and Kerala. It is difficult to comprehend that similar populations have been measured. And before proceeding, consider the differences in the female-to-male ratios in Table 7.3, which is referenced as a critical explanatory factor below.

Looking further into Table 7.3 we may ask: Why is Indian fertility twice as high as that in Kerala? Since low fertility is encouraged by high well-being, we may restate our question: Why is well-being low in India and high in Kerala? We look at the levels of literacy, infant mortality and length of life, and each begs a similar question. Why is literacy so much higher in Kerala than in any other part of India? Why is infant mortality in Kerala so low? Why do the men and women of Kerala live so much longer? Looking at each of these questions we see mirrored measurements integral to the well-being considered here as a unity, a human goal.

The reports of travellers and officials have long noted the higher status of women in Kerala. A 1875 census report for a part of the future Kerala included the comment, 'The partiality of parents in bestowing greater care on their female issues, will be hazarding an opinion based on insufficient data, though it is a fact that among [matrilineal] people a female child is prized more highly than a male one' (Aiya 1876). Looking back at India in 1999, data are no longer *insufficient*.

Table 7.3 Comparative data for three of India's twenty-five states, all-India and four Asian neighbours.

	Kerala	West Bengal	Uttar Pradesh	all-India	Bangla-desh	Paki-stan	Sri Lanka	China
1. Females per 100 males	104	92	88	93	94	92	99	94
2. Infant mortality rate	17	66	98	79	91	95	18	31
3. Female life expectancy	74	62	55	59	56	59	74	71
4. Male life expectancy	69	61	57	59	55	59	70	68
5. Female literacy rate	86	47	25	39	23	22	74	68
6. Male literacy rate	94	68	56	64	49	49	94	87
7. Economic growth	0.3	2.5	2.2	3.1	1.9	3.0	2.6	7.7
8. Total fertility rate	1.8	3.2	5.1	3.7	4.0	5.6	2.5	2.0
9. Population	29	68	139	884	114	119	17	1,162

Notes

1: Number of females per 100 males in the population.

2: Infant mortality rate (IMR) is the number of infants who die per 1,000 live births. This is the best composite measure of well-being in a society. IMR is a sensitive indirect measure of the quality of the food and water, the quality of the housing and clothing, the quality of health care, and the quality of the education in the whole society. By 1995 the IMR in Kerala had declined to 13 (see Parameswaran this volume).

3 and 4: Life expectancy is the average number of years a child born into a given society may expect to live.

5 and 6: Literacy is the percentage of the population over the age of 7 who can read and write.

7: Economic growth is a ten-year average of the annual growth of the economy (%).

8: Total fertility rate (TFR) is the average number of children borne by all females in their lifetime. In a population which has an equal amount of in- and out-migration, a TFR of less than 2 will create zero population growth within a generation or so. By 1995 the TFR in Kerala had dropped to 1.7

9: Population shows the most recent census count, given in millions.

Source: Drèze and Sen (1996).

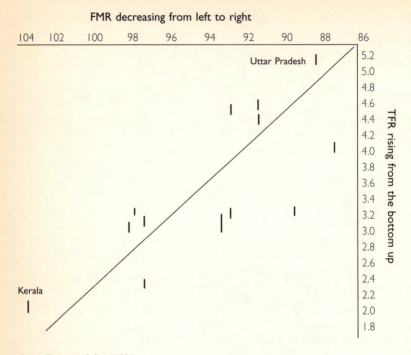

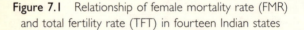

Source: Drèze and Sen (1996).

Figure 7.1 Relationship of female mortality rate (FMR) and total fertility rate (TFT) in fourteen Indian states

Female-to-Male Ratios

Probing into the history of India and Kerala reveals hard data that help to establish the gender equity explanation of caste demise, higher well-being, and lower fertility in Kerala. These significant measurements were revealed in the very first official enumeration of the Kerala population. For all India, typical of most non-industrial countries of that time, the number of males exceeded the number of females. Yet in Kerala, as was observed only in industrialized countries, the number of females was greater than the number of males.

An examination of a century of census data shows abnormal female-to-male differences to be persistent and increasing. The favourable ratio of females-to-males in Kerala in 1901 was 101 to 100 males. As in the industrialized countries, this female share had increased to 104 by 1991.

Table 7.4   Female-to-male ratios declining in twentieth-century India

Year	Females per 1,000 males		
	Kerala	all-India	Difference
1901	1,004	972	32
1911	1,008	964	44
1921	1,011	955	56
1931	1,022	950	71
1941	1,027	954	73
1051	1,028	946	82
1961	1,022	941	81
1971	1016	930	86
1981	1,032	934	98
1991	1,040	929	111

Source: Nanda (1991).

During the twentieth century the female-to-male ratio began in India at 97 to 100, and by 1991 had declined to 92 per 100 (Drèze and Sen 1996). Impaired female survival is typical of developing countries but the decline in female survival rates relative to males is abnormal.

A fundamental insight leading this analysis flows from the correlation between high fertility and low female-to-male ratios within the several Indian states. The fourteen major states of India are located in Figure 7.1 as vertical blips bisected by a trend line. The female-to-male ratios (number of females per 100 males) are shown as the declining numbers (left to right) across the top. The increasing total fertility rates (number of births per female) related to the decline of female-to-male ratios are shown (bottom to top) along the right side. This crude figure clearly shows the critical relationship – as female-to-male ratios decline, fertility goes up.

Figure 7.1, showing the significance of differential female-to-male ratios on fertility in the fourteen Indian states is based on 1991 census data. In a demographic transition a generation of delay is common before well-being improvements with decreasing death rates cause declines in birth rates. Therefore, to display the importance of female-to-male ratios through time let us look at the abnormal decline in female-to-male ratios in India through the twentieth century. Table 7.4 shows the abnormal twentieth-century decline in India and the normal (similar to industrialized countries) female-to-male ratios of Kerala.

Fatal Daughter Syndrome

Reports of female infanticide in twentieth-century India are rare. However, beginning in 1789 the officers of the British raj were reporting 'almost wholesale female infanticide'. Among 400 Jadeja Rajput households, there was 'not a single female child in any of them' (Vishwanath 1998). The Jadejas were the highest-ranking subcaste of this (Rajput) wealthy landowning caste. Family wealth was maintained by allowing sons to marry brides from slightly lower subcastes paying dowries. The four-wives rule of the Muslims accommodated the surplus daughter problem at the top of their social and wealth hierarchies. The monogamous Hindus of the highest ranked families practised female infanticide.

Opium and other poisons were sometimes used, but the newborn infants were so vulnerable that the 'refusal of the mother to feed the female infant or exposure to heat or cold were enough to finish them off'. In 1856 census officials reported that castes practising female infanticide were 'resorting increasingly' to neglect of their female children to escape the accusation of killing their daughters (Vishwanath 1998). Our current evidence shows that girl-child neglect, not infanticide, is the major cause of the low female-to-male ratios in India. The devaluation of females by the highest castes has diffused into the practices of all lower castes and communities. However, the force of the fatal daughter syndrome declines as we look down from the top to the bottom of the class–caste hierarchy.

Traditional discrimination in health care that produces lower male than female mortality has been shown in eleven villages in the northern Indian district of Ludhiana. These villages were the subjects of intensive observation in the Khanna Study (Wyon and Gordon 1971). Similar study methods were applied in the Mitlab project area in Bangladesh. In both areas, female mortality was lower than male mortality in the early months after birth, consistent with the female physiological advantage in survivorship over the entire span of life. In the latter part of the first year and thereafter female death rates were higher than male death rates (D'Souza and Chen 1980).

In the early interval after birth when the source of nutrition is predominantly breast-feeding, the normal female advantage prevailed. When hand feeding began, however, female death rates rose relative to male death rates. The more-sons incentive for the provision of better nutrition (other than mother's milk) for males is also shown in other studies. The higher female than male child mortality in the Khanna Study turned up particularly revealing evidence. The mortality of females under 5 who have no older sisters is little different from the male death rate, but the death rates of under-5 females who have an older sister is about 50 per cent higher than the rate for males (Das Gupta 1987).

This set of evidence indicates that higher female mortality is caused by a lower regard for female infants – less fatal when the new daughter does not have an older sister. Further evidence on the professional health-care side is provided by an investigation of medical attendance during fatal illnesses in the Khanna Study area, 1957–59. The overall death rate was much higher for females (19.6 per 1,000) than for males (14.8 for males) during these years. Fewer females than males had received medical care during the fatal illness, and the care received by females was attended by personnel of lower competence (Singh, Gordon and Wyon 1962).

A recent analysis of fatal daughter syndrome notes the slight numerical advantage of males at birth balanced by a slightly greater vulnerability of male infants, creating a parity between the sexes some time after the age of 5. We should expect the numbers of boys and girls between the ages of 5 and 9 to be about equal – as they are in Kerala. We may contrast Kerala with average girl–boy survivorship in the twenty-four adjoining districts in North India, parts of Haryana, Uttar Pradesh, Rajasthan, and Madhya Pradesh. The evidence of fatal daughter syndrome is extreme. The reduction of the numbers of girl children to 77 per 100 boy children was characterized as *gender cleansing* in this study (Harriss-White 1999).

Indian Family Structures

Indian census data allow us to identify districts with low and very low female-to-male ratios caused by fatal daughter syndrome. We may look within these districts to observe an all-pervasive class system marked by the ranking of the extended families which characterize the Hindu culture. These extended families are the repositories of social power, economic power and political power – a power combination related to *familialism*, described above. Competition among these families to maintain their rank order in the comprehensive hierarchical family systems of India is the essential motivation for fatal daughter syndrome. This competition is managed and supervised by a patriarch or his agent within these extended families.

Muslims and Christians living in the same localities are accorded a kind of proportional class standing within the overall Hindu culture. Those districts with the lowest female sex ratios are clustered in the northern states adjacent to New Delhi where the dominant caste is often the Rajputs. Although Rajputs are not dominant in most Indian census districts, naming a caste is important because marriages are not allowed (by hard-line religious and social traditions) across caste lines or into the Muslim or Christian communities.

Among the Rajputs (and other high-ranking patriarchical castes) the purity of the male lineage, father to son, is a highest value consistently protected. The sexuality (physical beauty, demeanour, manners and skills) of a female may be her means of self-expression and thus a part of her power relative to others, particularly males. This sexuality is systematically suppressed by family institutions, disempowering females. Although more extreme in India, the struggles of females to avoid disempowerment in Western patriarchical families have been a familiar plot central in countless novels in the West. In India every opportunity for expression of a female's sexuality, excepting only in her husband's bed, is circumscribed or denied.

All marriages are arranged by family elders; girls are seldom allowed any role in these negotiations. Maintaining and improving the class status of the family is seen as the central goal of each marriage arrangement. A bride's function is to serve in the maintenance of her husband's family lineage. The arranged marriages among the royal and other high-ranking families of Western experience often had this power-maintaining function. The basic marriage rule is: outside of family and within caste. The critical problem in marriage arrangements flows from the need to maintain or improve the class standing of the extended family. If a daughter should be married into a family lower in the class ranking, the daughter's birth family loses status. On the other hand, a son may marry down provided the bride's family can afford a large dowry. Inasmuch as class ranking is based on the somewhat interchangeable elements of wealth and social power, a significant infusion of wealth into the groom's extended family could maintain or even improve a family's class standing. Within a family at the peak of the class hierarchy (no marrying up possible), wealth is the only means of increasing status.

As we compare the family structures in Kerala below, it will be important to note that at marriage in North India the bride moves into the household of her husband. The daughter-in-law arrives as the least significant member of her new family, rather like a servant to her husband and his mother. She is also cut off from her birth family by distance and restricted visiting customs. As an outsider in her new extended family, she may be denied female support, and may exercise influence in family decisions only through the intervention of her husband speaking on her behalf. Even here she is disempowered. Husbands are discouraged from forming affectionate bonds with their wives – such attachments diminish the husband's allegiance to the family patriarch and attention to his first responsibility, his extended family.

It is many years before the bride's status may be established by the birth of sons bonded to her and later speaking up on her behalf. Before puberty daughters are helpful to mothers, but at marriage their value to their mother's household disappears as they devote themselves to their husband's welfare, producing sons for the benefit of his family lineage, and caring for his parents. Anthropologists have a word for this female-disempowering family structure: hypergamy – brides marrying socio-economically upward within caste into richer and more esteemed extended families that require compensation for what would otherwise be a misalliance.

Kerala Family Structures

Looking for those census districts in India that display normal female-to-male ratios, we also discover different family structures and empowered females. None of the districts in the Indian state of Kerala displays the abnormality of low female-to-male ratios characteristic of India (Raju et al. 1999), and the family structures are matrilineal and matrilocal with patriarchical appearances honoured. At the same time, the extended families located in India as a whole (different from the nuclear families of Western societies) are common in Kerala.

The entire caste system of Kerala is quite different from India. The Nayars, the dominant caste group after the Brahmins, originated in Kerala. Matrilineal and matrilocal family structures found in Kerala are unfamiliar in the experience and literature of Western societies. Lacking a patri-archical identity, the Nayar family structure is most easily explained in terms of its joint family residence called a *taravad* (also spelt *tharwad*). A distinguished Indian jurist explains that a taravad

> consists of a female ancestor, her children, and all such other descendants, however remote, in the female line. The male descendants themselves are its members but their children are not. A person belongs to the Tharwad of his or her mother only and the Tharwad membership arises by birth in the family. A female member of a Tharwad does not change her family by marriage unlike the other systems which follow the agnatic line of descent.... Each member of a Tharwad acquires an interest in Tharwad properties by reason of his or her birth alone, and when any member dies, the interest of that member devolves upon the other members of a Tharwad. (Variar 1969: 2)

Taravads were the female-lineage joint families (with female-owned properties and residences) of the high-ranking Nayar caste of historic Kerala. Lawyers and jurists trained in English law brought the ownership of family property vested in females under concerted attack during the time of the British Raj. In addition, a Christian attack on the appearance of polyandry in the taravads, joined by a low-caste attack on caste restrictions generally, moved with force in Kerala during the early twentieth century. Both the religious and the legal foundations of the taravad institutions were severely undercut (Jeffrey 1992).

The description of Indian family structures above featured a centuries-long diffusion of the patriarchical customs and practices of a high-ranking caste group. The patriarchical customs of the Rajputs seemed to have diffused into the lower caste and class families in the regions where they dominated. On the other hand, it does not appear that a downward diffusion of family customs occurred in Kerala. The largest caste group, the Ezhavas, or Thiyyas as they are called in northern Kerala, also had taravads and matrilineal decent similar to the dominant Nayars. Rather than diffusion from the Nayars, the gender equity family structures indigenous to Kerala were conserved by the taravads. Although female-headed taravads were unable to maintain control over their large landholdings (against British courts steeped in primogeniture and the individual ownership inherent in British property law), the gender equity family structures of Kerala persisted and continue.

From early times the gender equity found in Kerala appears to have grown out of the attitudes and beliefs of the indigenous Malayalee population. Some of these became Nayars and some Ezhavas living in taravads. Unlike the high-ranking Rajputs noted earlier, the high-ranking Nayars of Kerala had an outlet for hypergamous marriages of daughters. The Nayars had a special kind of marriage of Nayar women with the very small, ritually high, landowning caste called Nambudiri Brahmins. The gender equity of the taravads was and continues to be found in all parts of the Malayalam-speaking population – among lower-caste Hindus, Muslims and Christians.

The experience of gender equity in the historic taravads has been described by anthropologist Kathleen Gough:

> [In Cochin] a woman might have six or eight husbands of her own or a higher subcaste, and a man, any number of Nayar wives of his own or a lower subcaste. Residence was duo local: spouses lived separately in their natal homes and a husband visited his wife in her home at night. Exact physiological paternity was, clearly, often unknown, and in any case a man had no rights in nor obligations to his children. Among Nayars of this area [the male-lineage] family was not institutionalized as a legal, economic, or residential unit. (Gough 1959: 161)

Male support, discipline and role models for each boy were provided by a mother's brother resident in the female-managed households.

The ritually highest caste of Kerala, Nambudiri Brahmins, practised an extreme form of primogeniture: only the eldest sons could marry within caste and carry on the family lineage. Excess Nambudiri daughters were relegated to lifelong seclusion and denied public opportunities enjoyed by Nayar daughters. Nayar women occasionally married men of the Nambudiri caste. The children of such marriages belonged to their mother and enjoyed the care of her tarawad. The numbers of Nambudiri Brahmins were small, less than 1 per cent, and remain numerically insignificant.

A well-known Nambudiri, a communist intellectual, E.M.S. Namboodiripad, rejected his feudal privileges and was elected the first chief minister of the state of Kerala in 1957. Fifteen years earlier he had written of the religiously sanctioned suppression of the sexuality of Nambudiri daughters – the 'disabilities of Hindu womanhood' outside Kerala.

> The absence of free marriage and the right of divorce, the existence of polygamy and compulsory purdah, the lack of economic rights and backward educational and cultural standards – all the disabilities of Hindu womanhood was the lot of Nambudiri women alone among the women of Kerala (Namboodiripad 1942).

The essence of the Nayar model of gender equity, which was a key factor that influenced the well-being of women of Kerala, is described by Ramachandran:

> Nayar women had greater personal freedom than most women to take decisions regarding marital and sexual relations. Nayar women played a crucial role in making household decisions, the decision-making role being invested with great authority – inheritance was through them, and it was they who were the bearers of the family name. The birth of a girl in a Nayar household was welcomed; it was far from being considered a disaster as in other parts of India. (Ramachandran 1997: 279)

Summary and Conclusions

This account of twentieth-century facts and events may be reviewed as an experiment in human behaviour. Two important characteristics distinguish the Indian laboratory from other parts of the earth. First, material resources available to Indians (in per-capita measurements) were low and have remained low throughout the century. The Kerala phenomenon appears to demonstrate the need for an economic theory which will display the higher efficiency of gender equity in the creation of well-being. Second, *familialism* has guided Indian class striving, as contrasted to the individualism motivating economic behaviour in the West.

Within these laboratory conditions, the citizens of India are divided into two experimental groups. The Malayalam-speaking peoples of Kerala become the normal or control group. The normal designation is based on the high well-being and low fertility of Kerala. The family structures in Kerala are intermediate between matriarchical and patriarchical extremes, which we call gender equity. The remaining Indian population is the abnormal experimental group. This vast experimental group are classified as abnormal in accordance with their low well-being measures and their high fertility. The family structures of this 96 per cent of the Indian population may be characterized as patriarchy.

During the twentieth century within the conditions of the Indian laboratory, the control (gender equity) and the experimental (patriarchical) families created different levels of well-being. At the end of the century we have measurements of well-being outputs. On every measure – life expectancy, infant mortality, literacy and fertility – the desired well-being outputs of the gender equity families have exceeded the patriarchical families by large margins.

As shown by several authors in this volume, several important religious, economic and political movements among the Malayalam-speaking peoples of India converged in a society-wide struggle, transforming Kerala from a tyranny of caste into an egalitarian democracy. The gender-equity family structures of Kerala were integral to and contributory to the successes of this magnificent struggle.

Looking into the well-being success of Kerala within abnormal India we defined *what*. Given the Indian shortages of resource and individualism, we have located a *why*, gender equity. Replication of the Kerala equity is a *how* question. Given the solid entrenchment of female suppression in the Indian culture outside of Kerala we may imagine how difficult the replication of gender equity within India may be.

One final note: the low consumption of earth resources within India plus the zero population growth of Kerala allow us to identify the Malayalees as a sustainable society. Lacking any working example of a large sustainable society in the First World, surely there are lessons in the Kerala experience for high-consumption societies, societies that will face shortages of earth resources in the twenty-first century.

8

Knowledge, Democratization and Sustainability: The 'Kerala Model' of Scientific Capacity Building

Wesley Shrum and Sundar Ramanathaiyer

(India)

ō15 ō2ō

ō17

How shall we build scientific capacity in less developed states? Such a question has a lovely simplicity, but conceals a complex array of concerns. The thrust of this chapter is that such simplicity is misleading if not pernicious for the process of capacity building itself, owing to the multiplicity of identities coupled to core research formations. In terms of policy, we must think hard about the kind of structures that we wish to 'build' when we 'capacitize'. An argument from contingency as it applies to developing countries suggests that more is at issue here than 'bringing the Third World up to scientific speed', more at stake than the development of equity between North and South, and more to be accomplished than the establishment of Internet access and Web pages.

For those of us who believe in the crucial role of science and technology in the contemporary world, advocacy and programmatic recommendations must be governed by a careful analysis of the nature and forms of knowledge one hopes to see generated, transformed and utilized. This imperative comes about in part because while capacity building in science[1] has constituted an unresolved set of issues for the past half century, it has only recently become contentious. The rise of alternative ideological and organizational paradigms has been central to the debate, even as there is general agreement on the importance of knowledge and of research processes to many aspects of economic and social development. Not only traditional leftist agendas but also feminism and environmentalism have left their mark on the debate, while demands for industrial modernization and conventional economic growth have not abated.

What emerges, as we hope to show, is a diverse set of research formations coupled in increasingly complex ways to projects such as sustainability and democratization[2] as well as the generation of knowledge for its own sake. But it would be well to make our theoretical biases clear from the start.

First, we consider capacity building in science to consist of *a process of increasing the ability of social entities to participate in the generation and development of scientific and technological knowledge through research formations.* Such a definition is neutral as to field and sector. Neither the kind of science nor its organizational locus is critical to the concept because capacity building is fundamentally a matter of research formations – that is, the embedding or decoupling of knowledge-producing activities in social organization. We are disinclined to believe we should pre-specify the contours of the science we wish to promote in the developing country context.

Our reluctance to specify is not entirely 'principled' but is in an important sense 'empirical'. It derives from an institutional examination of knowledge production in Kerala State in southwestern India.[3] The choice of Kerala is strategic and no claim is made that the region is *generally* representative of developing country contexts.[4] Indeed, it would be much easier to argue that Kerala is *un*representative for a variety of reasons. However, Kerala's unique combination of low economic and high social development renders it uniquely suitable for an examination of the contexts, the problems and the potentials for building research formations where democratization and sustainability are at issue.

Second, the principal conceptual contribution of recent studies of knowledge production is the analysis of science and technology in terms of the *circulation and transformation of technical stories through social networks.* Here the notion of 'locality' is convenient shorthand for the variety of processes that have been implicated both in the physical situatedness of knowledge-making and the translation of claims through a variety of contexts and interests. This development is a much-needed corrective to several tendencies in social studies of science. One is the problem of polarity in orientation to science: the proclivity to adopt attitudes that are either highly deferential towards science as a force for enlightenment and progress or the relativistic desire to demystify and critique it as a reductionist – even violent – patriarchal and imperialist conspiracy.

Crosscutting these approaches are alternative conceptions of the things that we should seek to incorporate in our vision of science and technology. While older paradigms in mainstream sociology of science tended to stress the internal dynamics of such basic sciences as physics and biology to the neglect of technology and applied science, the reverse was often the case for political economists. Here science was reduced to a material or productive force, with little consideration of the institutional processes that characterized knowledge-generating social formations. With many others, we believe that a mature view of science will transcend these dualisms, or 'straddle the quadrants' of such dichotomies (Buttel 1993: 23).

This pair of commitments concerning research formations and locality leads directly to the third and most important. It makes no sense to speak of building scientific capability in the abstract, but only in the light of particularistic contexts – a point that is invariant whether our objective is to create a worldwide network for the study of global warming or an improvement in artificial reef design for a village of fishermen. To that end we want to suggest that Kerala is a particularly good choice for detailed examination and future work on both scholarly and policy issues – owing to its historical combination of educational and democratic initiatives combined with their contemporary translation into sustainability issues. In the first part of this chapter, the social and economic character-istics of modern Kerala are outlined, with special attention to the value of education. In the second, the primary institutional locations for this production are compared with counterparts in two African states. Based on the results of a recent study, we review dimensions of difference, including educational qualifications, autonomy from the international scientific community, internal communication patterns, external profes-sional networks, and the distinctive role of NGOs.

Constructing the Developmental State

Locality is not the preserve of science and technology studies, but has grown pervasive in the developmental literature as well. First at the national, then at the community level, the multiplicity of settings and conditions in the developing world renders it folly to suggest more than the broadest trajectories of change. 'Lessons learned' in one place are often unlearned in another. Places are as likely as people to acquire repu-tations, which circulate widely owing to the sheer population of possible transmitters as well as the published media. It is well to be clear about our choice of a case study for capacity building. This section develops the argument that the historical and political characteristics of Kerala have produced a situation that reflects *both* the contemporary concerns of development *and* science and technology studies. These include (1) the preoccupation with knowledge, education and literacy; (2) development of state and university research institutes, as well as research activities in the NGO sector; (3) broad-based democratization and social change initiatives; and (4) concern with sustainability. Such features are – or are thought to be – descriptive of industrialized societies. What makes Kerala interesting is that they exist within a developing country context where *even by Indian standards* economic growth has performed poorly. In effect, Kerala may be considered a test case for scientific capacity building where democratization and sustainability concerns are important, but economic growth lags.

Over the past quarter century, Kerala's reputation as a state with a unique combination of high social and low economic development has been parlayed into the 'Kerala model of development', or, simply, the 'Kerala model'.[5] Although it would be too strong to say there is agreement on its specific features, two general traits are clear. First, the level of social development in Kerala (often defined as involving high literacy, long life expectancy and low birth rate) is much higher than the level of economic development would lead analysts to expect. Second, this combination is relatively unusual and represents a dramatic contrast with conventional models of development in which economic growth precedes social equity.

The contrast between social and economic development is apparent in a variety of ways: poor economic growth with relatively high physical quality of life, retarded industrial development with a decent standard of living, low per-capita income combined with high levels of consumerism (Sooryamoorthy 1997).[6] Often this is expressed in terms of scores on indices of the well-being of the population. On such measures as the Physical Quality of Life Index (PQLI) and the Human Development Index (HDI)[7] Kerala ranks above all other Indian states, though it ranks among the middle in economic terms. Using per-capita state domestic product to calculate a *predicted* PQLI, Ramanathaiyer shows that Kerala's *actual* PQLI massively exceeds the level expected based on its level of economic development (1996).[8]

Demographic and health statistics provide specific indicators of the meaning of social development here. Death rates and birth rates have declined so quickly that Kerala has already made the demographic transition ordinarily associated with industrialization – perhaps the most rapid on record (Bhat and Rajan 1990). Fertility has declined throughout the state, is near replacement even in rural areas, and had reached parity with developed country rates by 1993 (Rajan and James 1993). The child mortality rate of 4.6 per 1,000 in 1990 stands in striking contrast with an Indian average of 26.3 and a global average of 87 (WHO 1995), owing to the institutionalization of deliveries. Life expectancy is high – the average Kerala citizen will live a dozen years longer than the average Indian.[9] Perhaps the best measure of the general status of Kerala is the sex ratio of 1,036 females to 1,000 males. This is more similar to European and North American ratios favouring women than the deficit India reveals as a whole (927 females to 1,000 males), and strongly suggests the rarity of selective abortion, female infanticide and neglect. Some Kerala people may prefer sons, but they do not discriminate in favour of males in the most pernicious ways.

A wide variety of government interventions, redistributive measures and welfare provisions are associated with these positive indicators of social development (Herring 1983; Ramanathaiyer 1996; Heller 1995). Franke and Chasin characterize Kerala as an 'experiement in radical reform as a development strategy' (1994: 1), while Heller focuses on workers and peasants as active agents in economic and political change (1995 and 1996).

Kerala is a strategic place for the examination of capacity building in the context of democratization and sustainability concerns because of its developmental preoccupation with knowledge, the way this has been translated into state action and popular organization, and the contemporary need for the retention and utilization of knowledge workers for the economic betterment of Malayalees.[10] Scientific capacity begins with education and communication. Perhaps the most telling indicator of the latter – and an important component of technological status, particularly if we regard Internet access as an aspect of scientific capacity – is the distribution of telephones – Kerala has more than four times as many telephones per square kilometre than India as a whole.[11] Six radio stations in Kerala reach 98 per cent of the population, of whom 70 per cent have accessible television (Sooryamoorthy 1997).

It is being claimed by many scholars that Kerala has achieved 'total literacy'. In 1991 the state government declared that Kerala has achieved total literacy after the culmination of a highly successful Total Literacy campaign managed by the Kerala Sastra Sahitya Parishad (KSSP). While 'total' may be an overstatement, this is not far above the 91 per cent literacy estimated by the census in that year, and vastly exceeds the Indian average of 52 per cent.[12] Moreover, the literacy gap between males and females (which is high in India as a whole) has narrowed to seven percentage points in Kerala.[13]

But literacy is not a simple matter of 'modernization', and for purposes of capacity building it is a mistake to think of improvements in scientific education as *simply* enhancing the ability of a nation to solve technical problems or contribute to the global scientific knowledge base. Indeed, a specific social epistemology has proven important to twentieth-century Kerala: the linkage between socialist ideology, educational accomplishment and the social mobilization of the population. The central message here is that literacy and primary education went hand in hand with mobilization processes involving both high-caste organizers and lower-caste labourers and farmers. Social and political movements by peasants and workers, led by committed organizers of labour unions, caste associations and farmer groups have achieved an overwhelming significance in the life and politics of the state and have led many analysts to the characterization of the Kerala experience as participatory, 'bottom-up' change (Franke and Chasin 1994; Heller 1996), or as 'organized pressure from below, and politics of democratization from above' (Törnquist and Tharakan 1996: 2041).

Undergirding these transformations, the discourse of class largely displaced the discourse of caste in both public and private arenas, and notions of equality and social justice diffused widely owing to increasing literacy and the spread of public education.[14] Inequality was not viewed as a fated state of affairs, as it had been in traditional Hindu India, but rather as a question of categorical (class) memberships, exploitation and oppositional struggle.[15] Marxist ideology promoted science, scientific method and scientific thinking as key components of class struggle and the battle against the traditional restrictions of caste and religion.

Shaped by these movements, the pervasive influence of the state began in 1957 with the world's first free election of a Communist government. It proposed legislation to regulate private schools and introduce land reforms that eventually resulted in its dismissal by the central government. Communist-led governments (or those coalitions in which communist parties played a role) have frequently held power since Independence. The ideological balance in Kerala is shown by the fact that even the election platforms of conservative political parties support egalitarianism and government interventions (Ramanathaiyer 1996: 219). Educational spending has been a consistent priority of state government, and the proportion of state funds spent on education has generally ranked near the highest among Indian states. The demand for high-quality Westernized education is such that the number of private schools unaided by government has increased even with the reduction in school-age population caused by the declining birth rate (James 1995).[16]

Primary and secondary educational improvements soon led to demands for higher-educational facilities.[17] Based on government surveys, Kannan reports that even in the late 1970s 97 per cent of Kerala villages were located within five kilometres of higher-education facilities, compared to the all-India average of 21 per cent (1988: 18–21).[18] Such infrastructure translates into human capital. Measured in terms of personnel per 1,000 population, Kerala has more than twice as many science and technology personnel (5.9) as the Indian average (2.4).[19]

The problem of educated unemployment and underemployment is one of the most serious in Kerala (Mathew 1995).[20] In 1991 – the same year that total literacy was declared – 100,000 professional technical graduates and diploma holders (including medical, agricultural, veterinary and engineering graduates) registered in government employment exchanges for jobs. From 1985 through 1994 unemployment registration among professional graduates increased nearly 200 per cent (Ramanathaiyer 1996: 73–5). White-collar job preferences (in particular, for salaried government jobs) and aversion to manual ('menial') labour has led to labour shortages requiring migrant workers from neighbouring Tamil Nadu. The high rate of unemployment, rather than reducing the demand for education, actually increases it. With heavy subsidies for education, tuition fees are among the lowest in India. Government and private colleges are affordable for low-income groups and education has become a desirable *substitute* for unemployment (Mathew 1995).

The people of Kerala have placed great store in education since the last century. Their commitment to discussion, argument and political debate is consistent with the proliferation of schools, from primary schools to institutions of higher education. But while it seems likely that education in a 'progressive political environment can elevate the self-conceptions of the poorest … [to] participate more fully in the developmental process' (Franke and Chasin 1994: 47), it also (1) increases the potential for labour militancy to the detriment of external investment; (2) increases expectations and decreases job satisfaction among the educated; (3) creates greater demand among both men and women for high-quality professional and management positions, which are still scarce in the Kerala economy.

In sum, democratization processes have been consistently implicated in Kerala's social development since before Independence, in terms of both popular movements and state programmes. This is not to argue that democratization has been completely 'successful' – only that (1) democratization is a dominant ideological and organizational theme and (2) literacy and education were crucial to this development. The reason for scepticism is that land reforms, union organization, and the electoral success of the Communist Party were all products of radical political mobilization that viewed *central organization and state intervention* as requirements to vanquish feudal and capitalist forces. This casts doubt on ascriptions of democratization that imply decentralization.

In the 1980s, 'state-modernists', who remained in favour of the state-led industrialization within the framework of Kerala's worker organizations, were joined by 'popular developmentalists', a loose network of scholars and activists who believed that this approach had come to a standstill. They recognized that production had stagnated and, instead of state programmes, emphasized the greater sustainability of grassroots capacity to reorganize and improve production. To this end they promoted mass literacy campaigns, group farming and resource-mapping initiatives. Yet as efforts to increase democratization in any permanent way, there are questions about the extent to which they took root, not least owing to large number of already-institutionalized interest groups in Kerala.[21]

In the following section, we briefly review the primary research formations in Kerala. Next we contrast researchers with their counterparts in the African states of Kenya and Ghana in terms of their educational qualifications, relative autonomy, internal communication patterns, external professional networks, and the distinctive role of NGOs.

Research Formations in Kerala

It is difficult to overstate the degree to which science is esteemed in Kerala. Government departments never fail to attribute policies to scientific experts. The largest and best known NGO is the Kerala People's Science Movement (Kerala Sastra Sahitya Parishad, or KSSP). In newspapers – the most significant media in this highly literate state – perhaps the most common rhetorical tactic used by representatives of a multitude of groups is to condemn a policy or practice as 'unscientific': a spokesperson protests the 'unscientific dumping of garbage', agitations by unions are promised against 'unscientific development works' in a region, an allegation of 'unscientific' supports an objection to a ban on trawling during the monsoon season. In one sense, the respect accorded to science, scientific knowledge and scientific claims is encouraging if not remarkable. But in another, many of these uses represent the worst kind of scientism, an assumption that to say something is 'science' is equivalent to saying it is 'true'.

We take for granted that building scientific capacity in developing countries does not involve an uncritical acceptance of knowledge claims based on their source. But there is another sense in which 'science' is placeholder for 'valid', the one in which local technological change is regarded as sustainable, authentic and sound. At most, it is said to be 'scientific' because it is the product of observation, natural experiment and analysis. At minimum, it is a hypothesis that has been fowarded, a fit and worthy subject for formal R&D. It is this sense in which Achari faults the global scientific community for neglecting the 'small innovations of ordinary fishermen as science', and praises the 'traditional science conceived and nurtured by the artisanal fishermen' (1994: i). For the late John Fernandez, these fishermen accumulated a 'treasure of scientific knowledge on diverse marine ecosystems and fish behaviour' (1994: 1). These usages are not bizarre or idiosyncratic in the Kerala context, but common among scholar/activists such as John Kurien, who argue for the need to verbalize and systematize 'this artisanal knowledge – basically a people's science' (1996: 21).

The importance of these practices lies in contrast reduction between three types of social formations for the systematic production of knowledge, government research institutes, university departments, and the non-governmental organizations that are often committed to 'people's knowledge'. Fernandez does not simply contrast 'traditional' or 'indigenous' knowledge with modern science and technology, but stresses that 'the science and technology of artisanal fishermen … is not at all inferior to modern science and technology but based on their intricate knowledge of the oceanography and fish behaviour' (1994: 2). Kurien, likewise, seeks to place this knowledge 'on a par with what is considered today as "scientific"'. One reason frequently given for the need for the status enhancement of indigenous knowledge is to create confidence in local communities, a sense of empowerment, and thereby participatory involvement in development. There is, however, good reason to be sceptical of this as an empirical claim, given that this enhancement generally occurs, if at all, outside the local communities at issue. Farmers and fishers worry much less about whether their knowledge is scientific than about whether it is useful.

Although the labels carried by knowledge claims are important for status and transmissibility, they are not the most salient aspects of capacity building. To reiterate the definition given at the outset, capacity building in science consists of a process of increasing the ability of social entities to participate in the generation and development of scientific and technological knowledge through research formations. Such knowledge includes 'know-how' and 'know-why', technical information and the ability to organize it, expertise and skills. Hence, capacity refers not to the nature or labelling of the claims themselves, but rather to social formations dedicated to a process that *produces* such claims. Such process is conventionally termed 'research'.

As in most developing countries, research occurs in three general types of organizational context. Universities and state research institutes constitute the core of this effort, with non-governmental organizations a relatively recent addition. In some countries, international research institutes constitute a fourth – sometimes major – organizational presence, while in the Kerala context, a number of research institutes come under the jurisdiction of the central government of India.

Although a Scientific Policy Resolution was adopted by the government of India as long ago as 1958, an equivalent resolution was not passed in Kerala until 1977.[22] The national policy resolution, based clearly on a linear model, viewed technology as the key to national prosperity. Technology, in turn, 'can only grow out of the study of science and its applications' (Damodaran 1991: 2). The discursive commitment to a scientific approach was expressed in specific terms – only through their use could 'reasonable material and cultural amenities and services' be provided to every member of the community. Hence, early development of science was thought to make up for deficiencies in natural resources and reduce the drain on capital in the early stages of industrialization.[23]

Owing to the size and diversity of developing countries such as India and China, central government institutes are viewed as insufficient for research at the state level. The Council of Scientific and Industrial Research, founded in 1942 to promote research for national needs along the lines of the British model, consists of forty research laboratories and employs 6,000 scientists and engineers,[24] yet only a single Regional Research Laboratory is located in Kerala. In agriculture, however, institutional concentration is greater, with five of forty-six central government institutes in Kerala. Though none of the twenty primary crop science institutes is located in this area of South India, there are three central horticultural institutes and two fisheries institutes, owing to the importance of these products to the economy of the state (ICAR 1996).

Organization of science and technology began in earnest at the state level in 1972 with the constitution of a State Committee on Science and Technology, the first state-level body of this kind in India (Damodaran 1991). The Committee was charged with 'constant review' of scientific and technological policies in relation to the objectives of the Five Year Plans that formed the basis of state planning activities, with a membership representative of all state S&T bodies as well as those from the Central Government Laboratories working in Kerala. Ten years later the Committee designated a full-time chairman and in 1984 added the environment to its mandate after a debate over whether environmental issues required a separate department, as they have in the central government. A professional secretariat was established within the Planning and Economic Affairs Department and upgraded in 1987 to the Department of Science, Technology and Environment within the Secretariat.[25] The Committee itself, with up to eighteen task groups (standing committees), had grown to fifty-four members and was streamlined with an Executive Committee of fifteen.[26]

The promotion of 'science for its own sake' was never the principal aim of the Committee or the Department. Major functions were to advise government on S&T issues, to identify problems in appropriate technology selection in the corporate sector, to plan for wider dissemination of S&T in traditional industries, to encourage training for special problems in agriculture, to advise on environmental issues, and to identify areas for application of S&T to the developmental needs and objectives of the state. Further, it was to advise on projects of S&T for Women and

Weaker Sections.[27] The Committee and associated task groups organize and sponsor symposia – including a Kerala Science Congress each January that generates a hundred papers and provides postdoctoral fellowships to unemployed PhD degree holders. A Scientific Research Fund has provided assistance for projects and travel since 1976. An officer for Science Communication was appointed in 1984 to engage in popularization of science and offer an award scheme for popular science literature. The Department of Science, Technology and Environment serves as a technical secretariat, with a staff of ten engaged in research administration. It provides the organizational locus for most of the autonomous research institutions sponsored by the state government.[28]

Relative to the state organization for science and technology, universities require and utilize more resources. The Kerala Agricultural University, established in 1971, was the fifteenth agricultural university established in India and has formal responsibility for the conduct of the agricultural research in the state as well as extension education. Research departments and institutes are located on six teaching campuses supplemented with twenty-three research stations. In addition, work by ICAR and commodity board stations focuses on specific crops. Until 1982, KAU also engaged in crop-based research. The National Agricultural Research Project introduced the idea of multi-disciplinary stations that would address research problems at the level of the farming system. Monocrop research stations were reorganized into a three-tier system including Regional Research Stations, Special Stations, and Substations for location-specific problems.[29]

Because universities and state institutes constitute the core research sectors, most work on science and technology for development neglects non-governmental organizations. NGOs became increasingly important actors in the development process during the 1980s owing in part to the increasing disenchantment of donors with corrupt and inefficient states. NGOs took on adversarial roles in development programmes, and were accurately characterized as 'reluctant partners' whose role was to disseminate the knowledge generated by state institutions they frequently did not support (Farrington and Bebbington 1993). In Kerala, NGOs play a small but significant role in research as well, often in the area of environmental work. As organizational contexts they are typically smaller in size and less complex than core research organizations.[30] However, one aspect of Kerala NGOs is unique by virtue of the social context in which they operate. Against the background of powerful Communist governments and radical reform movements, left-leaning NGOs do not face a climate of ideological hostility. Themes of participation and democratization frame discourse across the spectrum of organizational entities.

To grasp the ways in which these three research sectors differ from each other, as well as the ways they may differ from similar contexts in other developing countries, scientists in Kerala may be contrasted with researchers in Ghana and Kenya, based on a recent survey.[31] Including African scientists, a total of 293 structured interviews were conducted.[32] Several points of contrast emerge that bear particular note in the context of the Kerala model. First, Kerala exhibits substantial research productivity, in terms of work on local problems and autonomy with respect to the world scientific community. Kerala scientists display high publication rates compared to African scientists, averaging 1.35 times the rate of Kenyans and 2.8 times the rate of Ghanaians on a measure based on a count of appearances in international bibliographies (Shrum 1997). But an even larger difference is apparent for domestic articles, where researchers publish more than one article per year in local journals, a rate more than six times that of Kenya and more than eight times that of Ghana. In Kerala, those who are oriented to the international scientific community are more likely to publish research in domestic journals as well, a relationship that is not present for Africans.[33] This fact seems especially relevant when we consider that international research attention is more focused on Africa. Compared to Kenya and Ghana, countries that have long elicited a high level of donor interest, Kerala research is primarily the province of researchers of Keralan origin. Bibliometric methods allow us to examine the ratio of publications *within* a location to publications *about* a location that are authored elsewhere.[34] This functions as a measure of international interest, or, alternatively, the degree to which research within a location is produced locally. The ratio of internal to external publications shows that, relative to the others, research on Kerala is much less dependent on the international community. While more than half of research on Ghana is conducted elsewhere and Kenyan research is about evenly split between work done inside and outside the country, work on Kerala is overwhelmingly produced in Kerala.[35]

Relative autonomy is also apparent with respect to the donor community. Overall, clients or users have the largest reported effect on problem selection. For all three locations, reported influences on problem selection were relatively similar: national priorities, clients or users, and the director of the organization. There is a significant exception to this, however. For Kenya, the country that has elicited the most donor interest, donors are still considered very important in setting research priorities, while for Kerala, in the more insular Indian research environment, these influences are less significant.

The reported influences on the selection of research problems do not vary a great deal between sectors in Kerala, even in terms of the orientation to clients or users. One might expect greater influence of clients among NGOs than other sectors, but that is not the case. NGOs are slightly (but not significantly) less likely to report influences from donors. However, there is one interesting difference regarding the impact of the director of the organization and the respondent's immediate supervisor which tends to be more salient in NGOs. This is precisely due to the smaller size of NGOs, which may be less bureaucratic but therefore offer greater opportunity for personal influence. It tends to confirm the view that NGOs can be dominated by a single individual, who sets the agenda and has a strong hand in most activities.

A second, notable feature of the Kerala research system is that all sectors reflect the high levels of education that characterize the state overall. While the PhD was the highest degree for fewer than half of African researchers (Kenya 45 per cent; Ghana 39 per cent), nearly 80 per cent of researchers in Kerala have PhDs. Indeed, the proportion of PhDs among NGO researchers is Kerala (58 per cent) is higher than the sample as a whole (57 per cent). Differences are equally large in other sectors. Excluding NGOs, about half of the scientists in other sectors have PhDs, compared with three-quarters of governmental researchers and 90 per cent of university scientists in Kerala. When we include Master's degrees, virtually *all* Kerala researchers, including those in NGOs, are qualified. Human capital is significantly greater in the Kerala context than the African, a fact attributable to the general emphasis on education credentialling in the area.

The availability of educational opportunities is significantly higher in Kerala than in Africa. Kerala scientists are less likely to be trained abroad than African scientists, who are more often the recipients of scholarships and grants for higher education in the developed world. Training abroad is an inverse reflection of the level of scientific development, since Kerala researchers have on average only half years outside training, while African respondents have between three and four years each. Among university scientists, Ghanaians have nearly five years of higher education abroad, compared with about four for Kenyans, and less than a year for Keralan scientists.[36] The reason for this is the generally high level of donor interest in sponsorship of Africans for training abroad and the relatively large opportunities for Kerala scientists for training within India.

If professional contacts are a 'zero sum' commodity, or if international visibility is associated with increased attention to mainstream scientific problems, then sending researchers abroad for training might not be wholly beneficial. The reason lies in the fact that basic research – intendedly more global in orientation – is traditionally performed in university contexts, while applied and problem-oriented research is the purview of state institutes and, recently, NGOs.

Initially, we believed that researchers themselves might be aware of a reduced domestic orientation resulting from affiliation with the external scientific community. When scientists were asked about their priorities for improving the capacity of the research system, training abroad received very little emphasis.[37] This seemed to be consistent, and was true regardless of whether scientists were themselves trained in or outside the country. However, the reality is more complex, since nearly 60 per cent of Kerala scientists, as contrasted with only 25 per cent of Kenyans and Ghanaians, told us that sending people abroad for training was 'very important'. We now think it is important to consider the opportunity people have had for advanced work in order to interpret this result. The greater emphasis placed on outside training by Kerala researchers is probably due to the lack of personal opportunity and does not take into account the matter of local or global orientation. As we saw above, there does not seem to be as large a distinction between domestic and international orientation to publication in Kerala as in the African locations. A third aspect of the differences revealed in the Kerala context involves supervisory behaviour and internal communication practices. Fourth, Kerala researchers do not have large professional networks – the average number of individuals reported as important professional contacts is *smaller than* in either African country.[38]

Finally, as Parayil and Shrum (1996) have shown, NGOs contribute distinctively to the mix of research formations in Kerala.[39] The different orientation to research is evident in publication productivity. NGO scientists publish approximately the same number of reports and bulletins as other researchers – documents that are disseminated locally. Their rate of publication in national journals is higher than for researchers in government institutes, but in international journals it is lower. In general, NGO respondents report spending more hours at work per week than those in other sectors, and spend more hours on research than university professors, a finding that confirms our own impressions about the high level of commitment to work in this sector.

These individuals were less likely to be married with children than others. This is explained by the fact that one group of NGO scientists is relatively young, while another group consists of active researchers who have reached the mandatory state retirement age of 55 and have fewer family responsibilities. The presence of retired scientists is an important factor in the capacity of Kerala NGOs. Many have had successful careers in government research institutes, retain linkages with their former employers, and are by no means ready to retire from research.

Some even use the laboratory facilities in institutes or universities through informal arrangements or with the permission of their former colleagues. It may demonstrate that an ideal configuration for NGOs with research interests consists of a combination of active retirees with recent graduates in a 'mentoring' relationship.

The high level of training and prior employment histories for NGO scientists results in strikingly high levels of involvement in professional activities such as office holding in professional associations and membership of government advisory groups. These individuals are just as likely as professors and twice as likely as those in state institutes to have served on editorial boards of journals. Indeed, they personally subscribe to more journals than either group. Our NGO scientists averaged seventeen professional meetings in five years, compared with ten for institute researchers and eight for academics. This difference is also apparent in the finding that NGO scientists spend more than twice as much time away from their home organizations than others – nearly two months per year.[40]

Discussion

The distinctive features of the Kerala research system, as contrasted with cases from West and East Africa, are relative productivity and autonomy with respect to the donor community, a distinctive and highly qualified NGO sector, and collegial internal relationships but smaller professional networks. What emerges is a picture of differences rather than similarities. If Kerala is indeed a model for development, its differences must be highlighted within the wider social context. To the extent that the context is unique, the term 'model' may be appropriate, but not in the sense of unmediated applicability. Where the production of knowledge is concerned the picture is blurred by complexity, even as there is a great paradox in the relative democratization of Kerala public life, which purchased sustainability at the price of low economic investment and growth. The proliferation of voices and interests leads to constant flux but gradual change.

One area that should receive more attention is the relationship between core research sectors and NGOs. From the standpoint of many state officials, the problem with universities and often state institutes is the questionable relevance and continuity of their research. A standard plea is for scientists to become more involved through affiliation with NGOs. Yet in spite of the high level of familiarity with NGOs in Kerala and support for the work of KSSP, we found that academics and NGO scientists had mutually low opinions of each other.[41]

A recent initiative by the International Council of Scientific Unions views building scientific capacity as enabling nations and regions to make use of science and technology for the well-being and culture of their citizens.[42] The stress on utilization as against production is slightly different from the definition with which we began, which viewed capacity building as a process of increasing the ability of social entities to participate in the generation and development of scientific and technological knowledge through research formations. The emphasis here is on the development of research formations, regardless of field or sector, rather than the 'utilization' of knowledge from elsewhere.

The already high levels of literacy in the state make Kerala an excellent site for fostering primary science education. Indian educational institutions have often been criticized for focusing on degrees rather than skills, owing to rigid and outmoded syllabi, a system of examinations based on rote learning, and the absence of laboratory facilities (Bhagavan 1995). The fact that Kerala has achieved an advantage in literacy and primary education over most other states does not mean it is exempt from these criticisms (Mathew 1995: 328).[43] Science education may be considered in large part an aspect of 'post-literacy' and raises important questions about the relative effectiveness of different forms of organization for capacity building that will facilitate and maintain gains. Electronic communication involving Internet applications is clearly a trend for the foreseeable future, and the widespread availability of telephone lines in Kerala leads us to predict rapid Web spread.

Yet there are risks involved, and the case of Kerala libraries serves as an example (K. Kumar 1994). During the immediate post-war period there was a campaign to set up community libraries. It flourished so well that within three years there were over five hundred. Nearly every village had one within the decade. But after the state takeover of the federation in 1977, sufficient support was not extended and the library system has deteriorated badly. Not only village libraries but even the Trivandrum State Library have fallen into disrepair. The lesson should not be lost even as we move towards electronic libraries based on Internet applications. A functioning library system is important to the capacity to produce and manipulate knowledge.

In conclusion, scientific capacity building in Kerala is a product of the historical and political circumstances that characterize a remarkable trajectory of development, which is exemplary in many respects. It may not be totally impossible to replicate many of these circumstances in other developing states. However, it is hard to come up with a workable heuristic for replication. Kerala's development experience is a double-edged sword, and that is no less true for scientific capacity building than for the paradox of strong social and weak economic growth. What captures the imagination of the policymakers and scholars is the emphasis on education – not the problem of educated unemployment, the high rate of female literacy, the dominance of men in the scientific professions, the quality of the technical workforce, or the low level of investment in its infrastructure.

These questions aside, we must admit to a similar fascination. It is hard to think of an example of any place on the planet where knowledge is such an embedded value, so taken for granted as a desirable aspect of life. It is likewise difficult to think of a place where, owing to the ideological comfort of participatory practices, science-as-truth has such an immediate resonance with the view of capacity building privileged here, a process that increases the ability of social entities to develop their own forms of scientific and technological knowledge. That social epistemology, still in the process of realization, may be the most important factor for sustainability in the twenty-first century.

Notes

This chapter was conceived for the Workshop on Social Scientific Contributions to Capacity Building in Science (Baton Rouge, Louisiana, 29 January 1999), sponsored by the US National Science Foundation. Early versions were presented at the Energy Management Center at the request of V.K. Damodaran, and at the University of Kerala in June 1997. Sincere thinks to Sreevasudeva Bhattathiri for his assistance.

1. Unless otherwise noted, 'science' refers to both science and technology – that is, to 'technoscience'.

2. Democratization is here viewed in terms of procedure. The argument that certain outcomes are in essence undemocratic and therefore unjust even if approved according to democratic procedures is not considered.

3. India is an interesting case for capacity building questions owing to the fact that it has long been a scientific leader among developing countries, yet has recently experienced an apparent decline in scientific output and impact, as indicated by data from the Science Citation Index (1981–95). A decline of 32 per cent in the Indian share of world scientific output is the most severe of any nation with the exception of the former Soviet Union (Raghuram and Madhavi 1996).

4. One objection to the use of Kerala as a case study is that it is a state rather than a nation, and thus it is subject to the political and economic policy context of the central government. In view of the argument from locality, this would appear to be an advantage in the Indian context. Moreover, the benefit of national statistics allows us to make reasonably precise comparisons within this national context.

5. See, for instance, Govindan Parayil's (1996) account. A secure origin of the term is not yet known. A 1975 study by K.N Raj and colleagues of the Center for Development Studies for the United Nations may have been responsible (CDS 1975), but did not use such phraseology (Raj 1994). Sometimes it is even termed the 'Kerala miracle' (Thomas 1994: 7).

6. Sooryamoorthy extends the analysis of Kerala's 'modernized' levels of social

welfare to the consumption of durables, showing high levels relative to India as a whole and comparable levels to the richest states. Remittances from Gulf employment led to a consumerism 'predominantly determined by status considerations rather than utility' and has affected the lower- and middle-income classes as well as the affluent (1997: 26).

7. The PQLI combines measures of infant mortality, life expectancy and literacy, while the HDI includes life expectancy, literacy and income adjusted for purchasing-power parity. Kerala's high rank on these indices is even more impressive given India's relatively low position among developing countries as a whole. In 1993 India ranked 134th out of 173 countries on the HDI according to the UNDP's Human Development Report and has generally low levels of spending on health and education as a percentage of total government expenditure (EPW 1994a).

8. The positive difference between actual and expected values of the PQLI is more than five times larger than that of Gujarat, in second place.

9. Among many Kerala paradoxes is a health paradox – relatively low rates of mortality combined with the highest levels of morbidity in India, which leads to the question of whether the low death rates mask unhealthy features of living there. High morbidity could be a statistical illusion, a perceptual phenomenon, or 'real' illness. Rajan and James make a persuasive case that diseases of affluence are substituting for diseases of poverty, that a shift has occurred from infectious diseases to chronic degenerative diseases, and that low mortality/high morbidity is common among developed countries where health consciousness is high (1993).

10. Malayalam is the local language of Kerala.

11. While India as a whole has 1.05 telephones per square kilometre (5.06 telephones per 1,000), Kerala has, on average, 4.5 phones (or 7.1 phones per 1,000 persons).

12. On a railroad overpass in Thiruvanathapuram, an elderly man sits with his begging bowl, too engrossed in his morning newspaper to bother with active solicitation. Such a sight is not common in other parts of India and is a justifiable source of pride for Malayalees, who boast the highest newpaper consumption in the country and an active publishing industry.

13. The superior literacy of Keralan society is not new. Even at the turn of the century the literacy rate was twice as high (11 per cent) as the rest of India (5 per cent) and this difference has remained roughly constant (Franke and Chasin 1994: 47–8). Early Christian missionaries were responsible for expanding education beyond village schools for upper-caste members, a perceived threat to the rulers that was countered by establishing local government schools. However, universal literacy for all members of society came about only after the formation of the developmental state.

14. Facilitating ideological diffusion was not only literacy but the relatively high density and even distribution of population throughout the state. See Mencher's (1966) classic comparison of Kerala and Madras on settlement patterns. It is difficult to overstate the degree to which the discourse of class now permeates not only the mass media but also the everyday social interactions of most people of Kerala. Rickshaw drivers will debate class membership ('I am not a proletarian') while bargaining over the fare with their white-collar customers ('we are all members of the working class'), but these class categories are flexible and strategic.

15. Administrative classifications facilitate the realization of particular class analyses by encoding class concepts in a bureaucratic structure – for example, in the categorization of households by the extent of land holding. Landlords, owner

cultivators, tenants and landless households were 'agricultural classes' identified by theory and institutionalized by Marxist governments (Kannan 1988; Morrison 1997).

16. James discusses the closure of sixty-seven 'uneconomic' schools by government during the early 1990s, and the likelihood of surplus schools and teachers in the coming decade (1995).

17. In 1964–65 alone fifty new junior colleges opened in the private sector (Woodcock 1967).

18. In 1993 there were 174 Arts and Science colleges (41 government; 133 private), with 154,000 university students and 13,541 teaching faculty (GOK 1993: 8).

19. With the second highest state (Karnataka) at 4.1, no other state is close (CMIE 1991).

20. Woodcock discusses a then recent survey in Trivandrum showing that a majority of municipal bus conductors were BAs and even MAs. 'The consequence of the unbalanced development of the Keralan educational system is that the physical distress of the half-literate fishermen is paralleled on another level by the mental frustration of the educated unemployed' (Woodcock 1967: 282).

21. Törnquist and Tharakan (1996: 2042–3) attribute the failure of the popular developmentalist project in Kerala to 'centralization, compartmentalization, factionalism, vested interests, and locked political conflicts'.

22. A National Technology Policy Statement was not developed until 1983.

23. Not until the Fifth Five Year Plan was S&T viewed as a separate sector, and by the Seventh Plan it was again removed, the argument being that S&T should be incorporated in planning for all economic and strategic sectors.

24. In terms of the global contribution of Indian science, papers from CSIR scientists constitute 15–20 per cent of those appearing in SCI journals (Damodaran 1994: 120).

25. The importance of the Department is symbolized by the fact that the director reports directly to the chief minister.

26. It is noteworthy for the interconnection of science sectors in Kerala that the director of the department for ten years was formerly a president of the KSSP, an NGO noted for the promotion of 'people's science' and its leftist ideology.

27. Kerala is progressive in terms of the number and treatment of women scientists. This is unsurprising, given the relatively favourable gender demographics described above.

28. The number of centres under the Department has varied. In the mid-1990s they included the Centre for Earth Sciences Studies, the Centre for Water Resources Development and Management, the Tropical Botanic Garden and Research Institute, the Kerala Forest Research Institute, the National Transportation Planning and Research Centre, and the Agency for Non-Conventional Energy and Rural Technology. Each centre is supported primarily by the state government, with a typical professional staff size of forty to fifty.

29. It should be noted that although monocrop research was now considered outmoded, each station was to have a 'lead function' based on a 'cropping system'. Pilicode Regional Research Station for the North specializes in coconut-based systems; Pattambi (Central Region) specializes in rice-based systems; and Vallayani (Southern Region) specializes in tuber crops. Ambalavayal (High ranges) functions as the leading centre for horticultural crops, and the Kumarakom station in the 'Problem Area' focuses on integrated crop–livestock–fish farming.

30. All of the NGOs in the study reported here were small, with the notable

exception of KSSP.

31. The study was sponsored by RAWOO (Advisory Council for Scientific Research in Development Problems) for the Dutch Ministry for Development Cooperation with assistance from the International Service for National Agricultural Research (Shrum 1996). The methodology of the study has been described elsewhere (Shrum and Beggs 1997). Responses from Kerala were based on 101 individuals, each of whom was engaged in some research activity, representing forty-nine organizations in three sectors.

32. Seven of these are NGOs, twenty-two are national institutes, and twenty are university departments. A total of 57 per cent of respondents were affiliated to national institutes, 31 per cent to universities, and 12 per cent to NGOs, but several respondents whose primary affiliation was academic or governmental were members of NGOs as well.

33. These measures are based on self-reported productivity.

34. I searched seventeen internationally available databases for the 1992–93 period for each of the three locations. Publications 'within' the state were those authored by individuals who were affiliated with Kerala organizations. Publications 'about' the state used aspects of the location as subject matter, collected data there, and so forth, but were authored by scientists who were not based in Kerala. The first indicator was developed by using the corporate source fields of each database, which indicate the organizational affiliation and location of the author(s). The second file was developed by searching the basic index (title, abstract, keywords) for the country of interest, then eliminating all those items that were also identified in the corporate source search. This remainder gives items on or about a location that do not originate there.

35. The ratio of internal to external items is 0.86 for Ghana, 1.1 for Kenya, and 2.7 for Kerala.

36. For scientists at national institutes, Africans (both Kenyans and Ghanaians) average 3.5 years of education abroad, while Keralan scientists average less than half a year.

37. Training and hiring personnel received the lowest ratings out of a list of twenty factors.

38. This is confirmed by an analysis of organizational linkages, wherein Kerala researchers report slightly lower rates of contact than Africans.

39. The following three paragraphs are based on data reported in Parayil and Shrum (1996).

40. Also somewhat surprising was that in terms of several basic infrastructural resources (telephone, fax, personal computer, secretaries), NGOs are comparable to core research organizations, and even work with about the same number of professionals and technicians. But they do not have equivalent access to specialized research instruments and materials.

41. NGO scientists in Kerala gave university contributions to agriculture and natural resource management the *lowest rating* any sector gave to any other sector in our entire study, while universities gave themselves the *highest rating*. This suggests significant difficulties inhere in bridging the gap and greater possibilities for relations between NGOs and state institutes.

42. The three principal components of the ICSU initiative are the improvement of science education in schools (beginning with the primary level), the promotion of public understanding of science, and the reduction of the isolation of scientists.

43. M.V. Pylee, formerly vice-chancellor of the University of Cochin, notes in

his review of higher education that one-third of colleges and universities are closed at any given time and rife with political activism. He contrasts the 180 day curriculum prescribed by the University Grants Commission, with an effective teaching period of 100 days per year owing to closures, strikes and work stoppages (1995: 19–20).

9

The Kerala Model:
Its Central Tendency and the 'Outlier'

John Kurien

When people allude to the 'Kerala model' of development they are referring to the apparent paradox of high quality of life in the state despite
its very low income. This high quality of life, for the population of
Kerala taken as a whole, is represented by the 'central tendency' of the
distribution of such indicators as literacy, infant mortality, life expectancy
and so on (CDS 1975; Ratcliffe 1978; Rajeev 1983; Panikar and Soman
1984; Franke and Chasin 1989; Drèze and Sen 1989; and Jeffrey 1992).
However, as in all distributions, the 'Kerala model' also has its 'outliers':
communities that seem to have been left out of the domain of public
action from what Drèze and Sen have referred to as 'capability building'
(Drèze and Sen 1989). Obtaining insights into the factors that explain
the context of the outliers in this distribution therefore acquires importance. This is particularly so since the credit for Kerala's achievement of
a high quality of life is attributed to development priorities driven by
enlightened, and presumably uniformly applied, state policy and public
action rather than market-led, individual initiatives.

The purpose of this chapter is thus twofold: first, against the background of the 'central tendency' of the Kerala model, it attempts to
provide some of the statistics of an 'outlier' in Kerala's economy – its
marine fishing community. For this community the indicators of the quality
of life pose no paradox of the kind noticed when considering Kerala
State as a whole. Instead, one observes the 'normal' relationship of low
incomes with the associated poor quality of life. Second, it makes a
preliminary attempt towards an understanding of why the factors which
fostered public action for 'capability building' in Kerala as a whole did
not permeate into the state's marine fishing community. This may pro-

vide some modest insights for those who wish to emulate and attempt to replicate the Kerala model.

The Kerala Model: Its Central Tendency

The history behind the statistics of the 'Kerala model' is replete with a wide variety of forms of public action. These start intensively from the era of British colonialism in India, which had its influence on the region that presently constitutes Kerala State. The reform movements among several of the lower castes and communities were matched by actions of the native rulers of the region, who responded to these demands by providing basic social services to a wide section of the population. These initial social movements laid the foundation for the emergence of more secular movements along class lines among the peasants and workers, which were led by radicals with leftist leanings. In the post-Independence period this resulted in the creation of political history when a democratically elected Communist government came to power in Kerala State in 1957. The government initiated progressive public action measures in the agrarian sector. These included measures such as land reforms, abolition of tenancy, granting of homestead rights, ensuring minimum wages and the improvement of working conditions. This gave a big fillip to the physical conditions of life and created a great upsurge and assertion of self-respect and dignity among the vast masses of the agricultural labourers and small peasants in Kerala.

The success of the agricultural labour movement in safeguarding their rights and enhancing their social welfare had a very strong influence among other occupational groupings both in agriculture and in traditional industry. The success of the toddy tappers, the cashew and coir workers, the beedi rollers, to name a few, in undertaking adversarial collective action which resulted in the enhancement of their socioeconomic position is an example of the positive demonstration effect. They resorted to a variety of measures and pressures to maintain and expand the control they exercised in their respective occupations. The outcome of this pressure from below was that the state had to undertake various 'protectionist' measures. For example, it curbed mechanization in the coir-processing sector to prevent the large-scale displacement of low-paid women coir workers. The state was also compelled to support the organizational efforts of the workers. For example, the cooperatives of the beedi workers were provided with credit and assurances of supply of raw materials at concessional rates. The state also had to recognize the rights of self-employed workers like toddy tappers to form trade unions. These actions greatly enhanced the 'exchange entitlements' of these

Table 9.1   Some development indicators: Kerala and India (1991)

	Kerala	India
Per-capita GNP (Rs.)	4,200[a]	6,290
Literacy rate (% for over 6 years)		
male	94	64
female	87	39
Life expectancy (years)		
male	69	59
female	74	59
Infant mortality (per 1,000 births)		
urban	13	53
rural	17	85
Birth rate (per 1,000)		
urban	18	23
rural	18	31
Sex ratio (females to 1,000 males)	1,040	929
Population growth rate (%)[b]	1.31	2.11
Mean age at marriage (years)		
males	28	24
females	22	19
% of villages with direct access to:[c]		
drinking water	96	93
electricity	97	33
metalled roads	98	45
primary school	99	90
health dispensary (within 2 km)	91	25
fair price shop (within 2 km)	99	35

[a] Excluding foreign remittances. Some authors (see Thomas Isaac 1992) claim that foreign remittance could be up to 40 per cent of this figure.
[b] 1981–91.   [c] 1989.

Sources: GOI (1992 and 1995); Zachariah and Irudayarajan (1997); Census Commissioner of India (1992); Director of Census Operations (1992); Franke and Chasin (1989); GOK (1996c), CMIE (1998).

workers. On the one hand this politicization and the awareness generated by their struggles against oppressive socioeconomic forces protected their occupations and prevented a drastic fall in their incomes. On the other hand it resulted in the generation of well-articulated demands from the communities for the expansion of social services which contributed to their basic needs of life – food, education, health and housing.

The present higher quality of life in Kerala is thus not merely the result of provisioning of services by the state in the form of physical facilities – schools, health centres, fair price shops, metalled roads, post offices, public transportation and so on. It is equally important to recognize the growth of awareness among the masses and concerted collective action by them to ensure that these facilities were utilized fully and well.

The results of such a pattern of development are highlighted in the following indicators: a generally high literacy rate and more particularly a high female literacy rate; a low infant mortality rate; lower population growth rates and high life expectancies; and greater accessibility to essential services like health, water, electricity, public distribution shops and roads. These indicators are important because they point to attributes which must be both widely available to, and enjoyed by, a large section of the population to show up significantly when measured on a spatial or per-capita basis.

It is apparent from Table 9.1 that the quality of life in Kerala is much better than in the rest of India despite the fact that the per-capita income of the state is far lower than that of the country as a whole. However, what we wish to highlight in this chapter is that even with such a development model, disparities can exist between the mainstream and some sectors of the economy which fall on the far adverse side of the above-mentioned positive indicators of social well-being.

The Fisheries Sector: The 'Outlier' of the Kerala Model

The marine fishery sector of the state provides an important case of the extent of disparities that can exist even within this model despite its heavy emphasis on equality. Fish and fisheries have a very significant place in the sociocultural fabric of life in Kerala. However, we are faced with a situation where fishing communities in Kerala have not benefited for many decades from the increased value of output in the sector or the state's overall efforts at improving the quality of life.

The marine fisheries sector has witnessed a substantial increase in the value of output over the decades. The data available for the period 1970 to 1995 indicate an increase from Rs. 252 million to Rs. 7,514 million. Until 1985 the growth was slow with value of output increasing by around 250 per cent (Table 9.2). Thereafter, following a substantial increase in the harvest and the price, the value increased by over sevenfold between 1985 and 1995.

Table 9.2   Output, price and value of marine fish harvest in Kerala State

Years	Fish harvest (tonnes)	Price (Rs./tonne)	Value of harvest (Rs. million)
1970	392,000	642	252
1975	420,000	1,761	741
1980	279,500	2,971	837
1985	326,000	2,780	906
1990	662,900	7,980	5289
1995	532,000	14,120	7514

Source: Calculated from data in GOK (1975, 1981 and 1996c).

Incomes in the Fisheries Sector

The data pertaining to the state domestic product and the product of the fishery sector of the state further confirm unambiguously that the performance of the fishery sector from 1970 to 1985 was dismal. While the net state domestic product (SDP) increased between 1970/71 and 1985/86 by about 350 per cent, the fishery sector product (FSP) increased by only 260 per cent. The overall impact of this rather dismal performance of the fisheries sector can be gauged from the fact that the gap between the per-capita state domestic product and the fishery sector product per fisherperson had increased sharply between 1970 and 1985 from 15 to 49 per cent (Table 9.3). Part of the reason for this is that the population growth rate for the state as a whole was lower than the growth rate of the fisherfolk population for this period – 1.7 per cent as compared to 2.3 per cent, respectively. An equally important reason, as indicated earlier (see Table 9.2) is undoubtedly the fact that the value of output of the fishery sector had not increased substantially after 1970 due to the fall of physical output and a slower rate of increase of prices due to the harvesting of a larger share of the lower-valued species. The scenario changes in the post-1985 period with the differences narrowing down considerably following increases in fish harvests and changes in the government's technology and credit policy in the fisheries sector. This was in response to pressure from the newly formed fishworkers' trade unions during this period (see below).

Table 9.3   Total and per-capita state domestic product and fishery sector product

	1970	1980	1985	1990	1995
Net state domestic product (Rs. million)	12,546	38,227	56,372	121,735	22,0243
Fishery sector product (Rs. million)	257	774	932	3,719	6,286
Per-capita state domestic product (Rs.)	595	1,510	2,076	4,200	7,200
Fishery sector product per fisherperson (Rs.)	504	972	1,062	3,800	6,334
Percentage difference	15	35	49	10	12

Sources: GOK (1986 and 1996c); CMIE (1998).

Quality of Life in the Fisheries Sector

The poverty of the marine fishing communities is proverbial. Our data also indicate that it is a fact. Living as they do on the geographic margins of the land and depending exclusively on the sea for a livelihood, they have been left behind in the economic, and more sharply in the socio-cultural, progress which has been witnessed in the rest of the state. The only other occupational group in a similar circumstance are the tribal communities who live on the hilly fringes of the state and depend mainly on the forests for their livelihood. It is noteworthy that it is the communities which depend on natural common property resources and dwell on the fringes of the natural boundaries of the state – the sea and the hills – that face these adverse circumstances.

Land holding and housing

One of the paramount reasons for the poor quality of life and the sub-standard conditions of habitat of the marine fishing communities is the crowding of the whole community on a narrow strip of land along the length of Kerala's coastline. This is a result of the highly dispersed nature of the fishery resource and the consequent decentralized nature of fishing operations using beach landing craft. Every fisherman prefers to live on the seafront near the point where he lands his craft and from where he can observe the sea. There are 222 fishing villages located in a spatial

Table 9.4   Land and homestead ownership in Kerala and its marine fishing villages (% of households in 1979–80)

	No land	<5 cents	5–10 cents	11–100 cents	101–500 cents	>500 cents
Kerala	n/a	9	73	73	15	3
Fishing villages	16	32	28	23	1	n/a

Note: One acre = 100 cents.
Source: GOK (1980 and 1988).

continuum along the state's 590 km coastline. None of these villages is more than half a kilometre wide from the seafront. With a total marine fisherfolk population of 769,100 in 1996 and a residential area of 290 square kilometres (590 km × 0.5 km) the population density in marine fishing villages was around 2,652 persons per square kilometre. This is in comparison to the state figure of 742 per square km, which is already one of the highest in the country.

The major impact of this crowding is reflected in the land-holding patterns. In a state where every household is entitled to a piece of homestead plot (as per the Kerala State Homestead Act) varying between 2 and 10 cents (100 cents = 1 acre), we have data indicating that in 1979–80 as many as 16 per cent of the households in marine fishing villages did not possess even their own homestead plot (see Table 9.4). A large section of these households built thatched huts on land even beyond the cadastral survey (land beyond the cadastral survey on the seafront is under central government jurisdiction). Consequently they are always prone to the perennial risk of their huts being 'eaten by the monsoon sea'. This situation has changed marginally in the post-1985 period following the granting of title deeds to those who occupied public lands.

Similarly, larger numbers of households in the fishing villages have small land holdings. With partitioning this situation is likely to have become more skewed at present. Such meagre land holdings have an immediate bearing on both the spatial settlement pattern and the quality of housing and related amenities. The resultant settlement pattern is a clustering of houses closely resembling the urban slum configuration. This is in sharp contrast to the 'individual house and compound' stereotype for which Kerala State is well known. When households have no land (or title deed to the plot they occupy) and have to erect a shelter

Table 9.5   Housing and related amenities in Kerala (1979–80)

	Kerala	Fishing villages
Total households	4,065,895	118,801
Percentage of homes which are:		
thatched	24	48
mud and semi-thatched	4	36
brick and/or stone	72	16
electrified	24	10
with latrines	19	5
with water easily available	61	33

Source: GOK (1980 and 1988).

on public property, it is but natural that they have to opt for some sort of temporary thatched roof and wall structure. Thatched roofing is very common in Kerala given the numerous coconut palms, but thatched walls characterize the housing of the very poor. The stark differences in the quality of housing for Kerala as a whole and the fishing villages is evident from Table 9.5.

The basic amenities related to housing such as electric lighting, toilet facilities and access to water were also at far lower standards in the fishing villages when compared to the state as a whole. There has been significant improvement in the post-1985 period with regard to the quality of the housing following the commencement of a large number of low-cost housing programmes.

One difficulty of providing toilet facilities in coastal villages is that septic tanks do not function effectively because of the high water table in the sandy soil and the risk this entails of leaching of sewage into wells used for drinking water. Consequently, the men use the beach as a toilet all the time and the women use other secluded places, only well before dawn. The health implications of these circumstances are obvious.

Health conditions

This lack of basic facilities, the use of the beach as a public toilet, and the excessive crowding caused by the cluster-settlement pattern, give rise to strong negative reciprocal externalities between households. This is certainly not a feature of the other parts of rural Kerala. Contagious diseases in fishing villages spread very rapidly under these sordid physical conditions. This is at the root of the much reported poor health conditions in fishing communities.

A study of the health status of Kerala State (Panikar and Soman 1984), which delves into the paradox of economic backwardness and a high level of health development in Kerala taken as a whole, points to the *lack* of this paradox in the coastal areas. This study shows that respiratory and skin infections, diarrhoeal disorders and hookworm infestations are much more prevalent in the coastal areas of the state.

Infant mortality and population growth rate

One important proxy measure for the level of basic amenities and hygiene is the infant mortality rate (IMR). Kerala State prides itself on the sharp decline it has achieved in IMR, which in turn has had the strong indirect effect of reducing the population growth rate. At the all-Kerala level the infant mortality rate was 40 per 1,000 live births in 1981 and has dropped to 17 per 1,000 live births in 1991. The population growth rate declined from 1.9 to 1.3 per cent per annum in this period. The corresponding figures for the fishing communities as a whole are not available, but data for one southern district revealed an IMR of 85. The population growth rate was 2.3 until 1981 but has probably come down slightly to 2.1 per cent thereafter.

Gender bias

There is also a strong gender bias in favour of male children in fishing communities, as evidenced in the sex ratio of 972 females to 1,000 males in 1981. This again is contrary to the all-Kerala situation where females outnumbered males by 32 per 1,000 in 1981 and by 40 per 1,000 in 1991. This gender bias in favour of males is all the more significant in the context of studies of fishing communities, which reveal that the pattern of sex differentials in infant mortality show the expected higher incidence of male mortality over females in the neonatal period (Vimala Kumari 1991). Consequently, we must infer that the higher mortality of females is in later childhood. It is well known that where the life expectancy at birth is low (under 50) and most childhood deaths are caused by infection and parasitic diseases, girls die at higher rates than boys because they are less well fed and cared for than male children (Kumar 1989). This seems to be a plausible explanation in the context of the fishing communities, where the male members are indispensable in the fish-harvesting operations at sea which provide the main source of income for the family. Consequently, the 'extended entitlements' of male members in the food

Table 9.6   Literacy rates in Kerala and its marine fishing villages, 1981

	Male	Female	Total
All workers	89	70	85
Fishworkers	67	44	66

Source: Director of Census Operations (1986).

distribution within a fishing household are very strongly entrenched. When we add to this the lack of privacy and the unhygienic sanitary conditions, which result in morbidity and mortality from a plethora of reproductive-system infections, the sex ratio is made more adverse even at higher age groups. Using the method adopted by Drèze and Sen (1989), we estimate that, given the male population in the fishing community in 1981 and the sex ratio of Kerala State, the number of 'missing women' in the fishing communities was about 18,500. This was about 6 per cent of the female population in 1981.

Literacy levels

Literacy and education are the hallmark of Kerala's social advancement. On this count also marine fishing communities lag behind the state as a whole. We have comparable data for literacy of the working population of the state and the fishworkers in the state for 1981 (Table 9.6).

The literacy levels of the fishworkers of the state, though they are significantly lower than that of Kerala as a whole, are higher than the literacy rate for the country. It has, however, recently been observed (Thomas 1989) that while literacy rates are above the Indian average, the adverse socioeconomic conditions of marine fisherfolk are perpetuated more by their poor and low standards of educational attainments when compared to the rest of the state's population (more on this below).

Why is the Fishing Community an 'Outlier'?

Having examined the status of the 'quality of life' indicators for the fishing community of Kerala State, there should be no doubt left in the mind of the reader that this is a community which is an 'outlier' in the scenario of sociocultural progress made by Kerala State. Using the terminology of Drèze and Sen we may say that some of the economic, social and cultural characteristics specific to fishing communities have placed restrictions on its members achieving a level of 'capabilities' commensurate with that of members of other communities in Kerala.

Resolving the paradox of the poor 'capability building' conditions in the fisheries sector in a state that boasts a very high quality of life requires an understanding of a few closely interrelated economic, social and cultural characteristics specific to the fishing communities, which provide an explanation for its outlier position.

Mode of Resource Use and Awareness of Deprivation

It is well known that consciousness is closely related to the modes of production and resource use. Among land-based workers in agriculture and other terrestrial natural-resources-based sectors in Kerala, one objective factor became important in the process of understanding deprivation. This related to the restrictions they experienced with regard to access to land or raw materials necessary for earning a livelihood. It is this awareness that in turn led to a consciousness about class contradictions in society. This has been one of the important planks in the mobilization of the rural proletariat in Kerala for 'capability building' public action (Kannan 1988).

For the fishing community, the sea was traditionally viewed as their 'community property' to which individual fishermen had 'open access'. This resulted in a greater degree of equality between them and gave the impression of a barrier-free access to resources. This fact, combined with the context of a perpetual (though fluctuating) harvest from the sea, has been an important deterrent in creating a consciousness of their class position. Together with this, there is a strong element of chance and uncertainty in their occupation. Fishermen with the same quantum of fishing gear, fishing in the same part of the sea for comparable periods of time, can end up catching totally different amounts of fish. Such outcomes defy logical explanation. They are rationalized by religion, which explains good and bad yields as the will of the gods.

Fishermen cannot live by fish alone. The compulsion to barter or exchange the produce of their labour comes even at a very low level of the development of the productive forces. Once a fisherman nets more than a few fish he has a 'surplus'. This, being highly perishable, must be disposed of soon, thus creating a greater dependence on persons specializing in trade. Also, considering that the beach sands on which the fishermen live are not conducive to the growth of plants (other than coconut palms), the dependence on the market for all forms of food and even fire wood is virtually total. This greater degree of penetration of the market into every aspect of their daily lives made them vulnerable to a variety of market-related conditions. They were reduced to 'price-takers' on every front: for all the inputs required for life and livelihood and for the produce of their hard and risky labour.

Merchants and middlemen, however, point out to fishermen that the fish in the sea are a 'free good' which fishermen harvest daily for very little initial investment and negligible recurring costs. The merchants and middlemen claim that it is because they finance the investment and arrange for the distribution and sale of the fish that this 'free good' acquires value. For as long as fishing was undertaken without using any form of mechanical propulsion, and despite the high level of 'cooperative conflict' in their relationship with merchants and middlemen, fishermen were prone largely to accept this argument. Even after the introduction of modern technologies, and the greater influence of capitalistic relations of production on many fishing units, one distinguishing feature of fishing has been the continued absence of a system of wage payments and the dominance of the income-sharing system between fishermen crew and craft owner. This has continued to mask the contradictions in the production relations.

The above factors acting in unison have been powerful elements in depriving the fishing community of a collective awareness of their deprivation and a consciousness of the material basis of their socioeconomic exploitation. This state of affairs is further reproduced by the role of religion, as well as their position in Kerala society at large.

The Role of Religion and Position in Society

Religion constitutes one of the main elements of the culture of fishing communities everywhere in the world. It influences the way they represent themselves, nature and society. Artisanal fishing in tropical seas is basically a hunting-and-gathering activity in which those who labour are directly confronted by the raw forces of nature. This fact and the strong element of chance in deciding the outcome of their labours (mentioned earlier) play an important function in legitimizing the role of a 'supernatural' element in their lives and give a strong sense of religiosity to the community. Before the ninth century, all the fishing communities in Kerala were in a tribal type of social organization, different from the tributary mode of production that characterized agrarian communities. The totem symbolized the identity of the group. Although all the marine fishing communities have over the centuries adopted Hinduism, Islam or Catholicism, their prior social status and the nature of their occupation continued to bestow on them a low status even within their respective new religious groupings (Houtart and Nayak 1988).

Hindu fishermen

The present-day Hindu fishermen (the majority of whom live in the central districts of Kerala state) were very gradually, and only negatively, integrated into the caste structure of local Hinduism. They remain at the bottom of the social structure because of both their origin and the nature of their economic activity, which involves the destruction of animal life. The Hindu religious organization, with its specific religious agents (*poojaris*), has therefore not interfered excessively with these communities. No attempt was made to impose orthodoxy of beliefs, rituals or ethics. Consequently they continued to reproduce their tribal kinship social organization (*karayogam*), which has remained quite democratic and flexible. The 'Hinduism' of these fishermen is deeply influenced by their traditional pre-Hindu religiosity (Houtart and Nayak 1988).

Muslim fishermen

The Muslim fishermen belong to the second generation of converts from among the marginalized tribal groups in the merchant-dominated society of the Sultanates (1100–1400 AD) of the present northern districts of Kerala State. Islam has always functioned through specialized religious agents (*imams*), who played a major role in shaping the social reproduction of the group using various forms of ethical regulation, which gradually resulted in changes in the kinship structure of these communities. This was replaced by a more rigid conception of God as master of history, thus inducing a certain immobility of social organization. Cohesion within the community is strictly maintained by the mosque councils, although they do not interfere with the economic activities of the community but may deliberate on which political party the community should support (Houtart and Nayak 1988).

Catholic fishermen

The origins of the Catholic fishermen go back to the Portuguese colonization of the fifteenth century, which had its pervading influences in the southern districts of Kerala. *En masse* conversions took place principally among the minority social groups excluded from the mainstream of the rigorous caste society. Roman Catholicism was founded on a highly centralized institution based on authority and one religious agent (the priest), who also became the central social leader. Being a marginalized and vulnerable minority community to start with, it affirmed its identity by the religious institution. It was almost as if the function of the totem was replaced by the conspicuously large church buildings which are the hallmark of the poverty-stricken Catholic fishing villages. The Church controls a good deal of the mechanism of social reproduction at the local level. Granting moneylenders and merchants – who exercise economic control over the labouring fishermen – a special status in parish responsibilities is an example of this. The rights to collect the 'church tithe' (the *kuttaka* or monopoly), which is often as high as 5 per cent of the value of the daily fish catch, is auctioned out to such persons. No fisherman can ever default on this tax: it would be collected by the priest before the defaulters' burial if necessary. Questioning the ways of the Church or deviating from its fiat can result in an *ooru velekku* (banishment from the parish) and even more stringent punishment like being lashed to a cross and beaten. This kind of ghetto control tends to reinforce a minority complex as well as the fear of influence from the power of other ideological or social groups.

Religion therefore played a major social role in defining the group's identity above the kinship structure. Being Hindu, Muslim or Catholic was a basis of differentiation among fishermen, who were otherwise fundamentally similar. Even today, Muslim and Catholic fishing communities continue to be regarded as 'inferior' within their own larger religious groupings. Having been forced to give up their earlier tribal or kinship social organization in the face of the value systems and ethics propagated by organized, centralized, male-dominated religious structures, their continued inferior status only reinforced the social and cultural disabilities they had historically faced. Consequently the discrimination meted out to them from the larger society continued unabated. This is particularly strong among the Catholic fishermen, making them the most socially and culturally disadvantaged among the 'outlier' fishing communities of Kerala. The social stigma attached to these communities is evident from the oft-encountered reluctance of government servants to serve in schools, health centres and other such social-service facilities extended to these coastal areas by state public action.

Low Educational Attainments

We have seen that the literacy levels of fishworkers were lower than those for other workers in Kerala. A more important disability that continues to hamper social change within these communities has been the low and inferior level of educational attainment of the community. Going to school implied keeping away from fishing. Most of the 'art' of fishing, particularly using the traditional craft and gear, could only be picked up through a process of 'learning-by-doing' from a very young age. Schooling, particularly for the male members, meant pulling them out of their traditional occupations.

It is of interest to note that such compulsions were strongest among the Catholic fishermen, who use *kattumarams* – a raft made by tying logs together, the use of which requires a high degree of skill as well as the ability to swim. To the extent that there had been no change in this mode of production, its reproduction could be assured only by a conscious non-participation in formal education. Consequently it is among the Catholic fishermen using *kattumarams* (restricted to Trivandrum District) that we find the lowest level of educational attainments. A study of the *kattumaram* fishermen undertaken in 1991 by this author tends to confirm this. It revealed that between fishermen who had a range of fishing experience as wide as twelve to fifty years, the average time spent in school was not significantly different: it was between three and four years.

A study (Thomas 1989) that examined three marine fishing communities in Kerala from three geographic regions and the three religions concluded that certain occupational, cultural and religious barriers do account in part for the low level of educational attainments (as distinct from literacy) of youth from the fishing communities. However, the study argues that the more compelling reason for the low attainment seems to be the grossly inadequate associative conditions required to do well in school: the lack of funds to buy books and clothes for school, poor habitat resulting in inadequate facilities for study, and inadequate parental attention and encouragement. Consequently the youth from the fishing communities are not in a position to compete successfully with their colleagues from other socioeconomic backgrounds for jobs in other sectors of the economy.

It is also appropriate to note that despite the remarkable contribution of both Muslims and Catholics to facilities for high-quality education in Kerala, the benefits of these have not percolated to their own fishing communities. In a highly literate society, basic education plays a major role in making information available to people on questions of life and living and also leads to greater utilization of public facilities. Those with some basic education go about provisioning themselves in a more informed manner. Educated mothers are the best assurance for children's education. We must also take cognizance of the fact that in Kerala it was mainly through the written word that a critical awareness of the world around was obtained by the less privileged in society. The fishing community at large had been deprived of all this because of their low educational attainments.

Pattern of Development as a Cause of Poverty

With the largest potential marine fishery resource in the country, Kerala had hoped to give the fisheries sector a major thrust in its planned development efforts. The pattern of development in the fish economy of the state was different in form and content when compared to that of the other comparable sectors of the economy. As mentioned earlier, under the active pressure of an organized workforce, in the other sectors of the economy the government implemented techno-economic policies and welfare measures which resulted in a different pattern of development in those sectors. In agriculture and the traditional land-based industries like coir spinning, toddy tapping, cashew processing, beedi making and so forth, no labour-displacing technologies were introduced. There were also a fair number of social-security and welfare measures that acted as a safety net which prevented a substantial marginalization of these workers and their families. Equally important was the fact that institutional initiative among these workers in the form of cooperatives and trade-related organizations met with considerable success.

Being unorganized, the marine fishermen did not benefit from such 'protectionism' against labour-displacing and ecologically inappropriate technologies. Also, the top-down, state-sponsored, institutional initiatives in the sector, particularly in the form of cooperative societies, were a total failure. They hardly benefited the fishermen, who were often even unaware of their existence (Kurien 1980). These cooperatives became instruments to strengthen the hands of the merchant class, who utilized these 'pocket societies' to usurp large amounts of government funds and facilities meant for the welfare of the fishermen. Another overriding factor that is important in accounting for the poorer socioeconomic conditions of marine fisherfolk was their inability to legitimize and establish their traditional, but unwritten, claim to custodianship of the coastal waters as the 'common property' of their community. Consequently, when the state began to play an active role in promoting modern fisheries development in the 1960s it created an open access regime in the coastal waters where *anyone who had the capital resources could freely enter*. This was a feature not obtaining in any of the other sectors of the economy, where there were more clearly defined property rights and several barriers to entry for both capital and labour from outside the respective sector. This led to the unregulated entry of capital into the coastal fishery and the rampant use of fish-harvesting technologies that initially raised the output, but in the long term resulted in destruction of the coastal ecosystem. The externalities imposed by this technology choice resulted in the reduction of the output for *all fishermen irrespective of the nature of the technology they used*.

The initial stream of benefits from this situation were very unevenly distributed: the investors from outside the fishing community who entered the fishery became wealthy, and the traditional marine fisherfolk who had no employment options other than fishing were the most adversely affected by the ensuing ecological crisis (Kurien 1992).

Social Movements and Political Mobilization

The social movements of the nineteenth and early twentieth centuries in Kerala were largely restricted to the Hindu communities in the agrarian setting. The material basis of the social movements was often to be found in the crisis of the institutional and economic moorings of agrarian society. The mode of twentieth-century political rhetoric in Kerala has to a large extent been conditioned by this. In the post-Independence era, the compulsions of a parliamentary democratic system made political parties anxious to see their efforts at politicization of social causes pay off in the form of votes. As a result, irrespective of their position on the political spectrum, all the parties were involved in taking up a variety of causes which focused on the issues in the agrarian and related natural-resource sectors and the populations involved therein. Two communities were left out of this: the tribal people of the hills on the high eastern fringes of the state, and the fishing communities on the western coastal front.

In the case of the fishing communities – particularly the Muslims and Catholics among them – the control by religious interests and the economic domination by merchants and middlemen from within the communities, who in turn had considerable influence over organized religious affairs, gave credibility to the perception held by political parties in the state that fishing communities were 'vote banks' to be wooed *only* at election time. The conservative parties, which generally got the open backing of organized religious forces and the economically powerful, were able to rest assured of the fishing community votes, come what may. Consequently they considered it unnecessary and even unwise to undertake any form of direct mobilization work among the actual fishermen. They strictly preferred to approach them always through their religious leaders or the influential persons in their communities (generally non-fishermen and often merchants). On the other hand, the more progressive political parties with secular policies and working-class concerns considered traditional artisanal fishermen, who were largely 'petty producers', an unstrategic group to mobilize. Also, given the circumstances described above, they could hardly hope to get their votes. This suspicion was confirmed as early as 1959 following the exhibition of the mesmerizing power wielded by the Catholic Church in inciting its 'faithful flock' of fishermen to come out *en masse* onto the streets in support of a 'liberation struggle' against the first Communist ministry in Kerala State. The paradox was that the main plank of this 'liberation struggle' was to protect the rights of minority communities to run their own educational institutions, the portals of which the majority of the fishermen would hardly have the fortune to enter! The end result of this was that, with the exception of a few pockets in central Kerala, where Hindu fishermen were in the majority, and in north Kerala, where the production relations in artisanal fisheries among the Muslim fishermen were capitalistic in nature, the progressive, democratic, political processes had little influence in these communities.

Beginnings of Collective Action

All the above-mentioned factors, which are both very specific to the fishing communities and a reflection of larger structural features, have been serious stumbling blocks to fostering collective public action within the fishing community for 'capacity building' up until the 1980s. Consequently, despite a common and committed public policy in Kerala for education, health, land reforms, essential commodity distribution, housing and so on, the fishing communities could not take advantage of these services.

A sea change occurred in the early 1980s. The fish catch in the state dropped drastically (see Table 9.2). The grossly deteriorating socio-economic conditions resulting from this spurred several social activists who had been working with these communities for over two decades to spearhead a socioecological movement, with the fishing community being mobilized as 'fishworkers'. A new genre of independent trade unions of these fishworkers led the struggles against users of destructive fishing technology – such as trawling – which they considered the cause for the destruction of the marine ecosystem. These unions also initiated efforts to safeguard the means of livelihood of the artisanal fishworkers by asserting their 'historic and traditional' rights of access to the coastal fishery resource. This was contested by the capitalist interests promoting trawling on the grounds that their freedom to undertake a business activity was curbed. That such traditional rights, which are intended to safeguard livelihood, should be accorded priority over other freedoms and claims was accorded approval by the highest court of the country. The verdict gave a boost to this new independent movement – an anathema in Kerala politics. In a state with numerous coastal electoral constituencies, this restiveness among the fishing community about their marginalization and the awareness of their rights made them indispensable to the plethora of political parties. By 1985 every party in the political spectrum of Kerala's politics had formed a fishermen's trade union. They did not wish to allow an opportunity for political gain to slip into the hands of a non-political party formation (Kurien 1992).

The political unions actively joined in the movement, which also sought to correct the inequalities experienced by the fishing community in relation to its access to the social welfare measures provided by the state. The initial successes of these actions over the last decade have created a widespread awakening in the fishing community which has cut across religious barriers and narrow political considerations. These actions have already begun to make significant changes in the socioeconomic conditions of the community. The primary reason for this has been the total reorientation of state policies in fisheries from 1985, providing an explicit bias to support of the artisanal fishworkers. Technologies and organizational structures more appropriate to their needs were introduced. This was supported by massive infusion of credit in favour of this small-scale sector. New welfare schemes which sought to provide incentives for children of the community to attend schools and not drop out were initiated. A scheme for bestowing land titles on those with hutments on public lands and a massive low-cost housing programme were initiated, along with a coastal sanitation and water supply project. No proper assessment has yet been made of the impact of these public policy initiatives on the quality of life of the community. Some case studies conducted by voluntary organizations in the southern districts provide hope for the future. They indicate greater participation of children in schools and positive steps in the realm of utilization of health and sanitation services.

Conclusions

Can another state in India today replicate the Kerala model? If a state government provides the financial allocations for particular public provisions that are essential to ensure a high quality of life – schools, health centres, public distribution systems for essential items and so forth – will this alone ensure that deprived sections of the population take advantage of these services and raise their standards of living? Does the experience of differential access and use of the 'support-led security' strategy of Kerala provide any clue about the nature of the challenge before those who wish to emulate the Kerala model?

The relative developmental success of a few countries such as Costa Rica, Sri Lanka and China, together with the influential writings of social scientists like Amartya Sen, seem to have created a 'paradigm shift' among large sections of public opinion on how a state can provision a high quality of life for its people. The earlier opinion that it can be achieved only by increases in the overall affluence of society has been replaced by the belief that public action by the state is indispensable for social security and capability building.

Our analysis of Kerala State – the central tendency as well as the context and condition of the outlier – serve to highlight another important but less emphasized facet in this paradigm shift. State-led public action guaranteeing widespread access to the basic facilities required to attain a high quality of life is never adequate. Without genuine people's participation in the form of collaborative and/or adversarial collective action such well-intended actions serve little purpose. It does not matter what comes first, the facilities or the collective action. The point is that without the latter, even radical and committed action by the state alone will remain a sterile challenge. For those who wish to emulate the 'Kerala model' we consider this to be the main insight from this chapter.

Note

This is a revised and updated version of a paper presented at the International Congress on Kerala Studies held at Thiruvananthapuram in 1994 which later appeared in *Social Scientist* 23(1–3), 1995: 70–90.

10

The Kerala Model:
Some Comparisons with
the Sri Lankan Experience

Rex Casinader

Among the few developmental states, one state that can compare favourably with Kerala's exceptional social achievements is its neighbour, Sri Lanka. Sri Lanka shares with Kerala the achievement of remarkable social indicators, in terms of literacy, life expectancy, fertility decline, low infant mortality and so on, as indicated by Tables 10.1 and 10.2. Like Kerala, this achievement is made more remarkable because it occurred in the context of slow economic growth, albeit better in the 1980s and 1990s than Kerala's record of economic growth. In fact, the Kerala model has been referred to as the Kerala–Sri Lanka model by some analysts (Timberg 1981).

In recent years Sri Lanka has been moving away from this model. This departure flows from some of the initiatives of the right-wing government of the United National Party (UNP) 1977–94, and their liberalization policies and adoption of the World Bank/IMF Structural Adjustment Programme.[1] These liberalization policies included dismantling of some subsidies and the social welfare package that had earlier provided food subsidies and equitable access to health care and education to the poor. These public measures are critical ingredients of the Kerala–Sri Lanka model. While this policy change may have contributed to the slightly better economic growth in Sri Lanka in the 1980s and reflected in relatively higher per-capita GNP (Table 10.2), it was nonetheless at the cost of growing disparities of income. This was a reversal of an earlier trend of reducing income disparities from the 1950s to 1970s in Sri Lanka,[2] which was perhaps another feature of the Kerala–Sri Lanka model. This may have been further compounded by the ethnic strife and violence that has scaled up in Sri Lanka during the past two decades.[3] But it is a testimony to the human capital that the Kerala–Sri Lanka model

Table 10.1 Comparative social indicators: Kerala and Sri Lanka (1991)

Social indicators	Kerala	Sri Lanka
Life expectancy at birth (years)		
female	74	74
male	69	70
all	72	72
Infant mortality rate (per 1,000 live births)	17	18
Crude death rate (per 1,000 pop.)	6	6
Crude birth rate (per 1,000 pop.)	19	21
Total fertility rate (per woman)	1.8	2.5
Adult literacy rate (%)		
female	86	85
male	94	94
all	90	89
Females per 100 males	104	99

Source: Drèze and Sen (1996).

creates that in spite of the difficult times Sri Lanka is going through, its HDI remains remarkably high (Table 10.2) and sustained (UNDP 1990).

A comparative examination of Kerala's and Sri Lanka's development experience may work towards an understanding of the model. To start with Sri Lanka's experience undermines the argument put forward by Jeffrey (1987b and 1994) that Kerala's matrilineal past is a critical factor in the emergence of the Kerala model. For, unlike Kerala, Sri Lanka does not have a matrilineal past. So the claim that the matrilineal past is a catalyst of the Kerala model appears flawed as it fails to explain the Sri Lankan experience. However, one can not rule out the possibility that different causal factors could lead to the seemingly same outcome. In Sri Lanka, the Sinhalese and a majority of the Tamils do not have a matrilineal past. There is a small Tamil Mukkuwa community on the east coast of Sri Lankan that had a matrilineal past. But ironically this community is among the few pockets that lag behind the high Sri Lankan national averages in the social indicators referred to earlier.

Radical Parties in Mainstream Politics and Government

While there are significant differences between the political economies of Kerala and Sri Lanka, a significant commonality is the presence of

Table 10.2   Development indicators: Kerala and Sri Lanka compared with selected Indian states, South Asian countries and selected other countries

Country/region	HDI	GDI	per-capita PPP$
Kerala (highest HDI and GDI in India)	0.651	0.565	829
Sri Lanka	0.789	0.660	2,053
Uttar Pradesh (lowest HDI and GDI in India)	0.292	0.293	787
Bihar	0.306	0.306	625
Maharashtra	0.532	0.492	1,348
Punjab	0.586	0.424	2,143
India	0.439	0.388	1,053
Pakistan	0.423	0.360	1,585
Bangladesh	0.318	0.334	883
Nepal	0.273	0.310	722
China	0.716	0.578	2,124
Japan (highest global HDI)	0.996	0.896	13,135
Sweden (highest global GDI)	0.987	0.919	13,780
Afghanistan (lowest global GDI)	0.212	0.169	1,000
Niger (lowest global HDI)	0.116	0.196	452

Notes

HDI = Human Development Index (1987/1990).

GDI = Gender Related Development Indicators (1990/95).

PPP$ = adjusted SDP/GNP per capita (1987).

Following Kumar, UNDP Reports have been used for HDI, GDI and per-capita PPP$ for all countries in this table. As other authors have shown, Kerala's development indicators increased considerably during the 1990s, while Sri Lanka's may have suffered due to the civil war and IMF/World Bank-led liberalization drives. Although the social indicators of Kerala and Sri Lanka are more or less similar, Sri Lanka's higher HDI is due to its higher per-capita income, which accounts for one-third of the weight of the HDI composite index.

Sources: For Indian states, Shiva Kumar (1991 and 1996). For all other countries, UNDP (1990 and 1995).

Marxist/radical parties in mainstream politics; a common feature that suggests the legitimacy of the analysis of the Kerala model put forward by Franke and Chasin (1992). An unpacking of this commonality, with some critical variations inscribed within it, may contribute to the discourse of making the Kerala model a little more intelligible. This unpacking may also provide some insights into the Sri Lankan development experience being in recent times increasingly convoluted and problematized by its ethnic pluralism.

Since the formation of the state of Kerala, governments have alternated between the Communist Party of India–Marxist or CPM-led Left Democratic Front (LDF) and Congress-led United Democratic Front (UDF). In Sri Lanka, too, since its independence in 1948, governments have been alternately held by the right-wing United National Party (UNP) and a centre–left coalition led by the centrist Sri Lanka Freedom Party (SLFP). This alternation in parliamentary government and electoral process has, in the Sri Lankan case, been broken only once by the unusually long hold on electoral power (1977 to 1994) by the UNP. This period saw ethnic relations become more violent and intense; it was perceived to be a period of erosion of some of the democratic institutions and decline of the strong trade-union movement. This was also the period that saw the changes in economic and social policies, including liberalization, referred to earlier. Nevertheless Sri Lanka was adequately politicized to have the capacity, even amidst a civil war, to change the government by ballot in 1994. The emergence in Sri Lanka from the 1920s/30s of strong organized labour, politicized and linked to Marxist/radical parties, is in part the genealogy of politicization in Sri Lanka. This parallels the Kerala experience of the symbiotic birth of trade unionism and radical political parties during the same period. There are, however, critical differences, which will be considered later.

The Sri Lankan left parties that developed during the 1930s included the Trotskyite Lanka Sama Samaja Pakshaya (LSSP) and the Communist Party (CP) of Sri Lanka; both have been partners in the centrist SLFP-led electoral alliance/coalition governments since 1956. This fits in with Franke and Chasin's (1992) argument that the Kerala model was driven by left-wing political parties and ideologies. It should be recognized that even during periods of right-wing government, the policy trends continued (until 1977 in the case of Sri Lanka), because such governments sought to pre-empt further radicalization by continuity/non-reversal of the social welfare package in health care, education, food and public transport subsidies. This is exemplified by the critical place of rice rations/subsidies in Sri Lankan electoral politics and manifestos until 1977. This further strengthens the argument that the critical factor for the Kerala–Sri Lanka model is the presence of radical political parties in mainstream politics and governance.

Educated Youth Unemployment and Political Movements

A significant problem that the Kerala–Sri Lanka model faces is the prevalence of high unemployment among educated youth. The economies of both Kerala and Sri Lanka were unable to absorb increasing numbers of young persons, most of whom were educated in an increasingly accessible education system. This may have been compounded by the phase of the demographic transition of both regions, also brought about by the health care features of the model, which saw an increasing youth component in the age profile of the population. This phase may be ending now as a result of the decline in fertility and population growth rate. Imbalances within the education system between technical and non-technical education/curricula may have intensified the problem of matching employment opportunities to job seekers.

Among the explanations put forward for the ethnic conflict in Sri Lanka are youth unemployment, competition for jobs and access to post-secondary education. The last is increasingly seen as a prerequisite for competitiveness in the job market. These explanations have been extended to account for the youthful character of the Liberation Tigers of Tamil Eelam (LTTE), the Jatika Vimukthi Perumuna (JVP) and other similar groups. In the case of the JVP the conflict engendered by the economic competition is primarily of a class character, though an ethnic element is present. Given that the job search is predominantly for white-collar and professional jobs, the youth movements have also been characterized as petty bourgeois, reflecting the social mobility aspirations involved. There is an element of stigmatization here: the unemployed and underemployed tend to be seen as backward-looking and politically reactionary, and not the historical bearers of social revolution.

Of significance, then, in a comparative examination of Kerala and Sri Lanka is the intense competition for employment, particularly among educated youth, and its potential implication for ethnic conflict. Yet there is a notable difference between the two. For prospective Kerala entrants to the labour force the job market extends beyond its state boundaries. The net out-migration from Kerala since the 1930s (Zachariah 1965) supports this observation. In contrast, in Sri Lanka the job market is largely contained within the small island character of the country. However, in the last decade there has been labour migration to the Middle East. Kerala, too, has made use of this employment opportunity; indeed, the highest number of labour migrants from India to the Middle East is from Kerala.

Labour Market and Gender

An issue that needs to be investigated is whether the labour market in Kerala is more segmented by gender than in Sri Lanka. Were this so, it follows that, by relatively greater exclusion on the basis of gender, the job market would be rendered less competitive. However, the data in

Table 10.3   Some indicators of the status of women: Sri Lanka, Kerala and selected Indian states (1981)

	1	2	3	4	5	6	7	8
Sri Lanka	10.1	24.4	17.1	33	12.2	88	49.1	48.5
Kerala	14.1	21.8	12.8	32	9.4	90	48.5	47.9
Punjab	14.4	21.1	3.1	5	2.2	65	45.0	39.5
Maharashtra	38.2	18.8	24.4	44	3.8	55	43.4	36.4
Uttar Pradesh	60.7	16.7	6.0	11	2.2	33	33.3	26.7
Bihar	63.9	16.5	9.2	18	2.4	34	29.7	21.3

Columns

1: Proportion of females married in age group 15–19.
2: Singulate mean age of marriage for females.
3: Female work participation rate.
4: Female workers as % of male workers.
5: Percentage of females in non-agricultural activities.
6: Female literates per 100 male literates.
7: Females as % of total school enrolment, grades 1–5.
8: Females as % of total school enrolment, grades 6–8.
Sources: For Indian states, Vaidyanathan (1989). For Sri Lanka, Department of Census and Statistics (1982, 1983a and 1983b).

Table 10.3, which are relevant to this issue, do not suggest the likelihood of a markedly differential gendered access to the labour market between Kerala and Sri Lanka.

The differing levels of the indicators on the status of women listed in Table 10.3 neatly reflect the differing scale of social development obtaining in selected states within India together with Sri Lanka. The selected Indian states apart from Kerala are Bihar and Uttar Pradesh, the two most socially backward states in India; Maharashtra, the most industrialized state; and Punjab, the agriculturally most developed state in India. Some of the listed indicators like the age of marriage, female literacy and education have also been seen as contributing to other social development processes such as the fertility decline observed in Kerala and Sri Lanka.

The common trends of Kerala and Sri Lanka are striking and substantiate their being classified as one type of development. Furthermore, the data do not suggest a significantly more gendered access to the labour market in Kerala than in Sri Lanka. However, slightly, but consistently, higher women's status indicators for Sri Lanka, other than in literacy (column 6), are observable.

Of particular interest for examining any gendered access to the job market is the female work participation rate and the percentage of females in non-agricultural activity. The higher rates prevailing in Sri Lanka suggest that women have a slightly more open access to employment than in Kerala. More rigorous analysis is required, breaking down the work participation by occupation, to identify what contribution gendered occupations such as certain household industries, nursing and so on make to the overall participation rate in both regions. This also needs to be done with data more recent than 1981. The issue of the invisibility of some of the productive economic activities of women in census and other statistical data must also be examined. This would identify whether the barriers to women's access to the job market differ between Kerala and Sri Lanka. Appearances suggest that there are relatively fewer barriers to women entering the job market in Sri Lanka than in Kerala. The presence of a large female work force in the Sri Lankan free trade zone, female labour migrants to the Middle East, female car-park attendants, policewomen, and even bus conductors for a limited period,[4] in Sri Lanka are evidence of this – and stand in contrast to the situation in Kerala. Females are negligible among the labour migrants to the Middle East from Kerala, being confined to some health-care professionals. There is no free trade zone in Kerala, and female non-agricultural participation in work appears to be in gendered occupations like nursing, education, clerical work, the coir industry, cashew processing, textiles, and beedi rolling.

What all this suggests is that there may be relatively greater constraints, some of them cultural, to female labour force participation in Kerala than in Sri Lanka, particularly in occupations that were formerly male preserves, such as bus conductors and the police, that educated young persons can perform. In Kerala, then, there may be a relatively greater gendered access to job opportunities, which privileges males. If women's access to the job market is more limited than in Sri Lanka, then women are taking more of the brunt in job-market competitiveness, and are made to opt out to become home makers. If this is so then the job market in Sri Lanka is apparently more intensely competitive than in Kerala because, relatively speaking, a section of the population is not kept out of the job market on the basis of gender.

There is no doubt that women in Kerala occupy a better position relative to all other regions in India. Indeed, one may argue that the broad north–south distinctions within India in terms of gender relations and position of women improve on the southeast-to-southwest axis as well. Southwest South Asia, meaning Kerala and Sri Lanka, may thus be one of the regions where the position of women is relatively better in the context of South Asia. It must be stressed that this value is indeed relative

– there are a number of issues that clearly show that women are subordinated in Kerala and Sri Lanka. This relatively better status of women appears in many ways to be comparable to the position of women in some Southeast Asian countries. It may be significant in this context to note that similarities in political history and organization have been observed between Southwest India and Southeast Asia (Subrahmanyam 1986). Dale claims that 'Certain aspects of the history and political organization of Kerala are more intelligible when the area is thought of as one of the Hinduized states of Southeast Asia rather than as an integral part of the South Asian subcontinent' (1980).

Dale sees historical parallels between Kerala and Southeast Asia in ecology, transport systems, cash crops and commerce. He claims that Kerala shares most of the characteristics of the 'Southeast Asian personality'. Franke and Chasin (1992), while not drawing parallels, argue that the Kerala model is influenced by its unique ecology, maritime culture and role in the maritime history of the Indian Ocean – which latter features it shares with some of the Southeast Asian states and Sri Lanka, particularly the southwestern quarter, the most densely populated region. Sri Lanka and Kerala also have aspects of political economy in common, albeit with some critical distinctions (discussed below).

In this regard it may be noted that Thomas Issac's (1986) use of a neologism in Malayalam, *gragara* – *gra-* from *gramam* (rural); *-gara* from *nagara* (urban) – to describe the mix of urban and rural landscape and economy in Kerala has striking similarities to *desakota* (McGee 1991) in the Javanese context. *Desakota* is almost an identical neologism coined in Bahasa Indonesia – *desa* (rural) and *kota* (urban) – to describe a similar sociospatial landscape that exhibits an intense mix of urban and rural features.

Though there are dangers of historical geographical determinism in such comparisons and analysis, the acknowledged central role of the political economy of capital–labour conflict and radical ideology in Kerala–Sri Lanka is justification in this case. What this discussion seeks to determine is whether that part of the historical/geographical/ecological contextualization seemingly shared by Southeast Asia and Southwest South Asia may include the nature of gender relations/definitions and the status and position of women within them. It is perhaps this feature, and not the specificity of its matrilineal past, as claimed by Jeffrey, that influences Kerala's social history, including the Kerala model.

Competition for Post-secondary Education

Competition for access to post-secondary education may also be more intense in Sri Lanka relative to Kerala, due to the fact that the Sri Lankan educational system, up to the secondary level, is the more open. In the early 1960s all schools in Sri Lanka that were run by religious organizations but aided financially by the state were nationalized. Shortly afterwards all English medium schools were progressively converted to Sinhala and/or Tamil medium schools. A handful of private fee-paying schools run by Christian organizations were not state aided and so not nationalized. But they too had to fall in line with government regulations on the medium of instruction. In Kerala, on the other hand, remnants of elitism persist in the private education sector. Although there is a system of state schools, the colonial school system of state-aided but privately managed, predominantly Christian schools continues to exist. The medium of instruction was not regulated by the state; consequently many of the schools retain English as the medium of instruction to cater for the needs of the elite.

The CPM-led LDF governments in Kerala did attempt educational reform, which if successful may have corrected some of the elitist features and brought the system closer to the kind of educational system that has emerged in Sri Lanka. But the Christian Church, as a major actor, opposed the move. The Congress Party in Kerala, the main electoral and parliamentary opponent of the LDF, was pro-Church. Given the Congress Party's position at the centre for a number of years, and the constitutional and other powers that resided there, as well as considerations of electoral and party politics, these reforms were never pushed through.

Kerala students had the advantage that they could seek admission to post-secondary institutions throughout India. In Sri Lanka, the fact that admissions were restricted to the national system made competition for places intense. Such competition had implications for ethnic conflict given the plurality of the society. The use of the vernacular languages as the medium of instruction, though an apparently progressive measure that removed some of the elitism from the educational system, was complicated by the linguistic duality of the society. A number of studies that focus on ethnicity and post-secondary education in Sri Lanka reflect the deep implications of the issue for ethnic conflict. The intense competition for post-secondary education is in fact a reflection of the intense competition that exists for jobs. It is also the consequence of a development process that made access to education more equitable. Yet it was also a development process that produced an economy that was unable to absorb the human capital it created.

Such comparative assessment helps account for the absence of ethnic or ethno-religious conflict in Kerala and its presence in Sri Lanka. The competitiveness intrinsic to Sri Lanka's relatively open educational system through to the secondary level, followed by fiercer competition for jobs, contrasts sharply with the situation in Kerala. In an island nation of ethnic and religious plurality such severe pressures can produce conflict.

Kerala is also a plural society: in religious terms, next to Punjab and Kashmir, it has the highest concentration of minorities (Muslims 21.2 per cent; Christians 20.6 per cent) in India. This pluralism, too, is not without its frictional moments and, indeed, implications for Kerala's political economy. Nevertheless, compared to Punjab, Kashmir and Sri Lanka, Kerala is a benign and tolerant civil society. Let us explore this critical distinction by examining the differences in the multiple genealogies of radicalism in Kerala and Sri Lanka. It is important to recognize that pluralism in Kerala, Punjab and Kashmir exists only as a religious fact; linguistically, they are relatively homogeneous societies. Pluralism in Sri Lanka, however, is both a religious and a linguistic fact. Furthermore, the bicultural divide between the Sinhala Buddhists and Tamil Hindus has been seen as central to the politicization and ethnic violence in Sri Lanka. Events of the last few years, however, indicate that the Muslims are no longer merely an audience; hence biculturalism may no longer be a valid characterization of Sri Lanka. The linguistic divide makes dialogue difficult (except for the few who are bilingual); there is little scope for developing a capacity to listen to the 'other'.

Reform Movements and Political Economy

The colonial experiences of Sri Lanka and Kerala have many common-alities; nevertheless their responses were textured by distinct religious contexts. An important historical feature of Sri Lanka's island nation character is the retention of Buddhism as the religion of the majority of its people. In Kerala's case, the presence of two Hindu princely states, Travancore and Cochin, is significant. Some aspects of their responses appear relevant to the processes that have shaped the political economy of each. The colonizers often, in order to legitimize the colonial encoun-ter, presented their actions as a 'civilizing mission'. The indigenous re-sponse was varied, but it included counter players who were both religious reformers and anti-colonial activists. As Ashish Nandy characterizes them in the Indian context, they 'borrowed their fundamental values from the Western world-view and, in spite of their image as orthodox revivalists, were ruthlessly critical of the Hindus. They also took the position that the Hindus had been great in Ancient times and had fallen on bad days because of their loss of contact with textual Brahminism' (Nandy 1983). The resistance came from religious reformers in all parts of India.

In Kerala of the late nineteenth and early twentieth centuries, one social-cum-religious reformer was the charismatic figure of Sri Narayana

Guru (1854–1928). He was not a privileged or *savarna* caste elite seeking to reform from above. He was a member of a subaltern or *avarna* caste, the Ezhavas, and was challenging Hindu, or more precisely Brahmanic, orthodoxy from below. It was an anti-Brahmin-establishment movement from within the Hindu community, and not led or orchestrated by Christian missionaries as in some other parts of South India.

The Sri Narayana Movement[5] sought to remove overt discrimination against Ezhavas on the basis of caste, such as prevention of access to public roads, entry to temples, employment in the state bureaucracy and so on. Resistance took the form of reference to the legitimizing authority of Hindu texts, which testified to the inappropriateness of these discriminatory restrictions; and of social activism, such as *satyagraha* at temple entrances and caste association as a lobby and pressure group. In the former tactic the charisma and learning of Sri Naryana Guru was invoked. By his active participation in the reform movement he gave a moral and textual authority to reform Brahminic Hinduism.

The Sri Narayana Movement became the most sweeping mass movement in Travancore in the period of the late nineteenth and early twentieth centuries. What is significant is that the Movement was a reform movement engendered not so much by the colonial encounter as by the context of Brahminic and caste domination in ideology and praxis. It may have been influenced by missionary efforts at caste reform, and reform from above, but basically it was a very successful attack on Brahmin orthodoxy from within Hinduism, and it came from below, from the *avarna/* subaltern castes who were the victims of that orthodoxy. This anti-Hindu-establishment stance had a liberating influence on the Kerala society of that time.

The Ezhavas were occupationally concentrated in the coir industry, where the trade-union movement in Kerala was pioneered in the 1920s (Thomas Issac 1982, 1983a, 1983b and 1985). There occurred, through them, a positive transference of the ethos of legitimate social and moral protest from the temple floor to the factory floor. The egalitarian ideology embedded in Sri Narayana Guru's teachings and its implication for radical ideology and politics is seen in his neat turning of the slogan 'one caste, one God, one religion' into 'no caste, no God, no religion'! The Sri Narayana Movement can be seen as part of the historically and ideologically rooted contestation between Brahminism and Sramanism (Thapar 1989). In this contestation Buddhism is of great historical significance.

Let us now briefly examine the nature of Buddhist revivalism in late-nineteenth- and early-twentieth-century Sri Lanka, and specifically the revivalism led by Anagarika Dharmapala (1864–1933). In contrast to the Sri Narayana Movement, the Buddhist revivalist movement has to be

contextualized in the colonial encounter. It was a response to the hege-
monic position of Westernization and the Westernized elite. In this there
was an implied depreciation of the indigenous and the vernacular, and
this included Buddhism. The revivalist language contained elements of
the language of ethnicity – a language that has been described as emotional
and passionate, with affinities to the concepts of resentment, shame,
honour, pride, dignity, insult, inclusion or exclusion, humiliation or recognition (Cairns 1991). The important point to stress here is the quite
distinct context of the two movements, Sri Narayana and Anagarika
Dharmapala. It followed that the character, responses and language of
the movements were also very different.

Each movement had implications for the political economy of its
region. The *avarna* activists who confronted Brahminic orthodoxy and
orthopraxis as well as deracinated *savarna* caste youths contributed to the
beginning of the radical political tradition in Kerala. In Sri Lanka, among
the participants in the Buddhist revivalist movement were the vernacular
intelligentsia, which included the Buddhist Sangha (bhikkus or Buddhist
clergy).[6] The vernacular intelligentsia nurtured the movement and was at
the same time nurtured by the movement. This process involved growing
anti-imperialistic attitudes and sentiments. Yet they failed to find a political
niche for their anti-imperialism, for the Ceylon National Congress[7] was
for them too elitist, comprador and insufficiently militant and anti-
imperialistic. These qualities the vernacular intelligentsia was to find in
the Lanka Sama Smaja Party (LSSP), which emerged in the 1930s.

What is the significance of all this for the Kerala–Sri Lanka development model? Radicalization of politics, trade unionization, together with
electoral and parliamentary politics have undoubtedly influenced the
genesis and shaping of the model in both regions; as such they form
something of a common ancestry. In terms of radical politics, there is no
doubt about the centrality of Marxian ideology. The impact of such events
as the Russian Revolution and the emergence of the Labour Party in
Britain were also significant, of course. Yet it is in the genealogy of the
two reform movements, albeit in many different ways, as I have attempted
to show here, that clues may be found for the absence and presence of
ethnic conflict in Kerala and Sri Lanka, respectively.

Concluding Observations

In conclusion, it may be pertinent to comment on some aspects of cultural
nationalism in Sri Lanka in the broader context of South Asia. It has
been argued that despite the fact that cultural–linguistic regional diversity
within the Indian subcontinent in many ways parallels that in Europe, it

did not lead to the formation of nation-states, as in Europe (Embree 1985). This, it is contended, was principally due to three factors. First, an overarching Brahminic ideology, whose principal carriers were the privileged castes, further empowered by being the performers of the legitimizing rituals for the rulers/kingship. Second, the intrusion of two powerful alien civilizations, the Islamic and the European. This worked against the fusion of regional cultures and political power – a process that seems to have underlain the rise of nation-states and nationalities in Europe. Third, the dynastic powers in India were too peripheral to the regional cultures to facilitate a fusion of regional culture and political power.

It may be argued that in the South Asian context this fusion had occurred among the Sinhalese in Sri Lanka. What is significant in the Sinhala culture is the minimal presence, if not absence, of Brahminic ideology. The continuity of Buddhism provided a resistance. Regarding the influence of alien civilizations, while the European intrusion was equally felt in Sri Lanka as in other regions of India, this was not the case with the Islamic intrusion. Indeed, from the perspective of Sinhala-Buddhist culture it was the South Indian/Tamil presence that was the alien intrusion. And this was at the same time perceived as carrying the virus of a Hindu (= Brahminic ideology) intrusion – a force that could disintegrate the fusion of culture and political power that was occurring or had occurred among the Sinhalese. The culural nationalism of the Sinhalese has to be viewed in this context of a growing fusion of their culture and political power, along with a heightened fear of Tamil Hindus as an alien intrusion that could destroy this fusion and the nation-state. Recent separatist ideologies of the LTTE reiterate this fear.

Notes

This chapter is a revised and shortened version of the author's article 'Making the Kerala Model More Intelligible: Comparisons with the Sri Lankan Experience', *Economic and Political Weekly* 30(48), 1995: 3085–92. The author acknowledges the kind permission of the editor of *Economic and Political Weekly*.

1. For a summary discussion of the debates about the Sri Lankan policy change in 1977/78 following the change of government, see Dunham and Kelegama (1998).

2. Sri Lanka's post-colonial economic growth 'experience may be divided into two phases: 1948–78 and after 1978. Modest growth characterized the first phase, with per-capita GDP rising about 2.2% a year during 1960–70 and about 2.5% during 1970–80. But the distribution of income was fairly good, with Gini coefficient of household income falling from about 0.45 in 1965 to 0.35 in 1973. After 1978, per-capita growth accelerated to more than 3%, but the distribution of income worsened. Estimates of Gini coefficient for 1978 and 1982 are comparable to those of 1950s and early 60s: above 0.45. It can thus be said that Sri Lanka shifted from a regime of moderate growth with a good distribution of income

(before 1978) to one of better growth with a poorer income distribution (after 1978)' (UNDP 1990: 49). One of the concerns of the International Congress of Kerala Studies held in 1994 at the AKG Centre, Thiruvanthanapuram, was what implications the Indian liberalization trends/policies would have on the Kerala model. The Sri Lankan experience suggests one of the many possible outcomes.

3. It has been observed in the context of the conflict situation in Sri Lanka 'that promoting faster economic growth at the expense of equity – without effective social safety nets to protect human development, especially after a sustained period of good human progress – can damage the invisible bond between the people and the government and lead to considerable social and political turmoil' (UNDP 1990: 50). Compounding the Sri Lankan experience, apart from the social unevenness of the benefits of economic growth, is the geographical unevenness (rural/urban and regional) of such benefits.

4. The opportunity for women to be bus conductors was lost with the privatization of the nationalized bus transport system following the policy change in 1977/78. This is another outcome of the liberalization/SAP initiatives.

5. It is also referred to as the Ezhava Social Reform Movement or SNDP after Sri Narayana Dharma Paripalana Yogam (The Society for the Protection of Sri Narayana Doctrine or Teachings) (Thomas Issac and Tharakan 1986).

6. See for an illustration of the colonial encounter Wickremeratne's (1995) discussion of the decline of Buddhist temple schools (*privenas*) with the emergence of the colonial Christian-dominated educational system by the late nineteenth century and the implications this had for the Buddhist Sangha.

7. The Ceylon National Congress was, as the name suggests, modelled on the Indian National Congress. But it hardly matched the latter in terms of resistance to British imperialism or in the demand for independence. Independence for Ceylon was an inevitable outcome following Indian independence. At the time of Independence in February 1948 the Ceylon National Congress transformed itself into the United National Party.

11

Sustainability and the 'New' Kerala Model

René Véron

In recent years, Kerala has been increasingly winning attention for its achievements and deficiencies in regard to sustainable development. Recent studies have examined the sustainability of the Kerala model of development in regard to fiscal limits (George 1993) and environmental aspects (Parayil 1996). Researchers as well as politicians have generally acknowledged that economic problems threaten the sustainability of Kerala's welfare policies, and indeed the 'old' Kerala model. Despite this, a few environmentalists (e.g. Alexander 1994; McKibben 1995) have begun to call Kerala a model for environmentally sound, sustainable development. Indeed, Kerala fulfils some core objectives of environmentally sustainable development, such as low population growth rates and moderate industrial pollution. However, most of the few studies on Kerala's development and environment have tended to downplay some negative aspects of its environmental record. This chapter seeks to put the notion of a 'Kerala model of sustainable development' into perspective, considering both its present environmental condition and the adoption of sustainable-development policies by the state government and popular movements.

In the early 1990s, a 'new' Kerala model began to emerge: one that promises to integrate sustainable-development goals more successfully into policy-making, and to go beyond mere state regulation (setting and monitoring environmental standards) to include community-based strategies for environmental protection. The new policy approach comprises decentralized administration; participatory planning combining productive and environmental objectives; and collaboration between the state, NGOs and social/civil society movements. This far-reaching experiment may hold important lessons about opportunities and limitations of community-based sustainable development (as opposed to state regulation or market-based instruments).

The first section of this chapter clarifies the concept of sustainable development, and introduces policy approaches towards sustainable development, including the community-based strategy. The second and third sections present Kerala's indicators of sustainable development, and discuss the current policy trend towards a new Kerala model. The fourth section analyses community-based initiatives to achieve sustainable development in Kerala, including discussion of state action, the role of environmental NGOs, grassroots action and environmental ethics. The final section presents a discussion of the common failures of community-based strategies and 'community failures' (e.g. the failure to include people's participation in defining development priorities; to address the needs of future generations; to overcome conflicts between local interest groups; to reduce spatial externalities and consider broader political, economic and ecological structures), and how the new Kerala model addresses these shortcomings. In conclusion, I argue that the new Kerala model holds some important lessons for community-based sustainable development, but that failure to implement complementary regulatory and price instruments for environmental protection at the state level limits Kerala's ability to achieve sustainable development.

Sustainable Development

Economic, social and environmental sustainability

A widely accepted definition of 'sustainable development' put forward by the World Commission on Environment and Development (WCED) reads: 'Sustainable development is development that meets the needs of the present without compromising the ability of future generations to meet their own needs' (WCED 1987: 43). While the first part of this definition relates to conventional economic and social objectives of development, the second part incorporates a long-term view, including consideration of environmental issues.

Development theory has commonly acknowledged that economic and social development are interrelated, that economic development comes first before social development can occur. Economic growth is considered the key in providing the means to meet basic needs, to alleviate poverty, and to generate employment. However, growing GNP per capita does not automatically lead to development. For development, economic growth and access to resources must be distributed over all sections of society. If, on the contrary, there are strong economic inequalities, 'growth without development' as well as social and political unrest are likely to occur, signifying unsustainable development. Growth is a necessary, but not a sufficient, condition for sustainable development.

Social development, apart from representing an end in itself, is also a means to promote economic growth. Drèze and Sen (1997) argued that the expansion of social opportunity is key to development. Extension of basic education, better health care, more effective land reforms and greater access to provisions of social security would enable the marginalized sections of society to lead a less restrictive life and, also, to make better use of markets (Drèze and Sen 1997). The expansion of social opportunity calls for public action, but government services cannot be sustained in the long run if economic growth does not take place and financial resources are limited. NGOs and community organizations may not be able to replace state support completely. For sustainable development, therefore, both an active state enhancing social opportunity and a strong economic basis are needed.

The sustainable-development debate has drawn attention to the interrelation between socioeconomic development and environmental sustainability. Environmental sustainability includes the upkeep or improvement of essential ecological processes, biological diversity, and the natural resource base. Environmental sustainability is important for development because we humans are inextricably bound up with nature. Thus, the environment is important for our survival, health and social life (Véron 1998). In order to become sustainable, economic and social development should retain the ecological and resource potential to support future generations; and development of one group should have no adverse (environmental) effects on contemporaries. This implies that processes of sustainable development should not bear negative, either temporal or spatial, environmental externalities.

Mainstream concept

Although there are many conflicting interpretations of sustainable development, a clear mainstream understanding has evolved (Adams 1993). While environmentalists of the 1960s and 1970s drew attention to contradictions between development and environmental protection, the mainstream concept of sustainable development of the 1980s and 1990s assumes there is no inevitable contradiction between development and environmental protection. Indeed, the current debate is about how development and environment can be reconciled, and how sustainable development can be achieved (Lele 1991).

Proponents of the mainstream concept of sustainable development reject the notion that economic growth inevitably leads to environmental degradation. Rather, the outcome depends on the *nature* of economic growth; that is, to what degree growth implies the depletion of non-renewable resources and the overuse of renewable resources, including the 'sink capacity' (the regenerative capacity of the environment to absorb waste). To some extent, growth can be made more environmentally sustainable and resource-efficient through the development of appropriate technologies and substitutes for non-renewable resources (Pearce and Warford 1993). Yet sustainable development also suggests that many environmental problems might actually originate from the *lack* of development (i.e. that poverty might be a primary cause of environmental degradation) and that environmental degradation can, in turn, reinforce poverty (i.e. the poor, whose livelihoods are often directly dependent on natural resources, might be hit most severely by environmental degradation). High local and global inequality in wealth and access to resources can also lead to the unsustainable use of resources and to overconsumption by the affluent (WCED 1987). In sum, the concept of sustainable development suggests a potentially positive relationship between socio-economic development and environmental sustainability.[1]

Strategies for sustainable development

As indicated, one strategy to achieve sustainable development has been to develop environmentally friendly technologies in industry, agriculture, transportation and so on. The other conventional method to protect the environment is the application of regulatory instruments (or 'command-and-control' instruments), such as emission standards, permissions and prohibitions. More recently, OECD countries in particular have considered the introduction of price incentives and market-based measures, such as environmental taxes, tradable emission permits and *bonus-malus* systems. These measures are generally guided by the 'polluter pays' principle. For less developed countries, however, regulatory and market-based instruments tend to be ineffective because of state failure to control environmental standards, and market failure to give the right price signals.

As an alternative, the consensus emerging from the United Nations Conference on Environment and Development in Rio de Janeiro in 1992 recommended a community-based strategy (Leach et al. 1997). Sustainable environmental management can only occur where active local-level support and participation exist. Particularly in less developed countries, community participation is believed to be the most effective strategy because people depend directly on their local physical environment and thus have a genuine interest in protecting it (Ghai and Vivian 1992). Research on indigenous technical knowledge suggests that local communities are key to finding solutions for environmental problems. Often, local communities develop technologies that are well-adapted to local socioeconomic and environmental conditions. Thus, these communities are regarded as appropriate units to restore and manage their local environment.

The pursuit of community-based sustainable development also requires 'a political system that secures effective citizen participation in decision making' (WCED 1987: 65). Many organizations, therefore, advocate democracy; decentralization of administration and planning; more responsibility for local communities; and increased involvement of civil society, including NGOs and popular movements. Co-management of resources (i.e. appropriate sharing of responsibility) between local communities and the state is expected to promote sustainable development.

The state of Kerala has recently adopted elements of such a political system and has included environmental goals in its policy approach. It has been suggested that this state comes 'closest to the sustainable development ideal in practice' (Parayil 1996: 953). Before discussing policies, the following section attempts to indicate how close Kerala really comes to the sustainable-development ideal.

However, this qualitative appraisal may be deficient because of general methodological problems in measuring sustainable development. Spatial and temporal externalities are often concealed, and socioeconomic development and environmental sustainability are difficult to weigh against each other. The environmental demands of future generations remain an unknown factor in sustainable development, as demographic trends and technological progress are unpredictable. Measuring sustainable development also faces serious problems regarding collection, selection, quantification and comparability of environmental indicators (Steer and Lutz 1993). Furthermore, sustainability depends on the capability of different social groups to cope with environmental change. Actors may also perceive and value the same environmental process differently, and seek to define and prioritize environmental 'problems' according to their own agenda (Bryant and Bailey 1997). Environmental problems thus become social and political constructs in which differing perceptions often relate to class, gender, ethnicity and locality.

Kerala: Indicators of Sustainable Development

It has been widely discussed that Kerala's outstanding advances in the field of social development have failed to spur sustainable economic development. By contrast, comprehensive appraisals of Kerala's environmental condition are absent. But if one reads reports on India's environment (WRI 1994; CSE 1985), one gets the impression that Kerala suffers less than most other regions from environmental problems such as deforestation; industrial pollution of air, water and soil; loss of soil nutrients, groundwater depletion and pollution due to intensified agriculture; and salinization and waterlogging because of canal irrigation.

Some of these problems are less apparent in Kerala because of high rainfall, distributed more evenly between the seasons, and a topography that has hindered the wide expansion of Green Revolution technologies. Also, some irreversible ecological changes seem to have disappeared: massive deforestation in the highland and serious overuse and depletion of firewood resources no longer occur (Parayil 1996).

In general, however, environmental problems have become more apparent and have started to affect environmental sustainability. The most important environmental problems are caused by deforestation incurred in previous decades, ongoing paddy conversions and disruption of backwater ecosystems. Of growing concern also are the 'chemicalization' of agriculture, pollution of water and soils, urbanization and air pollution by growing traffic. A range of other more localized events, such as industrial pollution in particular areas, excessive sand mining and pollution of some rivers, and destruction of natural *shola* grasslands with eucalyptus plantations (*Hindu Survey of the Environment* 1991), also trouble Kerala's generally good environmental record.

Deforestation of natural rainforest was probably the most significant environmental change in Kerala until the mid-1980s. Based on satellite images and topographical sheets of the Survey of India, Chattopadhyay (1984) has concluded that Kerala's forest area declined from 28 per cent of the total geographical area in 1965 to 17 per cent in 1973, and 7 or 10 per cent in 1983, involving massive loss of biodiversity and genetic resources. Since then, deforestation seems to have stopped because of more effective law enforcement and increased public awareness. However, the deforested highland continues to affect the environment as well as people's livelihoods: it has enhanced soil erosion and laterization, has led to more frequent and more serious landslides and floods (which, in some cases, caused destruction of houses and made evacuation of people necessary) and, presumably, has induced changes in the local climate (Kannan and Pushpangadan 1988). Deforestation has also directly affected tribal populations, who formerly earned a significant part of their living from gathering forest products.

Kerala's cultivated wetlands are dwindling. Since the mid-1970s, about 40 per cent of the wetland under paddy cultivation has been converted into dryland. Farmers stopped or reduced paddy cultivation because it has become less profitable and is subject to the availability of agricultural workers around the clock, which has become difficult under new, formalized labour relations. Paddy conversions mean abandoning the sophisticated traditional wetland agrosystem. As a result, ecologically valuable wetland fauna and flora disappear and the biological food chain is disrupted. For farmers downstream, furthermore, conversion of higher-lying fields can render the continuation of paddy cultivation impossible because water does not overflow to the next field and becomes too scarce (Véron 1998). Moreover, the change of the wetland system results in lower water retention on the fields, and more surface runoff increases the probability of floods downstream. In fact, even under normal rainfall conditions, the cities in Kerala's lowland experience severe floods more often than in earlier times. As another consequence of floods, large fields become waterlogged more often and yields decline. Paddy conversions have also contributed to the decline in the groundwater table. Many household wells in Kerala are drying up and need to be dug deeper and deeper.

Kerala's coastal ecosystems are threatened. The almost complete destruction of mangroves in coastal areas as well as the reclamation and pollution of backwaters have not only hampered a unique ecosystem but have also affected the livelihood of the fisherfolk. Commercial maritime fishing by mechanized trawlers caused overexploitation of fish stock, leading to violent conflicts between trawler owners and artisanal fisherfolk (Kurien 1993).

Although this listing of environmental problems may suggest otherwise, Kerala does not face a severe ecological crisis, and generally has a comparatively good but mixed environmental record. Also, the low population growth rate and relatively equal land distribution may help to reduce the risk of environmental degradation. The following section discusses how environmental concerns have been adopted in state policies and popular movements.

Development of the 'New' Kerala Model

Kerala's well-documented economic stagnation has resulted in an increasing scarcity of financial resources to pay for costly welfare schemes such as pensions, unemployment relief and the public distribution system of food (George 1993). The fiscal crisis together with the underdevelopment of productive sectors and the high reliance on Gulf money have threatened the sustainability of the old Kerala model with its redistributive policies and radical reforms. The emerging consensus among scholars and politicians in Kerala suggests that the current development priorities are to strengthen the production basis and to realize economic growth in order to overcome unemployment and to sustain the outstanding social achievements made in the past. For example, both the late E.M.S. Namboodiripad (1995) and A.K. Antony (1995), who represent Kerala's main rival parties, the Communist Party of India–Marxist and the Indian National Congress, stated that Kerala cannot prosper in the long run without industrialization, and stressed the need for the development of infrastructure, particularly in the power sector.

Yet Kerala's educated and skilled workforce could be a good basis for economic growth. In turn, achievements in the spheres of social justice, redistribution of assets, education and health may ensure that increased attention to productive aspects would not lead to 'growth without development' but to equitable development so that Kerala can become a real example of development.

Indeed, recent policy trends, including increased attention to productive needs and decentralization of development planning, may constitute the beginning of a 'new' Kerala model. Local self-government and decentralized planning were imposed by amendments in India's constitution in 1992, but Kerala has taken these national directives more seriously than other states. Under the Kerala Panchayat Raj Act of 1994, local elections were held in 990 village-level panchayats, 152 blocks and 14 districts in 1995, and power was formally handed over to the local bodies. The administrative decentralization included a provision to ensure participation of panchayats and municipalities in the formulation and implementation of development plans. Remarkable compared with other Indian states is that Kerala's left-coalition government decided to allocate 37 per cent of its budget for new development plans to projects designed by the local bodies themselves. After initial reluctance, the centre–right opposition has apparently consented to this policy. The new decentralized and democratic development planning also gives people's participation and non-governmental organizations a bigger role – at the expense of line departments and civil servants (George 1997).

The new model seems to rely on the same basics as the old Kerala model: development through public action by a responsible state and effective popular participation. However, unlike the old Kerala model, the emphasis of state policies is, to a certain extent, shifting from welfare to growth, and from top-down intervention to bottom-up planning. Furthermore, the 'new left'[2] is pursuing a different kind of popular participation than the previous class-based mobilization – which included the very successful land-reform movement of the 1960s and 1970s as well as the trade-union movement that has existed since the 1930s. Recognizing the economic contradictions of labour militancy, the left now seeks class compromises and corporatist arrangements (Heller 1995). New participatory development programmes try to overcome class conflict

and party politics at the local level by emphasizing joint productive interests, and so attempt to build up broad alliances and mediating bodies in
which different interest groups are represented.

Decentralized participatory planning explicitly aims at increasing production and productivity in agriculture; alleviating ecological problems,
including the depletion and pollution of resources; improving the quality
of social infrastructure; tackling gender injustice and deprivation of tribal
populations and fisherfolk. The challenge to accelerate industrialization
and to develop the power sector remains in the realm of the state and
central government (Thomas Isaac and Harilal 1997).

In sum, the new Kerala model pursues objectives of productive
development, social improvement and environmental sustainability, thus
representing a serious attempt to make development sustainable.

Towards Sustainable Development?

The imaginary Kerala model

Some scholars have transcended the standard arguments of the old Kerala
model to describe Kerala as a model for environmentally sound, sustainable development. Alexander (1994) called Kerala a prototype of 'efficient resource use' and 'sustainable human behavior'; McKibben (1995)
regarded Kerala as an example of 'living lightly on the earth'. However,
these authors did not look at actual environmental processes but only at
a few general indicators, including population growth and family size,
GNP per capita as a proxy for resource consumption, and the relation
between GNP per capita and social-development indicators as a proxy
for efficiency and sustainability – a simplistic and inadequate approach.

Resource and energy consumption may be useful indicators for global
comparisons that uncover excessive, possibly unsustainable, consumption
in industrialized countries. However, in a developing-country context,
low energy-consumption does not necessarily imply sustainability, but
can also mean scarcity and restricted access to resources. Iyer (1996)
argued that Kerala's presumed resource efficiency may relate more to the
poverty of many than to sustainability:

> Like anywhere else, the rich in Kerala live 'heavily' on the earth.... Those
> people who live lightly on the earth, 'sleeping on the floor', without many
> possessions, do so, not out of ecological consciousness, as one would like to
> believe, but because they cannot afford even the essential possessions. (Iyer
> 1996: 216)

As indicated above, ecological factors such as climate and topography,
rather than a particular model of development, have influenced environ-

mental sustainability. Also, the comparatively low level of industrial pollution is a consequence of industrial backwardness rather than of *clean* industries or effective environmental policies. Furthermore, increasing consumerism in Kerala and rising imports from other states, boosted by the influx of Gulf remittances, suggest that Kerala shows no pattern of 'sustainable human behavior', but increasingly *externalizes* environmentally unsound industrial production (to an extent that is, however, not comparable to North America, Europe or Japan).

The above-mentioned scholars were not able to demonstrate any reconciliation between economic development and environmental sustainability in Kerala's government policies or people's practices. Dismissing the economic component, they did not present a model of sustainable development in the sense of the mainstream concept. These authors have also failed to consider new policy trends in Kerala that may offer more meaningful lessons for sustainable development. The policies of Kerala's state government, NGOs and popular movements probably merit our attention more than the allegedly low level of resource consumption.

The new Kerala model: seeking people's participation for sustainable development

As indicated above, the new Kerala model includes decentralized development planning that, with the cooperation of non-governmental organizations and popular movements, aims at encouraging both economic development and environmental sustainability. The most comprehensive effort to implement decentralized participatory planning has been the 'people's campaign for the ninth five-year plan'. In August 1996, the newly constituted Kerala State Planning Board launched this five-month-long campaign. With the help of NGOs and researchers, more than 100,000 resource persons were trained to assist the panchayat and municipal bodies in designing their own development plans. This 'planning from below' started with thousands of meetings at the sub-village level in which nearly 3 million people discussed their local development problems. On the basis of these meetings, participatory rapid appraisals and a village-development seminar, people's representatives, officials and experts identified the main problems and drafted panchayat development reports. The reports were expected to contain a section on the environmental condition of the village. Based on these general reports, task forces in each panchayat – comprising local officials and activists – drafted twelve sectoral project proposals, which helped the village governments to formulate the panchayat plan. Finally, the more than 1,000 panchayat plans were integrated at block and district levels, and incorporated into the state's ninth five-year plan, 1997–2002 (Thomas Isaac and Harilal 1997).

The state government announced plans to increase untied funds to the village panchayats from 5 to 37 per cent of the total plan outlay in order to assist the implementation of the village development plans. The panchayats are asked to allot at least 45 to 50 per cent of their budget for productive projects in agriculture, animal husbandry, fisheries, small-scale industry; 30 to 40 per cent for social services (education, health, sanitation, drinking water supply, housing); and only 10 to 25 per cent for infrastructure. Furthermore, the State Planning Board expects a voluntary contribution of 25 per cent by the community in the form of labour, material and/or money (Bandyopadhyay 1997).

Although five months were probably too short a time to develop necessary rules for decision-making in participatory planning and to foster a new 'development culture' among the population (George 1997), first observations indicate that the campaign has been successful in gathering all-round support (Thomas Isaac and Harilal 1997). According to an informal assessment, 'planning from below' was carried out successfully in about 60 per cent of the panchayats (Bandyopadhyay 1997). More than 150,000 local projects have been proposed, from repairing irrigation ponds to developing cooperative vegetable gardens, to introducing water-sealed latrines, establishing women's enterprises, building houses for squatter families and reviving ritual traditions (see Franke and Chasin 1997). With regard to the adoption of sustainable-development principles, the impression is mixed. In those panchayats where NGOs and scientists/activists were closely involved, sectoral projects seem to have integrated environmental protection quite effectively (e.g. development of organic-vegetable farming, introduction of high-efficiency cooking stoves, construction of water-sealed latrines). This indicates that decentralized planning has expanded the scope for environmentally concerned organizations to implement sustainable-development projects.

It is premature to evaluate implementation and impact of the panchayat development plans, or even to conclude that Kerala can offer a new model of sustainable development. Also, decentralization barely affects two of the most inefficient state-level line departments, irrigation and electricity (*Economic and Political Weekly*, 16–23 August 1997). Furthermore, the new Kerala model leaves the responsibility for improving infrastructure and attracting private capital for large-scale industrialization to the state. However, prioritizing economic goals, the state tends to approve industrial or energy projects without proper environmental impact assessment. Also, Kerala's state institutions have not improved their performance in monitoring environmental standards (see Ramachandran 1998).

Therefore the chances of the new Kerala model achieving sustainable development relies to a great extent on popular movements and environmental NGOs. For example, Kerala's most influential NGO, the Kerala People's Science Movement (Kerala Sastra Sahitya Parishad, KSSP), has played a leading role in the campaign for planning from below, and has promoted environmental protection for the past twenty years. Its most significant environmental struggle was the campaign to halt the hydro-electric project in the rainforest area of Silent Valley, a battle that gained wide international attention (see D'Monte 1985). The KSSP has combined productive, social and environmental objectives in most of its political campaigns and development programmes, thus promoting sustainable development (Thomas Isaac et al. 1997). 'Purist' environmental movements, on the other hand, seem to be rather insignificant and restricted to the educated middle class. In most cases, environmental degradation has remained a 'problem' of natural scientists and social activists rather than of the wider population.

Environmental ethics and grassroots action

Environmental awareness may not be very widespread in Kerala because the region does not face a severe ecological crisis. As a consequence, most Keralites do not seem to pass ethical judgement on inefficient or unsustainable resource use. In other words, the normative concept of sustainable development has not yet become a general cultural value in Kerala. This may be contrasted with the ideas of social development, justice and equity, which, prompted by particularly extreme cast rigidities, became strong cultural values in the first half of this century in Kerala and facilitated the spread of education. Social and political awareness led to widespread popular participation that has supported and even pressured the state government to implement welfare policies and radical reforms. If the new Kerala model is to become a model of sustainable development, the strong sense for social justice and the political consciousness among Kerala's people must be complemented with more environmental awareness and an enhanced 'development culture'. In order to achieve this before a severe ecological crisis unfolds, initiatives by the KSSP and other environmental NGOs to spread people's environmental education and to provide ecological training of local planners will be crucial.

Although no general environmental awareness has yet evolved, people seem most concerned about specific environmental changes when these affect their livelihoods directly. 'Grassroots environmental action' (Ghai and Vivian 1992) that links environmental protection with livelihood issues is already common in Kerala. It often emerges as a consequence of conflicts over local resources. For example, neighbourhood groups have acted against excessive sandmining, which has enhanced river-bank erosion affecting human habitats and agriculture. Other groups have struggled against deep-soil mining, which has caused serious accidents (i.e. people falling into the deep ditches at night on their way home). In a few places, paddy farmers took action against wetland conversions upstream, which have affected water availability on their fields. Grassroots environmental action tends to meet favourable conditions in Kerala because people are politically aware and experienced with collective action.

Unlike First World environmentalism, grassroots environmental action links development issues with environmental sustainability. However, grass-roots action usually reflects a conflict between different local groups over resources rather than a united community-based struggle against environmental degradation. Moreover, it does not consider the 'needs' of future generations, which have no voice in current conflicts over local resources. In many cases, there is also a *trade-off* between ensuring a livelihood and protecting the environment. Like anywhere else, people in Kerala tend to prioritize their own immediate economic, social and political interests. Unless they see a close link between environmental protection and their own well-being, they do not care about environmentally sound practices. For example, the local population in a granite-mining area of south Kerala have even accepted the negative environmental and health effects of neighbouring quarries because such quarries give employment to their families.

Because it ignores intergenerational justice and environmental sustainability as such, grassroots environmental action has only limited scope to form the basis of sustainable development. On the other hand, it brings to light the fact that mainstream sustainable-development concepts tend to underestimate conflicts between different resource users and the possible trade-off that exists between livelihood security and environmental protection, as well as between present and future needs.

Previous community-based programmes

Prior to the campaign for decentralized planning, the KSSP and the state government had initiated participatory-development programmes with an environmental component. The most significant programmes were 'group farming' and the 'people's resource-mapping programme'.

The group-farming programme was initiated by the left-coalition state government in 1989 with the primary aim of improving agricultural growth and food self-sufficiency in Kerala. Group farming was expected to reduce production costs and raise productivity of paddy cultivation, thus preventing paddy conversions. The Department of Agriculture, providing financial and technical assistance through its newly decentralized local extension offices, motivated paddy farmers of the same micro-watershed to take up collective farm operations and to purchase jointly such farm inputs as chemical fertilizers and mechanical tillers. Furthermore, the farmers were asked to form committees, and local corporatist bodies comprising farmers, agricultural workers and bureaucrats were set up. However, group farming failed in most cases. Not only did interests between farmers and agricultural workers diverge, but common interests among fellow farmers usually did not go beyond receiving subsidized farm inputs via the group. And when these subsidies were withdrawn under the succeeding centre–right coalition government in 1992, most groups became inoperative and fell apart (Törnquist and Tharakan 1995).

In 1991, the KSSP launched the resource-mapping programme in collaboration with the Centre for Earth Science Studies (CESS) and with the support of the state government. The programme aimed at initiating more efficient and sustainable management of local resources. With the help of a checklist designed by the CESS, local volunteers, including teachers, retired and educated unemployed people, began to map local resources in cooperation with farmers. In doing so, it was intended that people would learn about their local resource potential and environmental problems, thus developing 'land literacy' and environmental awareness. In many panchayats, the KSSP built up organizations of local leaders and volunteers. These organizations were expected to draft an 'action plan' map that would identify environmental problems and potential sustainable-development projects. At completion of the programme in 1992, when a centre–right coalition came back to power in Kerala, mapping had been done in twenty of the twenty-five pilot villages, but only two villages drafted an action plan (Thomas Isaac et al. 1997).

Both group farming and resource-mapping were 'participatory' programmes initiated 'from above'. Local people were not invited to define their own problems or determine the area of action; instead the programmes reflected the perceptions of policy-makers, social activists and scientists. As a consequence, these programmes failed to gain the participation of farmers and agricultural workers; at best, they were able to mobilize volunteers from the middle class. This was because low efficiency of paddy cultivation, for example, was not an immediate or pressing problem for farmers as they can shift to other, more profitable, crops. Furthermore, most people did not share the concern of policy-makers and activists about the environment, and so prioritized environmental problems differently. Their views of 'rational' land use also differed from those of natural scientists. In addition, group farming overlooked differentiation by class, caste, gender, political affiliation and micro-locality within villages and micro-watersheds. People in these spatial units do not form a homogenous group, and may have only a few interests in common. Moreover, many farmers perceived group farming and resource-mapping as programmes of leftist political parties, and therefore refrained from participating.

In sum, the experience of previous participatory programmes suggests that the success of the new Kerala model will depend on the ability of local planners and popular movements to overcome deep-rooted political and class boundaries by convincing different groups of common productive interests and potential mutual benefits of cooperation. For environmentally sustainable development, moreover, increased environmental awareness among the population seems necessary.

Conclusions

The new Kerala model seems to address some of the general failures of community-based sustainable development that have been indicated above. For example, many community-based programmes do not invite sufficient local participation in defining problems, areas of action and project goals. Too often, 'participation' refers only to the implementation of schemes that were designed at higher levels. 'Co-management' may involve more responsibility for local communities without offering more rights and funds. Faced with fiscal constraints, many states welcome participatory programmes, including local voluntary contributions of labour, material and money. By contrast, the new Kerala model includes increased allocation of funds for village development plans, and decentralized planning that is targeted to involve people at every stage. People get a fair chance to express local development problems.

Still, decentralized planning cannot ensure empowerment. Village development plans may not reflect people's problems as expressed in local meetings because formal and informal rules of decentralized planning have barely developed yet. Moreover, conflicting interests within the village can impede compromises and solutions. Local-level development plans are thus likely to reflect the political power structure in the village rather than a 'common will'. The initiators of decentralized planning attempted to overcome deep-rooted political and class boundaries by stressing joint productive interests and by seeking the active involvement of opposition parties. But, in the recent past, most participatory initiatives have failed to overcome local party politics in rural Kerala.

Furthermore, community-based projects can support sustainable development only if people at the grassroots opt for environmental protection and consider the needs of future generations, which have no say in these projects. Although communities may depend directly on natural resources, environmental awareness cannot be assumed as there are often *trade-offs* between immediate livelihood needs and long-term environmental protection. In order to spread environmental awareness, the new Kerala model seeks the collaboration of NGOs that are engaged in environmental education. The KSSP and natural scientists promote the idea of 'ecologically efficient land use'. Some of their technical solutions, however, fail to consider the social reality of differentiated access to natural resources and conflicting individual and group interests. Because no common 'environmental interests' can be assumed and because most environmental resources are under private control, community-based management tends to have limited scope.

Village development plans made by locals themselves are likely to neglect spatial externalities as well as temporal externalities. Therefore these plans require coordination at higher levels, and some sort of top-down planning. This points to the inevitable conflict between popular participation and planning. For example, Kerala's State Planning Board gives distinct guidelines on what village reports should contain, and how much money village plans should allocate to the various sectors. Thus, some priorities are still set at the state level. For community-based development to succeed, it is crucial to define what the complementary roles of the state and of the community are. Clear rules are required in order to enhance accountability of the state, local civil servants, assisting NGOs and the community organizations. The new Kerala model has tried to integrate local civil servants into the process of decentralized planning, hoping to make them more responsible and accountable for the implementation of the village plans. Also, the allocation of development funds have been made transparent. However, clear rules and institutions of decentralized planning still need time to develop.

Finally, participatory initiatives at the local level have a limited reach because they take place in state and national political contexts, global markets and wider ecological systems. This implies that community-based sustainable development is no substitute for environmental planning and regulation at state and international levels. It must be recognized that there is also 'community failure' to protect the environment (as there is market failure and state failure). Yet community-based strategies may become an important addition to regulatory and price instruments if complementary roles of the state, the market and the civil society can be identified, defined and interwoven.

In sum, Kerala is certainly not yet a model of sustainable development: a careful appraisal of the environmental condition reveals a mixed record, and economic stagnation threatens the sustainability of social progress. However, the emerging new Kerala model includes policies towards community-based sustainable development. The new Kerala model has also tried to overcome some common problems of this policy approach (e.g. conflicts between local interest groups; lack of general environmental awareness at the grassroots).

Community-based sustainable development also meets the very conducive sociopolitical conditions in Kerala. The population is educated, informed, politically conscious and well organized to bring about necessary far-reaching social change. The current state government and opposition parties seem to back decentralized development planning. In order to achieve sustainable development with this participatory strategy, environmental awareness among the population is essential. As influential NGOs are engaged in environmental education, there is scope for sustainable development to become a general value in Kerala, as did social justice and equity in the first half of this century as a result of caste-based reform movements.

However, conflicting interests of groups differentiated by class, caste, gender, locality and political affiliation may remain an obstacle for community-based sustainable development. Furthermore, rules for participatory development planning and project implementation still have to be developed. Decentralized planning needs to become an iterative, continuing process in order to enhance accountability for all the involved actors. Though the state government is making a genuine effort to initiate community-based sustainable development, it fails to enforce environmental policies at the macro-level. For example, monitoring of environmental standards and use of environmental impact assessment have remained insufficient, and the introduction of environmental taxes have not been considered. This counteracts the efforts of decentralized environmental planning, and may limit Kerala's prospects considerably in achieving sustainable development.

It would be premature to draw conclusions about the success of the new Kerala model, but this community-based development experiment may well provide more lessons for environmental planners in developing countries. In particular, Kerala's attempt to foster environmental awareness through participatory planning and its performance in developing accountability of local bodies, NGOs and state agencies may deserve further research.

Notes

The writing of this chapter has been made possible thanks to a stipend from the Swiss National Science Foundation while I was an Academic Visitor in the Department of Geography at the School of Oriental and African Studies, University of London. I am grateful to Govindan Parayil, K.T. Rammohan and Antonito Paul for their invaluable comments on an earlier draft.

1. The mainstream concept of sustainable development has been criticized for its preference for reformist technical-economic solutions over more radical, structural and sociopolitical changes (Adams 1990). Furthermore, 'deep ecology' fundamentally rejects the compatibility of the modernistic project of development with environmental preservation (Sessions 1995).

2. I use the term 'new left' to describe new intellectual and political trends within Kerala's Communist Party to initiate participatory development beyond class boundaries, although established Communist leaders, including the late E.M.S. Namboodiripad, took an active part to design these new initiatives. With the term 'new left', I do not intend to suggest parallelism to Great Britain's 'New Labour' or the United States' 'New Democrats'.

12

What Does the Kerala Model Signify?
Towards a Possible 'Fourth World'

M.P. Parameswaran

Though it is right to reject millenarian hype as a limited Western indulgence, without validity for the majority of humanity that lives unconnected to the information superhighway, it is nevertheless a fact that for some time a feeling of uneasiness, of imminent change – and not for the better – has been growing steadily the world over. This sense of anxiety has arisen as a response to the spectacular ability of humans to transform nature through the amazing advances in science and technology. In fact, a clear warning about what was to come was given more than a century ago by Friedrich Engels, who noted:

> Let us not flatter ourselves over so much on account of our human conquest over nature. For, each such conquest takes its revenge on us. Each of them, it is true, has in the first place the consequences on which we counted but in the second and the third places it has quite different unforeseen effects which only too often cancel out the first. (Engels 1954)

Although this was written in 1876 and first published in 1896, the warning was not taken seriously for half a century. The world suddenly became aware of the destructive possibilities of science and technology during World War II, especially after Hiroshima and Nagasaki. The relative peace that then reigned, despite the Cold War, once again numbed the sensibilities of the people of the developed nations until Rachel Carson (1962) shocked Americans with her exposure of the horrors of pesticide- and industrialization-induced ecocide. Despite the subsequent proliferation of such revelations, the mainstream scientific community and the development establishment, by and large, ignored the warnings concerning unreflexive modernization and rampant industrialism.

We had the Stockholm Conference on the Environment in 1972; 'The Decade after Stockholm' in 1982; and the 'Earth Summit' at Rio de Janeiro in 1992. By the early 1990s, it had become impossible for the politicians and scientists to ignore the possibility that global ecological changes could make life on earth impossible. The existence of a *problem* was recognized. However, people were afraid or unwilling to think of any solution. The then American President George Bush haughtily declared at Rio that 'the American way of life is non-negotiable'! This foolish statement echoed the feelings of the majority of the people in the industrialized 'developed' nations.

The human species has survived and expanded through 'negotiations' both with itself and with nature. The ability to negotiate is a unique human quality. Loss of that ability will spell doom for the species. To speak of non-negotiability is absurd. Several scholars and authors have attempted to work out the terms of reconstructring human society under changed conditions, involving new relationships between humans and nature and changes in human nature. A few have tried to build up movements to put their ideas into practice. The most outstanding experiment involving such renegotiations was initiated in 1917 – the 'Great October Revolution' in Russia. It lasted for seven decades, but finally collapsed. An even more revolutionary project was proposed by Mahatma Gandhi, but it was never tried out. His closest followers undermined it. These experiments helped shape the first half of the twentieth century. The discovery of the human capability to transform nature and natural processes marked the second half, and especially the last quarter, of that century, amply demonstrating Engles's warning that 'nature takes its revenge'. This capacity of humans to transform nature, resulting in grave ecological destruction, gave rise to numerous social movements across the world that recognized the necessity of renegotiating the relationships between humans and nature. Yet practically none of them was able to comprehend and piece together the extremely complex nature of human life; none was able to achieve anything like the 'grand synthesis' of ethics, economics and politics that was attempted by a Karl Marx or a Mahatma Gandhi. Most of these movements are peripheral and one-dimensional. Arguably, the 'Green Movement' in Europe and the United States and the 'People's Science Movement' in India may possess a greater sweep and more depth than others. Nevertheless, these movements, to succeed in overcoming the present momentum of human 'development' towards self-destruction, must learn and build upon the experiences of the grand syntheses mentioned earlier – Marxism to build a genuine communist society and Gandhism to build an organic world union of self-reliant local communities. It is in this context that we explore the possibilities of developing a 'Fourth World': a 'participative and decentralized new people's democracy' based on the experience of the 'Kerala model'. The 'Fourth World' is a tentative concept of a new social contract. It is used here in the sense of an extension of the First, Second and Third Worlds. The notion is based on the failures of the First and the Second Worlds and the successes of a limited number of Third World states, especially that of Kerala in India.

The Kerala Experience

Kerala, the home of about 30 million Malayalees, as Keralans call themselves, was known to the ancient Chinese, Greeks, Phoenicians and others even before Christ. However, only in 1957 did it catch the attention of the world, when it elected a communist government to power, through the ballot box. Lately, it has become a subject of curiosity among world development experts because of its creditable achievements in various aspects of human development despite a very low per-capita domestic product. Table 12.1 provides an interesting comparison of Kerala with the wealthiest county in the world, the USA.

Table 12.1 encapsulates the features of Kerala society that have been intriguing scholars the world over. This feature of Kerala's development experience has been referred to as the 'Kerala model'. While famous scholars like Amartya Sen (see Drèze and Sen 1989) have praised it, many not so famous have condemned it (see Tharamagalam 1998a; Nossiter 1988; Panicker 1998). Yet some analysts have totally misunderstood it (see Shaw 1998). The term 'Kerala model' may be inappropriate because it is not the product of any explicit modelling. 'Kerala's development experience' is a more appropriate term.[1] Both developing and developed countries can learn some useful lessons from the Kerala experience.

First, the Kerala experience demonstrates that the essential elements of genuinely human development (see Table 12.1) can be achieved without squandering enormous quantities of natural resources − note the ratio of about 1:40 between Kerala and USA (that is, Kerala uses natural resources 40 times more efficiently than the USA). The nearly 6 billion people of the world and the forthcoming billions cannot aspire to consume the same per-capita resources as an average US citizen as there would not be enough to go around. In any case, such high consumption levels cannot be sustained for ever on this planet. What Kerala has shown is that Third World countries need not despair: that with per-capita resource availability less than 10 per cent of that of developed countries, it is still possible to achieve a high quality of life. The developed countries

Table 12.1 Selected indicators of USA and Kerala

	USA (1993)	Kerala (1995)
Area (1,000 km^2)	9,500	39
Population (million)	260	30
Per-capita availability of land (hectares)	3.6	0.13
Per-capita income ($US)	25,000	380
Per-capita energy consumption (KGOE)	12,000	<400
Life expectancy at birth (years)	76	72
Crude death rate (per 1,000)	8.8	6
Infant mortality rate (per 1,000 births)	9	12
Birth rate (per 1,000)	15.9	15
Total fertility rate	2.1	1.8
Adult literacy (%)	96	93
Average number of years of schooling	12.5	9

Notes: KGOE = Kilogram Oil Equivalent. Per-capita income of Kerala includes foreign remittances, which account for about 25 per cent.
Sources: USA from WRI (1997); Kerala from GOK (1998a).

can also learn a lesson from this; indeed, they must if they are to survive in the long run. Their present per-capita throughput of natural resources – depletion of resources and degradation of the natural environment through pollution – cannot continue for long.

Yet there are some negative lessons to be learnt from the Kerala experience, too. More than two decades ago, politicians, economists and social activists had pointed out that the achievements in human development could not be sustained for ever resting on a weak economic foundation. In summary form, these weaknesses are as follows:

- The Kerala economy has virtually been stagnating for over two decades. Its agriculture input is decreasing even in absolute terms. Its industry is not growing.
- Whereas unemployment has been increasing by leaps and bounds, major economic sectors like agriculture and construction have been experiencing considerable shortage of labour.
- A combination of factors, chief among them being education, has resulted in the development of a peculiar tendency on the part of the youth of Kerala to shun any form of physical labour and to vie only for white-collar jobs.

- Being 'integrated' into the global economy more than any other state (per-capita import to and export from the state is the highest in India), the people of Kerala have acquired a consumerist culture. This is unsustainable and may undermine Kerala's achievements.

It is important to resolve these inimical developments, not only for the Malayalees but also for the rest of the world. It is important to show that high levels of human development can be achieved and sustained at comparatively very low levels of resource throughput by means of a more judicious use of human labour power and by developing a new non-consumerist ethic. The experience of Kerala has to be provided with a theoretical foundation. Neither capitalism nor socialism – as it is under- stood and practised today – can provide this theoretical framework. The following thoughts regarding the formulation of a 'Fourth World Model' are intended as a contribution towards the development of such a theo- retical foundation, which must not only explain the present but also provide guidelines for the future. In essence, what follows is a synthesis of Marxian and Gandhian thoughts as applicable to the twenty-first century: the integration of politics, economics and ethics into one organic whole.

The Fourth World: The Concept of a New World Order

The Fourth World will be one built upon the experiences of human societies the world over. The term is not used, as it is by some writers, to denote a group of countries still worse off than countries of the Third World. Its motive force is neither 'private profit' nor 'desire for power', but rather 'social good'. It will be a new form of people's democracy – decentralized and participative. Its production relations – individual, family and social – and international relations will be different from those of twentieth-century capitalism and socialism. Of course, nobody can work out or project the final design of such a world order. All that can be attempted is an outline. Nevertheless, the outline should incorporate the theories and teachings of Marx and of Gandhi, not to mention ancient sources of knowledge.

Politics in the Fourth World

1. The new society can be termed either decentralized or participatory democracy (obviously democracy automatically implies participation and decentralization). Every able-bodied citizen will undertake, in addition to activities necessary for self or for family, responsibilities, small or large, in the day-to-day management of the community.

2. Each citizen has to acquire knowledge and capabilities to enable her/him to take up such responsibilities. Besides literacy and numeracy, each should acquire knowledge about local natural resources, science and technology, development planning and execution, administration, finance and so on.

3. Democracy should not simply be the casting of a vote in favour of one candidate or another, fielded by one or another political party. Today citizens lack the elementary right to recall those of their representatives who are not performing to their satisfaction. This system grants, in effect, an irrevocable power of attorney for five years. Absolute sovereignty is thus vested not with the people but with their 'representatives'. (In reality even this is notional.) This has to be changed. The right to recall representatives and easy procedures to enforce this right must be incorporated into the constitution. This would herald a new type of participative and decentralized people's democracy.

4. If people are to participate actively in day-to-day management of their societies, they should be aware of what is taking place, what is to be done and so on. Their right to know and the responsibility to learn should become fundamental.

5. As Gandhi and many other social activists and leaders have argued, human activities should be carried out on a human scale. The process of 'giantization', which was characteristic of both capitalism (First World) and socialism (Second World) has to be reversed. Very large steel mills, chemical complexes, power stations and so on are not ultimately controlled by human beings. They have a dynamic of their own and humans have increasingly become their slaves. Humans are to be liberated from this slavery to machines and capital.

6. The present political-economic power structure has to be inverted. Citizens and small groups – neighborhoods and village assemblies – should become sovereign. Only at that level does face-to-face democracy become possible. At larger levels of conglomeration – panchayat (group of villages), block, district, state and national levels – only representative democracy is possible. These levels should be, in the ultimate sense, responsible to citizens and small groups. That is, representative democracy should be subservient to face-to-face democracy. A new form of 'social contract', a new constitution, will have to be worked out to manage the economics and politics of the society at state, national and international levels.

7. The nature of political activities at the basic levels of sovereignty – the neighbourhood and village ward – must undergo fundamental change. They have become increasingly divorced from real class interests, and tied up with caste/religion/language/region/group loyalties. Instead

of the present united front political parties, which have become a means of sharing power, a united front of the people, representing their basic class interests, should emerge. This may lead to a transformation of the existing character of political parities or to the formation of new and more inclusive broad-based ones.

8. Thus the country (nation) can be compared to (as Gandhi had written) a set of concentric circles, with the neighbourhood and villages at the centre encircled by the village panchayat, block panchayat, district panchayat, state and national governments. They lie in a horizontal plane. Each level has its functions and these will change with time and place. The responsibilities and the rights at the different levels will be divided on the basis of mutual agreement.

Economy

1. Accompanying, and in many cases a prelude to, the changes in social structures there must be economic change. The economic order of the 'Fourth World' will of necessity be quite different to both the present capitalist and the erstwhile socialist worlds.

2. The 'Fourth World' might be considered a transitional phase. It will have markets and exchanges. It will have small-scale private enterprises. Yet even these latter will operate not for maximization of private profit but for maximization of social good, as Mohammed Yunus (1997) puts it. The intention will be to make social good and private profit mutually compatible.

3. The purpose of production will be chiefly to meet needs rather than commodities for profit. The present dictatorship of the producer over the consumer will be reversed.

4. Production enterprises should be economically, technically and ecologically sound and sustainable. Humans have achieved astounding success in transforming nature and producing goods and services. Yet the present application of science and technology in the service of private profit is leading to grave consequences. Furthermore, technologies that are viable only when harnessed to very large-scale production have been generally oppressive and exploitative. Thus, in the 'Fourth World' the aim will be to develop technologies that can make small-scale production economically viable and ecologically safe – that can make small beautiful.

5. Scientific and technological R&D now, as in the past, is aimed at creating large-scale production to concentrate economic and political power in the hands of a few. The problems that are selected for the S&T community to work on enrich this minority at the expense of the rest of humanity. In the new Fourth World, society will place before the S&T

community quite different sets of problems: how to guarantee the basic necessities of life such as food, clothing, shelter, health, education and recreation; how to make small-scale production more efficient; how to make local communities more self-reliant and self-sufficient.

6. Human habitats and the location of natural resources are not evenly distributed across the globe. Hence the transportation of goods and services cannot be avoided. Nevertheless, the historical tendency has been consciously to aggravate these mismatches and consequently expand the transportation of goods and services. Even the most ordinary items of our daily consumption are made elsewhere, even though most could be locally produced. Efforts will have to be taken to use local resources for local needs so that the need for transportation of men and material can be reduced.

7. The primary sector should meet basic needs like food, clothing and shelter. The majority of the products of the secondary sector – industry – are unnecessary for comfortable living. Yet its limitless expansion is necessary for the survival of capitalism. The same can be said of the tertiary sector. Local self-sufficiency in food and other products of the primary sector will be a characteristic of the Fourth World.

8. Energy is an essential component of all production processes. One of the greatest challenges facing the twenty-first century will be how to meet the demands for energy. Conventional sources like coal, oil and gas are limited and will quickly be exhausted, all the more if the presently developing countries increase their per-capita consumption to equal the developed countries. Nuclear energy, considered inexhaustible and a saviour in the 1960s and 1970s, has proved to be of the greatest danger to society. It is becoming increasingly clear that the only permanent and benign source of energy is the sun, whose radiation can be converted into both thermal and electrical forms.

9. The scientists and technologists are now presented with two tasks by the ruling class: (i) To strengthen and perfect weapons of mass destruction, such as nuclear bombs, missiles, chemical and biological agents. This effort is supported by the largest section of the secondary sector, the military-industrial complex. (ii) To expand indefinitely the already excessive array of consumer goods, most of which have no welfare value, though they may have exchange and even use value.

10. The exploited and impoverished majority, at whose expense the scientists carry out their R&D activities, must stand up and stop this unconscionable waste of human potential. Likewise, the scientists, as re-sponsible citizens, should make a stand and say no. Instead their R&D work should focus on the following: (i) How to collect, concentrate and convert solar energy into more useful forms of thermal and electrical

energy, and how to store it, in a decentralized and dispersed manner at affordable costs. (ii) How to extract useful metals and other materials from highly diluted sources, like ordinary soil and sea water (since the concentrated ores are rapidly being depleted), using only solar energy. (iii) How to convert present and future waste into harmless and, preferably, useful materials. (iv) How to combat and reverse the globally deleterious effects of deforestation and atmospheric pollution.

Culture

Such drastic changes in politics and economics will not be initiated unless the ideas grip the imagination of a sizable number of people. This can only be achieved through a cultural awakening. Some elements of this necessary new culture are outlined below. This can be materialized only if substantial changes take place in the political economy of all modern societies:

1. Human needs and desires are numerous, including both things that exist in the world and things that currently do not. Efforts to satisfy these needs and desires have been the motive force of human development. We have to accept, though, that physical resources available on this earth are limited; they may be sufficient to satisfy the genuine needs of all, but not the greed of even a small minority. We must develop the wisdom to differentiate needs from greed.

2. Human progress will have to be redefined. Increasing production and consumption of goods and services can no longer be construed as progress. Human progress, it must be realized, is something more fundamental. It consists of two essential components: physical quality of life and spiritual quality of life. The word 'spiritual' is here used to include moral, cultural and ethical elements, which are not to be considered the exclusive prerogatives of religion.

3. Physical quality of life can be defined in terms of three parameters: (i) *Biological quality* (BQ). High life expectancy at birth and low life-time integrated morbidity are the basic elements of BQ. High BQ may be quantified by low crude death rate, low infant mortality and low child and maternal mortality rates, low birth and total fertility rates, and low levels of malnutrition. (ii) *Human liberation*. Increased freedom from the basic (animal) aspects of existence such as the search for food and the demands of reproduction, and increased availability of time for intellectual and cultural activities. (iii) *Sustainability*. Liberation from the basic (animal) aspects of life is currently attained at the expense of nature, depleting non-renewable resources at unsustainable rates. True human development should be enabling. This would demand the use of natural

resources in a renewable manner. The consumption pattern should be changed only if contingencies that threaten human existence intercede.

4. Spiritual quality of life can be defined in terms of three elements: (i) *Social quality*, indicated by a continuous reduction in the suicide rate, in murder and crime rates, in the rate of consumption of alcohol and narcotics, in expenditure on police and military, in employment of child labour, in the abuse of women, and so on. (ii) *Cultural quality*, indicated by high literacy and levels of education, high reading rates, increasing participation in cultural and sporting activities. (iii) *Participation*. Human beings do not like to live on charity; the availability of work to earn a living is essential. Increased participation of all citizens in the economic and political activities of society is imperative. Full employment is thus not only an economic but also a spiritual necessity. Likewise, participatory democracy is not merely a political but also a spiritual demand.

Outlined above are some of the essential features of the concept of a Fourth World. Some of them may read like the stuff of dreams; nevertheless, they announce a definite sense of direction and purpose. Individuals and groups the world over share the hopes and aspirations that inform the concept. In Kerala, however, a major experiment is under way. It is a planned and conscious effort to achieve in practice some of the features of a possible 'Fourth World' described above. It is to this experiment that we now turn our attention.

The Kerala Experiment

Governmental initiatives

The state of Kerala came into existence in 1956. The first general election held in 1957 brought the Communist Party of India to power, and E.M.S. Namboodiripad became the first chief minister of Kerala. It was a great shock to Jawaharlal Nehru, the first prime minister of India and his colleagues in the ruling Congress Party. However, in 1958 H.D. Malaviya, a noted Congress leader, gave a glowing tribute to the new Communist government in Kerala. He noted that,

> The Communist Ministry, having realised the vital need of remoulding the administrative machinery, constituted an Administrative Reforms Committee soon after it came to power. The report of this committee was signed in July, and it was widely acknowledged that a major job was done in record time in just about nine months. The committee's report has not yet been published.... Democratic decentralisation is supposed to be the keynote of the recommendation. (Malaviya 1959)

This committee was headed by the chief minister, Namboodiripad. The Kerala Panchayat (village council) Bill was introduced on 9 December 1958 and the District Council Bill on 10 April 1959. However, before the state legislature could adopt the legislation the state government was dismissed in a most unconstitutional way by the president of India on the recommendation of Prime Minister Nehru, under pressure from the Congress leaders in Kerala. A decade of bureaucratic centralization and corruption followed. When in 1967 the Left Democratic Front was voted to power, the question of decentralization, together with many other shelved issues like land reform and educational reform, was put back on the agenda. The Panchayat Bill was reintroduced in the state legislature on 26 March 1969. This government, however, was also short-lived due to some partners in the coalition government defecting to the opposition camp. It was unable even to conduct the panchayat election that was due. The Panchayat Bill was again introduced in the legislature in August 1978 and was finally adopted with minor modification in 1979. In 1980 it received the president's approval. The issue of decentralization and local self-governance was revived in 1980 by the newly elected left democratic front (LDF) government, by which time the village panchayats were securely in place. An important seminar on decentralization was organized at the Centre for Development Studies in 1981, with K.N. Raj, among others, as a participant. However, before steps were taken to operationalize decentralization, the LDF government was again toppled.

In 1987, with an LDF government in power under the leadership of E.K. Nayanar, the project of decentralization was once again brought to the fore. A committee under the chairmanship of V. Ramachandran was formed to work out a detailed programme of action for effective decentralization of powers. (Ramachandran had been closely associated with the 1957 Administrative Reforms Committee.) He submitted his report in a record time of six months (Ramachandran 1987). The report recommended that 30 per cent of the Eighth Plan allocation should be set aside for projects initiated by panchayats, blocks and districts. However, under the combined weight of decades-long habits, the absence of elected bodies at block and district levels, and resistance from the bureaucracy and a number of political parties, this amount was ultimately reduced to the provision of a few thousand rupees to each panchayat as an 'untied fund'.

The idea of district councils, though it had been mooted at an earlier stage, could not be realized at first due to opposition within the LDF itself. However, by the end of the 1980s, the time was ripe for the reform, even though individual members of most parties still held reservations. By this time prime minister Rajiv Gandhi had introduced constitutional amendments to provide protection to panchayat raj institutions. Many of the provisions of these amendments were found to be in violation of state rights, and were therefore opposed by many political parties. In 1992, with the objectionable sections removed, the parliament unanimously passed the 73rd and 74th amendments to the constitution, which opened the way to the formation of panchayats (three-tier) and nagarpalikas (municipalities). It took another two to three years for the states to enact legislation on panchayats and nagarpalikas.

The absence of a holistic view on development had led to confusion on how best to mobilize panchayats. Even those limited programmes that the panchayats were empowered to undertake were not executed, to the neglect of the long-term interest of local communities. For the panchayats, 'development' meant roads, community halls, stadiums, marketing complexes, and so forth, all involving civil construction works. This 'contractor-dictated development perspective' may be the legacy of line department interests. No priority was given to projects leading to increased production and productivity.

Although most of these cosmetic changes in the operation of panchayats were taking place at the government level, there was little or no effort to educate the people, to mobilize them, to empower them and to transform the bureaucracy in form and content. Though grama panchayats had been in existence in West Bengal for more than fifteen years, they never became real 'local self-governments'. They were at best more effective and more transparent implementing agencies of vertically conceived bureaucratic programmes. It was only in 1996, when the Kerala State Planning Board took a decision to launch a massive campaign for the formation of the Ninth Five-Year Plan with people's participation, that the decentralization process experienced a qualitative change. It is significant that this took place in Kerala and not in West Bengal. By 1996, the people of Kerala were ready to rise to such a massive challenge. The credit for this goes back to a unique movement called Kerala Sastra Sahitya Parishad – generally known as the People's Science Movement. It has been assiduously preparing the people to take power and responsibility in their own hands for more than two decades.

KSSP and decentralized democracy

The literal meaning of Kerala Sastra Sahitya Parishad – KSSP as it is popularly known – is Kerala Science Literature Association. It was formed in 1962 by a group of science popularizers in Kerala with the objective of enriching science literature in the Malayalam language and taking science to the people. In the process of doing this it had continuously to enlarge its areas of activity, from merely that of enriching science literature.

First, science began to be understood in a broader way than usual, to include technology, social sciences and even liberal arts. Second, the KSSP began to look for science not only in the printed pages of books and journals but also in the hands, heads and hearts of the working people, artisans, technicians, engineers, peasants and physicians. In 1973, the KSSP adopted the slogan 'Science for Social Revolution'. It also took a decision to set up 'Rural Science Fora' in every village panchayat of the state. This contained within itself seeds of the ideas of decentralized development, people's planning.

'Science for Social Revolution' envisaged a qualitative change in the way people live, a reversal of the process of enrichment of a minority at the expense of the majority. Science is to become a weapon in the hand of the majority and its organizations to fight their impoverishment. The Rural Science Fora, consisting of locally available teachers, technicians, experts and other knowledgeable people who are more favourably inclined towards the poor than towards the rich, were conceived as centres of knowledge that is easily accessible to local people. Their aim was to develop what Gramsci referred to as 'organic intellectuals'. Three major areas of work were conceived: (1) Rural surveys; (2) Education of the people; (3) Welfare/constructive work.

The model by-laws of the KSSP Science Fora state the following as objectives: (i) to carry out construction activities useful for the village as a whole; (ii) to conduct discussion, seminars and classes on topics of common interest; (iii) to organize studies on agriculture and agrarian relations; (iv) to conduct studies within villages on industry, labour, raw materials, capital potential and so on; (v) to conduct surveys on unemployment and human resources; (vi) to organize programmes related to health-care delivery; (vii) to oversee activities related to education and educational institutions; and (viii) to campaign against illiteracy and ignorance.

Over the years, many of the features of the 'social revolution', and how exactly science or knowledge was going to help it, became better articulated. The essential elements are the following: (a) participative and creative democracy; (b) increasing the capacity of the people to participate and create; (c) an appreciation of the importance of environment and nature; (d) an understanding of the concept of development, different from the conventional understanding of 'developed countries', viewing development from the human perspective rather than from a free-market perspective of 'limitlessness' and 'abundance'; (e) constructive work as a method of learning through practice.

For nearly two decades now, the KSSP has been involved in educating the people, working to empower ordinary citizens through a variety of activities. These have included mass lecture campaigns; publications;

polemics; mass literacy campaigns; micro-level studies, including the Panchayat Resource-mapping Programme (the last two items are elaborated below).

In 1989, the KSSP launched the Ernakulam District literacy campaign, which mobilized nearly 30,000 volunteer teachers and 150,000 learners. In February 1990, Ernakulam became the first fully literate district in India. In 1990–91, the KSSP acted as the anchor of the Total Kerala Literacy programme, which mobilized more than 300,000 volunteers and more than 1.5 million learners. As a result of this massive campaign, Kerala became the first 'totally literate' state in India.

In 1990–91, the Integrated Rural Technology Centre (established in 1987 by the KSSP) and the Centre for Earth Science Studies together initiated the Panchayat Resource-mapping Programme, which was later to become an important tool in micro-level planning. The experience of the studies conducted by Rural Science Fora and the insights of J.C. Kumarappa's (1931) study of Matar Tuluka formed the basis of a comprehensive micro-planning experiment in 1991–92 in the Kalliasseri panchayat, located in northern Kerala. In 1995 a major action research group was formulated by the IRTC together with the Centre for Development Studies to carry out intensive local area planning with people's participation in five panchayats along with Kalliasseri. In addition, the concept of the Neighbourhood and Panchayat Development Society, piloted in Kalliasseri from 1993 onwards, was to be extended to twenty-five other panchayats.

All these schemes were forms of 'action research'; they were not part of mainstream planning or thought. However, it was hoped that in the future they would influence mainstream economic and political thought. That moment came much sooner than had been expected.

The People's Campaign for the Ninth Plan

The newly elected Left Democratic Front government of 1996 formed a State Planning Board, whose vice-chairman and members were committed proponents of decentralized planning and had been active in many action research programmes for more than a decade and a half. The Ninth Five-Year Plan was about to be drawn up and launched. They took the daring decision to invert the entire process: to start planning from the grama sabha (village council) and the panchayat upwards with people's participation, and thereby to arrive at a state plan. Many considered this decision rash. But the State Planning Board, which knew that if it was missed this opportunity may not have presented itself again, was able to convince the government to go ahead with the bold experiment. The decision was taken at the meeting of the full Planning Board held on 14

July 1996. The programme was launched formally on Kerala's New Year's Day of 1172 (Malayalam Era), 17 August 1996.

The approach paper released by the State Planning Board on 24 July 1996 stated as its objectives: (1) decentralization and people's participation; (2) 35–40 per cent of Plan funds for projects/schemes formulated and implemented by local bodies; (3) all departmental schemes to be implemented in consultation with local bodies; (4) local bodies to prepare and prioritize a list of projects; (5) maximum popular participation at every stage of the planning process; (6) to break the atmosphere of cynicism; (7) to tap new resources, both material and human; (8) to empower the panchayats and make them real local self-governments. In order to achieve these objectives the State Planning Board envisaged a number of structured stages of activity:

1. September–October 1996. Grama sabhas or ward conventions with mass participation to discuss the approach to the Ninth Plan.
2. October–November 1996. Panchayat/municipal-level development seminars to discuss the problems vetted by grama sabhas/ward conventions and the development report based on them, along with secondary data, and to constitute task forces of experts, officials and activists in each of the development sectors.
3. November 1996–March 1997. Formulation of a list of projects in each of the ten to fifteen development sectors, as envisaged and indicated in the development report.
4. March–April 1997. Finalization of the project document, discussion at grama sabhas and adoption at the panchayat council level.
5. March–June 1997. Block–district seminars, finalization of block and district plans, as well as the state Plan.
6. May–October 1997. Formation of a Voluntary Technical Corps (VTC) to evaluate technically the projects prepared by the task forces, improve them and make them financially viable, and later to assist the District Planning Committee in granting its technical sanction and approving the Plan.[2]

Grama sabha was a concept alien to Kerala. The distributed habitation pattern of Kerala is quite different from the conglomerate habitats of the rest of India. Extensive urbanization long ago obliterated community cohesion and traditions. Even old village names occurring in revenue records do not register any recognition by the population. The new generation has become accustomed to panchayats, blocks, towns and cities, the boundaries of which are redefined relatively infrequently. The panchayat forms the smallest political administrative unit. With an average area of 20–30 square km and a population of between 20,000 and

30,000, the Kerala panchayats are much larger than the average Indian panchayat, by a factor of between five and ten. The panchayats are divided into a number of wards, often quite arbitrarily. The number of wards varies from seven to fifteen. The Kerala Panchayat Act, for want of a better idea, defined the 'ward' as the equivalent of the 'village'; the voters made up the grama sabha or village council. This is too large a body, having anything from 1,000 to 2,000 members, for intimate discussion to be possible or for making truly collective decisions. The quorum for the grama sabha was kept at the absurdly low figure of fifty; the fear was that very few people would attend. Thus, neither legislators nor officials had faith in the functioning of the grama sabha. And it duly transpired that the people did not understand it. The first statutory grama sabha held was a farce.

It is, nevertheless, the case that the constitution granted a very important role to the grama sabha. It is the most basic unit of democracy, where every citizen can, and is expected, to act. It consists of sometimes a few dozen, at most a couple of hundred, households in most parts of India. In such circumstances, every family knows every other family, of course. It is in recognition of these circumstances that first the KSSP and later the State Planning Board arrived at the concept of neighbourhood – an informal grouping of betwen thirty and fifty households which are very close to each other. This concept, however, is still in its infancy.

The Sen Committee

The State Planning Board was all too aware that providing funds alone was not sufficient. The local bodies would need both unequivocal powers to act and people able to execute the new responsibilities. A number of acts, rules, statutes and guidelines would have to be amended or changed drastically. Vertically organized departments needed to be horizontally integrated at the various levels and brought under the control of the self-governments. This was far from an easy task. At the recommendation of the State Planning Board, the government set up a committee on decentralization, with Dr S.B. Sen as chair.[3] The Sen Committee presented its Interim Report in a record time of three weeks on 14 August 1997.[4] The death of Dr Sen soon thereafter affected the pace of the Committee's work. However, under the direction of the vice-chair, V.J. Thankappan, the Committee issued three reports: (1) on an internal audit of local and state government (LSG) institutions; (2) on the changes required to the Panchayat and Municipal Acts; and (3) on the redeployment of engineering personnel under the Irrigation, Public Works and Rural Development Departments.

The Interim Report of the Sen Committee emphasized the importance of grama sabha as the only body accessible to all citizens and stressed its function as the basic unit of democracy. It recommended that many statutory rights and responsibilities be granted to the grama sabha. It also proposed the formation of neighbourhood groups to assist the working of the grama sabha. The essential elements of the first report of the Sen Committee are as follows:

1. *Autonomy*: functional, financial and administrative. The various levels of the LSGs should not be hierarchically organized; they should be perceived as complementary units.
2. *Subsidiarity*: 'what can be done best at a particular level should be done at that level and not at a higher level. The process of transferring powers between levels should start from the level of the grama sabha and ward committees and go up to the union government.'
3. *Role clarity*: a clear understanding at each level of the LSG of its role in the development process.
4. *Complementarity*: functions should not overlap and double up, but should merge into an overall unity through a process of horizontal integration.
5. *Uniformity*: of norms and criteria for selection of beneficiaries, prioritization of activities, and so on.
6. *People's participation*: not to be limited to mere information giving, but should involve all stages of planning and implementation. Grama sabha and ward committees are the ideal vehicles for promoting direct decision-making.
7. *Accountability*: not to be left to the elections. There should be continuous social auditing of performance on the part of grama sabha and ward committees.
8. *Transparency*: freedom to the people to know every detail of how money is going to be spent both before a scheme is taken up and after completion. Procedures and language of administration need to be demystified and rendered people-friendly.

The report also made recommendations on the planning processes, implementation, people's participation, and steps to be taken to make local self-governments functional with regard to procedural matters, the role of officials and departments, and accounts. These recommendations formed the basis for the subsequent steps taken by the State Planning Board in the People's Campaign for the Ninth Plan. This is an experiment the like of which has never been attempted anywhere in the world. It is too early to judge the outcome. Table 12.2 provides an idea of what is going on.

Table 12.2   Resources available under the Ninth Plan

Human resource development (approximate)	
State level (persons)	1,000
District level (persons)	12,000
Local level (persons)	100,000
Departmental officers trained	10,000
Days of training	5–30
Training materials	
Handbooks for training	40
Additional reference books	20
Electronic media (minutes of video)	900
Financial resources of LSGs (Rs. billion)[*]	
1997–98	10
1998–99	12

* In earlier years the figure has never been higher than Rs. 400 million.

Bringing individual citizens to the centre stage of self-governance is an ambitious, perhaps an unrealistic, notion. The experience so far has been mixed, with more pain than pleasure.

The experiment has a large number of passive well-wishers. But its enemies – the vested interests of politicians, officialdom, contractors and lumpen elements – know the danger for them if the experiment succeeds, and have joined hands to stop it. Though most of the political parties formally 'stand by the people', no political party has made the struggle for people's power their real agenda. The furthest they are prepared to go is to advocate people's representatives. The small group in the State Planning Board and the few individuals in various political parties cannot engender participatory democracy on their own. The only mass-based organization that genuinely holds high the banner of people power is the People's Science Movement, the KSSP. As such, the entire movement is gearing up to fight the enemies of people's democracy; to struggle against the degeneration of decentralized democracy into multi-centred corruption; to strengthen local-level capacity to plan and execute, to monitor and correct; to encourage each and every citizen to participate in running the affairs of society; to make the local community more self-reliant, so that people will take their own welfare in their hands.

Notes

1. It should be noted that Sri Lanka and Costa Rica share some features of Kerala's social development. For a comparison of the 'Kerala model' with Sri Lanka, see the chapter by Casinader in this volume.

2. The VTC was not envisaged at the beginning of the campaign. It was introduced in response to certain ground realities and actual field experience.

3. Dr. S.B. Sen was the architect of the decentralization initiatives carried out at the panchayats in West Bengal state.

4. Sen Committee, *Interim Report*, GOK (1997).

Bibliography

Achari, Thankappan, T.R. 1994. 'Foreword'. In John Fernandez, *Artificial Fish Habitats: A Community Programme for Bio-diversity Conservation*. Trivandrum: Fisheries Research Cell, Programme for Community Organization: i–iii.

Adams, B. 1993. 'Sustainable Development and the Greening of Development Theory'. In F. Schuurman, ed., *Beyond the Impasse: New Directions in Development Theory*. London: Zed Books: 207–22.

Adams, W.M. 1990. *Green Development: Environment and Sustainability in the Third World*. London: Routledge.

AIDWA (All-India Democratic Women's Association). 1994. Fourth National Conference, *State Reports*, Coimbatore.

Aiya, V. Nagam. 1876. *Report on the Census of Travancore 1875*. Thiruvananthapuram, Travancore, India: Government Press.

Aiyappan, A. 1965. *Social Revolution in a Kerala Village*. Bombay: no publ.

A.K.G. Centre for Research and Studies. 1994a. *International Congress on Kerala Studies*, Abstracts, Volume 1, Thiruvananthapuram.

———. 1994b. *International Congress on Kerala Studies*, Abstracts, Volume 2, Thiruvananthapuram.

———. 1994c. *International Congress on Kerala Studies*, Abstracts, Volume 3, Thiruvananthapuram.

———. 1994d. *International Congress on Kerala Studies*, Abstracts, Volume 4, Thiruvananthapuram.

———. 1994e. *International Congress on Kerala Studies*, Abstracts, Supplementary Volume, Thiruvananthapuram.

Alexander, William M. 1994. 'Exceptional Kerala: Efficient Use of Resources and Life Quality in a Non-Affluent Society'. *GAIA: Ecological Perspectives in Science, Humanities, and Economics* 4(3): 211–27.

———. 1997. 'Exceptional Kerala, Efficient and Sustainable Human Behavior'. In Valentine James, ed., *Capacity Building in Developing Nations*. New York: Prager.

———. 1998. 'Female Sexuality Denied, Fatal Daughter Syndrome, and High Fertility Maintained'. *Michigan Sociological Review* 12 (Fall): 117–31.

Amin, Samir. 1991. 'Four Comments on Kerala'. *Monthly Review* 42(8): 28.

————. 1997. *Capitalism in the Age of Globalization: The Management of Contemporary Society*. London: Zed Books.

Antia, N.H. 1994. 'Kerala Shows the Way to Health'. In A.K.G. Centre for Research and Studies, *International Congress on Kerala Studies*, Abstracts, Volume 2, Thiruvananthapuram.

Antony, A.K. 1995. 'The Kerala Model'. *Hindu*, 25 September 1995, p. 5.

Arun, T.G. 1992. 'Growth and Structural Changes in the Manufacturing Industries of Kerala: 1976–87'. MPhil thesis, Centre for Development Studies, Trivandrum.

Bandyopadhyay, D. 1997. 'People's Participation in Planning: Kerala Experiment'. *Economic and Political Weekly*, 32(39): 2450–54.

Bates, Robert. 1989. *Beyond the Miracle of the Market: The Institutional Foundations of Agrarian Development in Kenya*. Cambridge: Cambridge University Press.

Bello, Walden, with Shea Cunningham and Bill Rau. 1994. *Dark Victory: The United States, Structural Adjustment, and Global Poverty*. London: Pluto Press.

Bhagavan, M.R. 1995. 'Technological Implications of Structural Adjustment: Case of India'. *Economic and Political Weekly* 30, 18–25 February: M2–M12.

Bhat, P.N. Mari, and S. Irudaya Rajan. 1990. 'Demographic Transition in Kerala Revisited'. *Economic and Political Weekly*, 25(35 and 36): 1957–80.

Bhattacharjee, P.J., and Shastri, G.N. 1976. *Population in India: A Study of Inter-State Variations*. New Delhi: Vikas.

Bose, Ashish. 1991. *Population of India: 1991 Census Results and Methodology*. Delhi: B.R. Publishing Co.

Bowles, Samuel, David M. Gordon and Thomas E. Weisskopf. 1990. *After the Wasteland: A Democratic Economics for the Year 2000*. Armonk, N.Y.: M.E. Sharpe.

Brass, Paul R. 1990. *The Politics of India Since Independence*. Cambridge: Cambridge University Press.

Breman, Jan. 1993. 'A Footloose Proletariat: Informal Sector Labour in the Rural and Urban Landscape of West India'. Manuscript. Amsterdam.

Brown, Lester R. 1998. 'The Future of Growth'. In Lester Brown et al. *State of the World: A Worldwatch Institute Report on Progress Toward a Sustainable Society*. New York: W.W. Norton: 1–20.

Bryant, R., and S. Bailey. 1997. *Third World Political Ecology*. London: Routledge.

Buttel, Frederick H. 1993. 'The Production of Agricultural Sustainability: Observations from the Sociology of Science and Technology'. In Patricia Allen, ed., *Food for the Future: Conditions and Contradictions of Sustainability*. New York: John Wiley: 19–45.

Cairns, Allan. 1991. *Disruptions: Constitutional Struggles, from Charter to Meech Lake*. Toronto: McClelland & Stewart.

Caldwell, J.C. 1986. 'Routes to Low Mortality in Poor Countries'. *Population and Development Review* 12(2): 171–220.

Caldwell, J.C., and Pat Caldwell. 1985. 'Education and Literacy as Factors in Health'. In Scot B. Halstead, Julia A. Walsh and Kenneth Warren, eds, *Good Health at Low Cost*. New York: Rockefeller Foundation.

Cameron, David. 1984. 'Social Democracy, Corporatism, Labor Quiescence, and the Representation of Economic Interests in Advanced Capitalist Democracies'. In John Goldthorpe, ed., *Order and Conflict in Contemporary Capitalism*. Oxford: Oxford University Press: 143–80.

Carson, Rachel. 1962. *The Silent Spring*. Boston, Mass.: Houghton Mifflin.

Casinader, Rex. 1995. 'Making Kerala Model More Intelligible: Comparisons with Sri Lankan Experience'. *Economic and Political Weekly* 30(48): 3085–92.

Census Commissioner of India, 1992. *Census of India 1991*, Series I, India, Paper I of 1991, New Delhi.

CDS (Centre for Development Studies). 1975. *Poverty, Unemployment, and Development Policy: A Case Study of Selected Issues with Reference to Kerala*. New York: United Nations, Department of Economic and Social Affairs.

Cereseto, Shirley, and Howard Waitzkin. 1988. 'Economic Development, Political-Economic System, and the Physical Quality of Life'. *Journal of Public Health Policy*, Spring: 104–20.

Chandramohan, P. 1981. 'Social and Political Protest in Travancore: A Study of the Sree Narayana Dharma Paripalana Yogam (1900–1938)'. MPhil dissertation, Jawaharlal Nehru University, New Delhi.

———. 1987. 'Popular Culture and Socio-Religious Reform: Narayana Guru and the Ezhavas of Travancore'. *Studies in History* 3(1): 57–74.

Chasin, Barbara H. 1990. 'Land Reform and Women's Work in a Kerala Village'. Working Papers on Women in International Development no. 207, Michigan State University, East Lansing.

Chattopadhyay, Sreeumar. 1984. *Deforestation in Part of Western Ghats Region (Kerala), India*. Trivandrum: Centre for Earth Science Studies.

———. 1985. 'Deforestation in Parts of Western Ghats Region (Kerala), India'. *Journal of Environmental Management* 20: 219–30.

Chekkutty, N.P., ed. 1997. *The People's Plan: A Debate on Kerala's Decentralised Planning Experiment*. Kozhikode: Calicut Press Club.

CMIE (Centre for Monitoring of the Indian Economy). 1991. Economic Intelligence Service, *Basic Statistics Relating to the Indian Economy*. Vols 1 and 2. Bombay.

———. 1993. *Basic Statistics Relating to the Indian Economy*, Vol. 2. Bombay.

———. 1996. *India: Social Development*. Bombay.

———. 1997. *Profile of States*. Bombay.

———. 1998. *1998 National Income Statistics*. Bombay.

Cohen, Joshua and Joel Rogers. 1992. 'Secondary Associations and Democratic Governance'. *Politics and Society* 20(4): 393–472.

Cohen, Marilyn. 1992. 'Survival Strategies in Female-headed Households: Linen Workers in Tullylish, County Down, 1901'. *Journal of Family History* 17(3): 303–18.

Cohn, Bernard S. 1971. *India: The Social Anthropology of a Civilization*. Englewood Cliffs, N.J.: Prentice-Hall.

Corrie, Bruce P. 1994. 'The Kerala Model of Development from the Perspective of the Dalit Child in Kerala'. Paper presented at the First International Congress on Kerala Studies, Thiruvananthapuram, 27–29 August.

CSE (Centre for Science and Environment). 1985. *The State of India's Environment 1984–85: The Second Citizens' Report*. New Delhi: Centre for Science and Environment.

Dale, Stephen F. 1980. *Islamic Society on the South Asian Frontier: The Mapilas of Malabar*. Oxford: Clarendon Press.

Daly, Herman E. 1990. 'Sustainable Growth: An Impossibility Theorem'. *Development* 3–4: 45–7.

———. 1996a. 'Sustainable Growth? No Thank You'. In Jerry Mander and Edward Goldsmith, eds, *The Case against the Global Economy and for a Turn Toward the Local*. San Francisco: Sierra Club Books: 192–6.

———. 1996b. *Beyond Growth: The Economics of Sustainable Development*. Boston, Mass.: Beacon Press.

Damodaran, A.D. 1994. 'Role of CSIR in Indigenous S&T Development'. In R. Ravi Kumar, ed., *Science, Technology, and Self Reliance*. Trivandrum: State Committee on Science, Technology and Environment: 119–27.

Damodaran, V.K. 1991. *Development of S&T Infrastructure in Kerala: A Database Construction*. Trivandrum: State Committee on Science, Technology, and Environment.

Das Gupta, Monica. 1987. 'Selective Discrimination against Female Children in Rural Punjab, India'. *Population and Development Review* 13(1): 77–100.

Department of Census and Statistics. 1982. *Population Tables. Preliminary Release No. 2*. Colombo, Sri Lanka: Dept of Census and Statistics.

———. 1983a. *Statistical Pocket Book of the Democratic Republic of Sri Lanka*. Colombo, Sri Lanka: Dept of Census and Statistics.

———. 1983b. *The Economically Active Population. Preliminary Release No. 4*. Colombo, Sri Lanka: Dept of Census and Statistics.

Deshpande, L.K. 1983. *Segmentation of Labour Market: A Case Study of Bombay*. Bombay: Orient Longman.

Devi, T. 1994. 'Sexual Abuse and Poverty: Tribal Women of Wayanad'. Paper presented at the First International Congress on Kerala Studies, Thiruvananthapuram, 27–29 August.

Deyo, Frederic C., ed. 1987. *The Political Economy of the New Asian Industrialization*. Ithaca, N.Y.: Cornell University Press.

Dharmadasa, K.N.O. 1992. '"The People of the Lion": Ethnic Identity, Ideology, Revisionism in Contemporary Sri Lanka'. *Ethnic Studies Report*, 10(1): 37–59.

Director of Census Operations. 1986. *Census of India 1981*, Series 10, Kerala Part III A&B (iii) General Economic Tables, B-21, B-22, Trivandrum.

———. 1992. *Census of India 1991*, Series 12, Kerala Paper 1 of 1991, Trivandrum.

D'Monte, D. 1985. *Temples or Tombs? Industry versus Environment: Three Controversies*. New Delhi: Centre for Science and Environment.

Dodds, Steve. 1997. 'Towards a "Science of Sustainability": Improving the Way Ecological Economics Understands Human Well-being'. *Ecological Economics* 23(2): 95–111.

Drèze, Jean, and Haris Gazdar. 1997. 'Uttar Pradesh: The Burden of Inertia'. In Jean Drèze and Amartya Sen, eds, *Indian Development: Selected Regional Perspectives*. New Delhi: Oxford University Press: 33–128.

Drèze, Jean, and Amartya Sen. 1989. *Hunger and Public Action*. Oxford: Clarendon Press.

———. 1996. *India: Economic Development and Social Opportunity*. Oxford University Press: Oxford and New Delhi.

———. eds, 1997. *Indian Development: Selected Regional Perspectives*. New Delhi: Oxford University Press.

D'Souza, Stan, and Lincoln C. Chen. 1980. 'Sex Differences in Mortality in Rural Bangladesh'. *Population and Development Review* 6(2): 257–70.

Dunham, David, and Saman Kelegama. 1998. 'Stabilization and Adjustment: Sri Lankan Experience, 1977–1993'. *Economic and Political Weekly* 33(24): 1475–82.

Dunn, Seth. 1998. 'Carbon Emissions Resume Rise'. In Lester Brown, Michael Renner and Christopher Flavin, eds, *Vital Signs 1998: The Environmental Trends that Are Shaping Our Future*. New York: W.W. Norton: 66–7.

Embree, Ainslee T. 1985. 'Indian Civilization and Regional Cultures: The Two Realities'. In Paul Wallace, ed., *Region and Nation in India*. New Delhi: Oxford

University Press, IBH Publishing House and American Institute of Indian Studies: 19–39.

Engels, Frederick. 1954. *The Dialectics of Nature* [1896]. Moscow: Foreign Languages Publishing House.

EPW (*Economic and Political Weekly*). 1990a. 'Kerala Economy at the Crossroads – I'. *Economic and Political Weekly* 25(35–36), 1–8 September.

———. 1990b. 'Kerala Economy at the Crossroads – II'. *Economic and Political Weekly* 25(37), 15 September.

———. 1994a. 'Social Indicators of Development for India – I'. *Economic and Political Weekly* 29, 14 May: 1227–40.

———. 1997. 'Kerala: Farm Workers' Agitation: Return to Politics of Confrontation?' *Economic and Political Weekly* 32(33–4): 2089–90.

———. 1994b. 'Social Indicators of Development for India – II: Inter-State Disparities'. *Economic and Political Weekly* 29, 21 May: 1300–1308.

Evans, Peter 1995. *Embedded Autonomy: States and Industrial Transformation*. Princeton, N.J.: Princeton University Press.

———. 1996. Government Action, Social Capital and Development: Reviewing the Evidence on Synergy. *World Development* 24(6): 1119–32.

Evans, Peter, and Dietrich Rueschemeyer. 1985. 'The State and Economic Transformation: Toward an Analysis of the Conditions Underlying Effective Intervention'. In Peter Evans, Dietrich Rueschemeyer and Theda Skocpol, eds, *Bringing the State Back In*. New York: Cambridge University Press.

Farrington, John, and Anthony Bebbington. 1993. *Reluctant Partners: Non-Governmental Organizations, The State, and Sustainable Agricultural Development*. London: Routledge.

Fernandez, John. 1994. *Artificial Fish Habitats: A Community Programme for Bio-diversity Conservation*. Trivandrum: Fisheries Research Cell, Programme for Community Organization.

Fox, Jonathan. 1994. 'The Difficult Transition from Clientalism to Citizenship'. *World Politics* 46(2): 151–84.

Franke, Richard W. 1992. 'Land Reform versus Inequality in Nadur Village, Kerala'. *Journal of Anthropological Research* 48(2): 81–116.

———. 1993. 'Feeding Programmes and Food Intake in a Kerala Village'. *Economic and Political Weekly* 28(8–9): 355–60.

———. 1996. *Life is a Little Better: Redistribution as a Development Strategy in Nadur Village Kerala*. Boulder, Colo. and New Delhi: Westview Press and Promilla.

Franke, Richard W., and Barbara H. Chasin. 1983. 'Asking the Critical Questions'. Development Watch Column in the *Global Reporter: A Journal of People, Resources, and the World* 1(1): 11. Boston, Mass.: Anthropology Resource Center.

———. 1989. *Kerala: Radical Reform as Development in an Indian State*. Food First Development Report No. 6. San Francisco, October.

———. 1992. *Kerala: Development through Radical Reform*, New Delhi: Promilla, in collaboration with the Institute for Food and Development Policy, San Francisco.

———. 1994. *Kerala: Radical Reform as Development in an Indian State*. 2nd edn. Oakland, Calif. and New Delhi: Food First and Promilla.

———. 1996. 'Female-supported Households: A Continuing Agenda for Kerala Model?' *Economic and Political Weekly* 31(10): 625–30.

———. 1997. 'Power to the Malayalee People'. *Economic and Political Weekly* 32(48): 3061–8.

————. 1998. 'Kerala: A Valid Alternative to the New World Order (Reply to Joseph Tharamangalam)'. *Bulletin of Concerned Asian Scholars* 30(4): 25–8.

Fuller, C.J. 1976. *The Nayars Today*. New York: Cambridge University Press.

George, Alex. 1990. 'The Militant Phase of Pulaya Movement of South Travancore: 1884–1914'. Werkdocument no. 22, Amsterdam: CASA.

George, Jose. 1980. 'Politicisation of Agricultural Workers in Kerala: A Study of Kuttanad'. M.Phil dissertation, Jawaharlal Nehru University, New Delhi.

————. 1997. 'Panchayats and Participatory Planning in Kerala'. *Indian Journal of Public Administration* 18(1): 79–91.

George, K.K. 1993. *Limits to Kerala Model of Development: An Analysis of Fiscal Crisis and its Implications*. Trivandrum: Centre for Development Studies, Monograph Series.

————. 1998. 'Historical Roots of Kerala Model and Its Present Crisis'. *Bulletin of Concerned Asian Scholars* 30(4): 35–40.

Ger, Guliz. 1997. 'Human Development and Humane Consumption: Well-Being Beyond the "Good Life"'. *Journal of Public Policy and Marketing* 16(1): 110–25.

Ghai, Dharam. 1997. *Social Development and Public Policy: Some Lessons from Successful Experience*. Discussion Paper No. 89, United Nations Research Institute for Social Development, Geneva.

Ghai, Dharam, and J.M. Vivian, eds. 1992. *Grassroots Environmental Action: People's Participation in Sustainable Development*. London: Routledge.

GOI (Government of India). 1984. *Report on the Working of the Minimum Wages Act, 1948, for the Year 1984*. Labour Bureau, Simla.

————. 1991. *Report of the National Commission on Rural Labour,* Vols 1 and 2. Ministry of Labour, New Delhi.

————. 1992. *Sample Registration System, Fertility and Mortality Indicators, 1992*. Ministry of Home Affairs, New Delhi.

————. 1994. *Health Information of India 1994*. Ministry of Health and Family Welfare, New Delhi.

————. 1995. *Family Welfare Programme in India, Year Book 1994–95*. Ministry of Health and Family Welfare, New Delhi.

————. 1997. *Selected Socio-Economic Statistics: India 1995*. Central Statistical Office, New Delhi.

GOK (Government of Kerala), 1975. *Economic Review*. State Planning Board, Thiruvanathapuram.

————. 1980. *Census of Fisherfolk of Kerala – 1979*. Department of Fisheries, Thiruvanathapuram.

————. 1981. *Economic Review*. State Planning Board, Thiruvanathapuram.

————. 1986. *Economic Review*. State Planning Board, Thiruvanathapuram.

————. 1987. *Estimates of State Income and Related Aggregates*. Department of Economics and Statistics, Thiruvanathapuram.

————. 1988. *Statistics for Planning – 1988*. Department of Economics and Statistics, Thiruvanathapuram.

————. 1990a. *Enforcement of Minimum Wages Act 1948 in Kerala*. Labour Department, Thiruvanathapuram.

————. 1990b. *Eighth Five Year Plan 1990–95 – Report of the Steering Committee on Industry and Mining*. State Planning Board, Thiruvanathapuram.

————. 1991. *Report of the Task Force for Review of Implementation of Plan Schemes under the Industries Sector*. State Planning Board, Thiruvanathapuram.

————. 1992. *Economic Review*. State Planning Board, Thiruvanathapuram.

————. 1993. *Economic Review*. State Planning Board, Thiruvanathapuram.

————. 1995a. *Economic Review 1994*. State Planning Board, Thiruvananthapuram.

————. 1995b. *Selected Indicators of Development – Kerala and India, 1961 to 1993*. Department of Economics and Statistics, Thiruvananthapuram.

————. 1996a. 'Power to the People. People's Plan – Ninth Plan: A Note, Training Programme for Resources Persons'. State Planning Board, Thiruvananthapuram.

————. 1996b. 'People's Campaign for 9th Plan: An Approach Paper'. State Planning Board, Thiruvananthapuram.

————. 1996c. *Economic Review*. State Planning Board, Thiruvananthapuram.

————. 1998a. *Economic Review 1997*. State Planning Board, Thiruvananthapuram.

————. 1998b. *Kerala Budget in Brief*. State Planning Board, Thiruvanathapuram.

Gough, E. Kathleen. 1959. 'Cults of the Dead among the Nayars'. In Milton Singer, ed., *Traditional India: Structures and Change*. Austin: University of Texas Press.

Government of West Bengal. 1992. *Report of the Education Commission*. Calcutta.

Grant, James. 1989. *The State of the World's Children: 1989*. Oxford: Oxford University Press for UNICEF.

Gulati, I.S., and T.N. Krishnan. 1975. 'Public Distribution and Procurement of Foodgrains: A Proposal'. *Economic and Political Weekly* 10(21), 24 May.

Gulati, Leela. 1993. 'Agricultural Workers Pension in Kerala – An Experiment in Social Assistance'. Paper presented at the conference of the Indian Association of Women's Studies, Manasagangotri.

Halliburton, Murphy. 1998. 'Suicide: A Paradox of Development in Kerala'. *Economic and Political Weekly* 33(36–37): 2341–5.

Haraway, Donna. 1985. 'A Manifesto for Cyborgs: Science, Technology and Socialist Feminism in the 1980s'. *Socialist Review* 80: 65–107.

Harriss, John, K.P. Kannan and Gerry Rodgers. 1990. *Urban Labour Market Structure and Job Access in India: A Study of Coimbatore*. Geneva: International Labour Organization.

Harriss-White, Barbara. 1999. 'Gender-cleansing'. In Rajeswari Sunder Rajan, ed., *Signposts: Gender Issues in Post-Independence India*. New Delhi: Kali for Women.

Heller, Patrick. 1995. 'From Class Struggle to Class Compromise: Redistribution and Growth in a South Indian State'. *Journal of Development Studies* 31(5): 645–72.

————. 1996. 'Social Capital as Product of Class Mobilization and State Intervention: Industrial Workers in Kerala, India'. *World Development* 24: 1055–71.

————. 1998. 'Problematizing the Kerala Model'. *Bulletin of Concerned Asian Scholars* 30(3): 33–5.

————. *The Labor of Development: Workers in the Transformation of Capitalism in Kerala, India*. Ithaca, N.Y.: Cornell University Press.

Hellmann-Rasanayagam, Dagmar. 1989. 'Arumuka Navalar: Religious Reformer or National Leader of Eelam'. *Indian Economic and Social History Review* 26(2): 235–57.

Herring, Ronald J. 1983. *Land to the Tiller: The Political Economy of Agrarian Reform in South Asia*. New Haven, Conn.: Yale University Press.

————. 1989. 'Dilemmas of Agrarian Communism: Peasant Differentiation, Sectoral and Village Politics'. *Third World Quarterly* 11(1): 89–115.

————. 1991. 'From Structural Conflict to Agrarian Stalemate: Agrarian Reforms in South India'. *Journal of Asian and African Studies* 26(3–4): 169–88.

————. 1992. 'Contesting the "Great Transformation": Land and Labor in South

India'. Government Department, Cornell University, Ithaca, N.Y.

Hindu Survey of the Environment. 1991. 'Environmental Hotspots, Kerala'. *The Hindu*, Madras.

Houtart F., and N. Nayak. 1988. *Kerala Fishermen: Culture and Social Organisation.* Louvain-la-Neuve: CETRI.

Huntington, Samuel. 1968. *Political Order in Changing Societies.* New Haven, Conn.: Yale University Press.

ICAR (Indian Council of Agricultural Research). 1996. *ICAR, Now and Ahead.* New Delhi: Indian Council of Agricultural Research.

James, K.S. 1995. 'Demographic Transition and Education in Kerala'. *Economic and Political Weekly* 30, 23 December: 3274–6.

Jeffrey, Robin. 1987a. 'Culture of Daily Newspapers in India: How It's Grown, What It Means'. *Economic and Political Weekly* 22(14): 607–11.

———. 1987b. 'Culture and Governments: How Women Made Kerala Literate'. *Pacific Affairs* 60(4): 447–72.

———. 1992. *Politics, Women and Well-Being: How Kerala became 'A Model'.* London: Macmillan.

———. 1994. 'Kerala's Story'. Review of Richard W. Franke and Barbara H. Chasin, *Kerala: Radical Reform as Development in an Indian State. Economic and Political Weekly* 29(10): 549.

Kabir, M., and T.N. Krishnan. 1991. 'Social Intermediation and Health Transition: Lessons from Kerala'. Paper prepared for a seminar on 'Health and Development in India', jointly sponsored by the National Council of Applied Economic Research and Harvard University Center for Population and Development Studies, New Delhi, 2–4 December 1992.

Kailasapathy, K. 1984. 'Cultural and Linguistic Consciousness of the Tamil Community'. In *Ethnicity and Social Change in Sri Lanka.* Colombo: Social Scientist Association: 107–20.

Kakwani, Nanak, Elene Makonnen and Jacques Van Der Gaag. 1990. 'Structural Adjustment and Living Conditions in Developing Countries'. PRE Working Paper No. WPS 467, World Bank, August.

Kane, Hal. 1993. 'Child Mortality Continues to Fall'. In Lester Brown, Hal Kane and Ed Ayres, *Vital Signs 1993.* New York: W.W. Norton: 96–7.

Kannan, K.P. 1988. *Of Rural Proletarian Struggles: Mobilization and Organization of Rural Workers in South-West India.* Delhi: Oxford University Press.

———. 1990a. 'Kerala Economy at the Crossroads?' *Economic and Political Weekly* 25(36), 1–8 September: 1951–6.

———. 1990b. 'State and Union Intervention in Rural Labour: A Study of Kerala, India'. Asian Regional Team for Employment Promotion. New Delhi: International Labour Organization.

———. 1992. 'Labour Institutions and the Development Process in Kerala, India'. Trivandrum: Centre for Development Studies.

———. 1993. 'Public Intervention and Poverty Alleviation: A Study of the Declining Incidence of Poverty in Kerala'. Trivandrum: Centre for Development Studies.

———. 1994. 'Levelling up or Levelling Down? Labour Institutions and Economic Development in India'. *Economic and Political Weekly,* 23 July: 1938–45.

———. 1995. 'Public Intervention and Poverty Alleviation: A Study of the Declining Incidence of Poverty in Kerala, India'. *Development Change* 26(4).

———. 1998. 'Political Economy of Labour and Development in Kerala'. *Economic and Political Weekly* 33(52), 26 December.

Kannan, K.P., and K. Pushpangadan. 1988. 'Agricultural Stagnation in Kerala: An Exploratory Analysis'. *Economic and Political Weekly* 23(39): A120–28.

Kannan, K.P., K.R. Thankappan, V. Ramankutty and K.P. Aravindan. 1991. *Health and Development in Rural Kerala: A Study of the Linkages between Socioeconomic Status and Health Status.* Integrated Rural Technology Centre, Kerala Sastra Sahitya Parishad, Palakkad and Trivandrum.

Karuna, M.S. 1994. 'Socioeconomic Status of Fishermen Families in Thiruvananthapuram District'. Paper presented at the First International Congress on Kerala Studies. Thiruvananthapuram, 27–29 August.

Kohli, Atul. 1987. *The State and Poverty in India.* Cambridge: Cambridge University Press.

Krishnan, T.N. 1976. 'Demographic Transition in Kerala: Facts and Factors'. *Economic and Political Weekly*, 11(31–33): 1203–24.

———. 1991a. 'Kerala's Health Transition: Facts and Factors'. Harvard Center for Population and Development Studies and Centre for Development Studies, Thiruvananthapuram, September.

———. 1991b. 'Wages, Employment and Output in Interrelated Labour Markets in an Agrarian Economy: A Study of Kerala'. *Economic and Political Weekly*, 29 June: A82–96.

———. 1994. 'Foreign Remittances, Consumption and Income'. Paper presented at the First International Congress on Kerala Studies, Thiruvananthapuram, 27–29 August.

Kumar, B.G. 1989. 'Gender, Differential Mortality and Development: The Experience of Kerala'. *Cambridge Journal of Economics* 13.

Kumar, Krishna. 1994. '"Battle Against their Own Minds": Notes on Literate Kerala'. *Economic and Political Weekly* 29, February 12: 345–7.

Kumar, Mohana S. 1989. 'Industrial Disputes in India 1951–1985'. MPhil thesis, Centre for Development Studies, Trivandrum.

Kumar, Rachel. 1994. 'Development and Women's Work in Kerala: Interactions and Paradoxes'. *Economic and Political Weekly* 29, 12 February: 345–7.

Kumarappa, J.C. 1931. *An Economic Survey of Matar Taluka.* Gujarat Vidyapith, Ahmedabad.

Kurien, John. 1980. 'Fishermen's Cooperatives in Kerala: A Critique'. FAO/BOBP Working Paper MICS-1, Madras.

———. 1991. *Ruining the Commons and the Responses of the Commoners: Coastal Overfishing and Fishermen's Actions in Kerala State, India.* Geneva: United Nations Research Institute for Social Development, Discussion Paper No. 23.

———. 1992. 'Ruining the Commons and the Responses of the Commoners: Coastal Overfishing and Fishworkers Actions in Kerala State'. In D. Ghai and J. Vivian, eds, *Grassroots Environmental Action: People's Participation in Sustainable Development.* London: Routledge.

———. 1993. 'Ruining the Commons: Overfishing and Fishworkers' Actions in South India'. *Ecologist* 23(10): 5–12.

———. 1994. 'Kerala's Marine Fisheries Development Experience'. In B.A. Prakash, ed., *Kerala's Economy: Performance, Problems, Prospects.* New Delhi: Sage: 195–214.

———. 1996. *Towards a New Agenda for Sustainable Small-Scale Fisheries Development.* Karamana, Trivandrum: South Indian Federation of Fishermen Societies.

Leach, M., R. Mearns and I. Scoones. 1997. 'Challenges to Community-based

Sustainable Development: Dynamics, Entitlements, Institutions'. *IDS Bulletin* 28(4): 4–14.

Lele, S.M. 1991. 'Sustainable Development: A Critical Review'. *World Development* 19(6): 607–21.

McCloskey, Donald N. 1985. *The Rhetoric of Economics*. Madison: University of Wisconsin Press.

McGee, T.G. 1991. 'The Emergence of Desakota Regions in Asia: Expanding a Hypothesis'. In N. Ginsburg, B. Koppel and T.G. McGee, eds, *The Extended Metropolis in Asia*. Honolulu: University of Hawaii Press: 3–26.

McKibben, Bill. 1995. *Hope, Human and Wild: True Stories of Living Lightly on Earth*. Boston, Mass.: Little, Brown.

———. 1996. 'The Enigma of Kerala: One State in India is Proving the Development Experts Wrong'. *Utne Reader*, March–April: 103–12.

Malaviya, H.D. 1959. *Kerala: A Report to the Nation*. New Delhi: People's Publishing House.

Mander, Jerry, and Edward Goldsmith, eds. 1996. *The Case against the Global Economy and for a Turn toward the Local*. San Francisco: Sierra Club Books.

Mathew, E.T. 1995. 'Educated Unemployment in Kerala: Some Socio-Economic Aspects'. *Economic and Political Weekly* 30(6), 11 February: 325–35.

Mayer, Adrian. 1952. *Land and Society in Malabar*, London: Oxford University Press.

Mencher, Joan P. 1966. 'Kerala and Madras: A Comparative Study of Ecology and Social Structure'. *Ethnology* 5(2): 135–71.

———. 1980. 'The Lessons and Non-Lessons of Kerala: Agricultural Labourers and Poverty'. *Economic and Political Weekly*, Special Number, 15(41–43): 1781–1802.

———. 1994. 'The Kerala Model of Development: The Excluded Ones'. Paper presented at the First International Congress on Kerala Studies, Thiruvananthapuram, 27–29 August.

Menon, S.C.S. 1979. 'Linking Annual Bonus to Production/Productivity: Employees' Viewpoint'. Mimeo. Cochin.

Mies, Maria. 1982. *The Lace Makers of Narsapur: Indian Housewives Produce for the World Market*. London: Zed Books.

Migdal, Joel S. 1988. *Strong Societies and Weak States: State–Society Relations and State Capabilities in the Third World*. Princeton, N.J.: Princeton University Press.

Mohan, V. Nanda. 1994. 'Recent Trends in the Industrial Growth of Kerala'. In B.A. Prakash, ed., *Kerala's Economy: Performance, Problems, Prospects*. New Delhi: Sage: 217–36.

Morrison, Barrie M. 1997. 'The Embourgeoisement of the Kerala Farmer'. *Modern Asian Studies* 31(1): 61–87.

Nag, Moni. 1983. 'Impact of Social and Economic Development on Morbidity: Comparative Study of Kerala and West Bengal'. *Economic and Political Weekly* 18(19–21): 877–90.

———. 1989. 'Political Awareness as a Factor in Accessibility of Health Services: A Case Study of Rural Kerala and West Bengal'. *Economic and Political Weekly* 24(8): 417–26.

Nair, P.R. Gopinathan. 1981. *Primary Education, Population Growth and Socioeconomic Change: A Comparative Study with Particular Reference to Kerala*. New Delhi: Allied Publishers.

———. 1994. 'Migration of Keralites to the Arab World'. In B.A. Prakash, ed., *Kerala's Economy: Performance, Problems, Prospects*. New Delhi: Sage: 95–114.

Nair, K. Ramachandran. 1973. *Industrial Relations in Kerala*. New Delhi: Sterling Publishers.

———. 1994. 'Trade Unionism in Kerala'. In B.A. Prakash, ed., *Kerala's Economy: Performance, Problems, Prospects*. New Delhi: Sage.

Namboodiripad, E.M.S. 1942. 'In Kerala Our Sisters Make History'. *People's War* 26.

———. 1984. *Kerala: Society and Politics: An Historical Survey*. New Delhi: National Book Centre.

———. 1985. *Selected Writings*, Vol. 2. Calcutta: National Book Agency.

———. 1992. Interview with V.K. Ramachandran. Thiruvananthapuram, April.

———. 1994. *The Communist Party in Kerala: Six Decades of Advance and Struggle*. New Delhi: National Book Centre.

———. 1995. 'Kerala Model is One of Deindustrialization'. *Hindu*, 11 September: 5.

Nanda, Amulya R. 1991. *Census of India 1991*, Series 1, Paper 1. New Delhi: Government of India.

Nandy, Ashish. 1983. *The Intimate Enemy: Loss and Recovery of Self Under Colonialism*. Delhi: Oxford University Press.

National Family Health Survey. 1995a. *Kerala*. Population Research Centre, University of Kerala, Thiruvananthapuram, and International Institute for Population Sciences, Mumbai, June.

———. 1995b. *India*, International Institute for Population Sciences, Mumbai, August.

National Sample Survey. 1991. 42nd Round, July 1986 to June 1987, Child and Maternity Care, *Sarvekshana* 14(4), April–June.

———. 1993. 42nd Round, July 1986 to June 1987, Results on Participation in Education for 8 Major States, *Sarvekshana* 16(4), April–June.

———. 1997. 53rd Round, January–December 1997.

Noss, Andrew. 1991. 'Education and Adjustment: A Review of the Literature'. PRE Working Paper No. WPS 701, World Bank, June.

Nossiter, T.J. 1988. *Communism in Kerala: A Study in Political Adaptation*. New Delhi: Oxford University Press.

Oberai, A.S., Pradhan H. Prasad and M.G. Sardana, 1989. *Determinants and Consequences of Internal Mogration in India*. Delhi: Oxford University Press.

O'Donnell, Guillermo. 1993. 'On the State, Democratization and Some Conceptual Problems: A Latin American View with Glances at Some Postcommunist Countries'. *World Development* 21(8): 1355–9.

Oommen, M.A. 1994. 'Kerala and the New World Order: Some Tentative Hypotheses'. Paper presented at the First International Congress on Kerala Studies, Thiruvananthapuram, 27–29 August.

———. 1979. 'Inter State Shifting of Industries: A Case Study of South India'. Manuscript, University of Calicut, Trichur.

Oommen, M.A., and R. Anandaraj. 1996. 'A District Profile of Human Development Index in India'. Unpublished paper, New Delhi: Institute of Social Sciences.

Panicker, Lalitha. 1998. 'Kerala Conundrum: Ugly Underbelly of the Miracle Model'. *Times of India*, 22 June.

Panikar, P.G.K. 1979. 'Resources Not the Constraint on Health Improvement: A Case Study of Kerala'. *Economic and Political Weekly* 14(44): 1803–9.

Panikar, P.G.K., and C.R. Soman. 1985. *Health Status of Kerala: Paradox of Economic Backwardness and Health Development*. Trivandrum: Centre for Development Studies.

Parayil, Govindan. 1999. 'Democracy at Work in Kerala, India'. *Bulletin of Concerned Asian Scholars* 31(1): 74–8.

———. 1998. 'The Perils of Trying to be Objective without Being Reflexive: The Kerala Model Revisited'. *Bulletin of Concerned Asian Scholars* 30(3): 28–31.

———. 1996. 'The "Kerala Model" of Development: Development and Sustainability in the Third World'. *Third World Quarterly* 17(5): 941–57.

Parayil, Govindan, and Wesley Shrum. 1996. 'Non-Governmental Research Organisations in Kerala'. *Science, Technology & Development* 14: 122–32.

Pearce, David W., and J.J. Warford. 1993. *World Without End: Economics, Environment, and Sustainable Development*. Washington, D.C.: World Bank.

Pearce, David W., et al. 1993. *Blueprint 3: Measuring Sustainable Development*. London: Earthscan.

Pillai, P. Govinda. 1994. 'Art and Literature in the Second Stage of Kerala Renaissance'. In A.K.G. Centre for Research and Studies, *International Congress on Kerala Studies*, Abstracts, Volume 1, Thiruvananthapuram.

Pillai, S. Mohanan. 1992. 'Social Security Schemes for Workers in the Unorganised Sector: A Case Study of Headload Workers Welfare Scheme in Kerala'. MPhil thesis, Centre for Development Studies, Trivandrum.

———. 1996. 'Social Security for Workers in Unorganised Sector: Experience of Kerala. *Economic and Political Weekly* 31(31): 2093–107.

Pinstrup-Anderson, Per. 1993. 'Economic Crises and Policy Reforms during the 1980s and their Impact on the Poor'. In *Macroeconomic Environment and Health: with Case Studies for Countries in Greatest Need*. Geneva: World Health Organization.

Prabhu, K. Seeta, and Somnath Chatterjee. 1993. 'Social Sector Expenditures and Human Development: A Study of Indian States'. Development Research Group, Study 6, Department of Economic Analysis and Policy, Reserve Bank of India, Mumbai.

Prakash, B.A. 1994. 'Kerala's Economy: An Overview'. In B.A. Prakash, ed., *Kerala's Economy: Performance, Problems, Prospects*. New Delhi: Sage: 15–40.

PROBE (People's Report on Basic Education in India). 1999. New Delhi: Oxford University Press.

Przeworski, Adam. 1995. *Capitalism and Social Democracy*. Cambridge: Cambridge University Press.

Putnam, Robert. 1993a. *Making Democracy Work: Civic Traditions in Modern Italy*. Princeton: Princeton University Press.

———. 1993b. 'The Prosperous Community: Social Capital and Public Life'. *The American Prospect*, Spring: 35–42.

Pylee, M.V. 1995. 'Reforming Higher Education'. *Kerala Sociologist* 23: 13–26.

Radhakrishnan, P. 1989. *Peasant Struggles, Land Reforms and Social Change: Malabar 1936–82*. New Delhi: Sage Publications.

Raghuram, N., and Y. Madhavi. 1996. 'India's Declining Ranking'. *Nature*, 17 October: 572.

Raj, K.N. 1992. 'Land Reform and Complementary Measures in Kerala'. *IASSI Quarterly* 10(3): 20–24.

———. 1994. 'Has There Been a "Kerala Model"?' In A.K.G. Centre for Research and Studies, *International Congress on Kerala Studies*, Abstracts, Volume 1, Thiruvananthapuram.

Raj, K.N., and P.K. Michael Tharakan. 1983. 'Agrarian Reform in Kerala and its Impact on the Rural Economy – A Preliminary Assessment'. In Ajit Kumar

Ghose, ed., *Agrarian Reform in Contemporary Developing Countries*. London and New York: Croom Helm and St. Martin's Press: 31–90.

Rajan, S. Irudaya, and K.S. James. 1993. 'Kerala's Health Status: Some Issues'. *Economic and Political Weekly* 28, 4 September: 1889–92.

Rajeeve, P.V. 1983. *Economic Development and Unemployment: Relevance of Kerala Model*. New Delhi: Asia Publication Services.

Raju, Saraswati, Peter J. Atkins, Naresh Kumar and Janet G. Townsend. 1999. *Atlas of Women and Men in India*. New Delhi: Kali for Women.

Ramachandran, K. 1998. 'Dubious Development: Petrochemicals Complex at Cheemeni'. *Economic and Political Weekly* 33(1–2): 14–15.

Ramachandran, V. 1987. *Report of the Committee on Decentralisation*. Trivandrum: Government of Kerala.

Ramachandran, V.K. 1997. 'On Kerala's Development Achievements'. In Jean Drèze and Amartya Sen, eds, *Indian Development: Selected Regional Perspectives*, Oxford and New Delhi: Clarendon Press and Oxford University Press: 205–356.

Ramachandran, V.K., and Madhura Swaminathan. 1996. 'Structural Adjustment and the Poor: The International Experience'. Mumbai: Indira Gandhi Institute of Development Research.

Ramachandran, V.K., Vikas Rawal and Madhura Swaminathan. 1997. 'Investment Gaps in Primary Education: A State-Wise Study'. *Economic and Political Weekly*, 4–11 January.

Raman Kutty, V. 1987. 'Socioeconomic Factors in Child Health Status: A Kerala Village Study'. MPhil dissertation, Centre for Development Studies, Thiruvananthapuram.

Raman Kutty, V., K.R. Thankappan, K.P. Kannan and K.P. Aravindan. 1993. 'How Socio-Economic Status Affects Birth and Death Rates in Rural Kerala, India: Results of a Health Study'. *International Journal of Health Services* 23(93): 373–86.

Ramanathaiyer, Sundar. 1996. 'Social Development in Kerala, India: Illusion or Reality?' M.Phil thesis, University of Hong Kong.

Rammohan, K.T. 1998. 'Kerala CPI(M): All That Is Solid Melts into Air'. *Economic and Political Weekly*, 3 October.

Ratcliffe, John. 1978. 'Social Justice and Demographic Transition: Lessons From India's Kerala State'. *International Journal of Health Services* 8(1): 123–44.

Richburg, Keith B., and Anne Swardso. 1996. '$2.28 a Day – On Track to Prosperity?' *International Herald Tribune*, 29 July.

Ross, Pauline. 1995. 'Female Education and Adjustment Programmes: A Cross-Country Statistical Analysis'. *World Development* 23(11): 1931–52.

Rudolph, Lloyd I., and Susan Hoeber Rudolph. 1987. *In Pursuit of Lakshmi: The Political Economy of the Indian State*. Chicago: University of Chicago Press.

Sample Registration System. 1994. Fertility and Mortality Indicators. Registrar General, India, New Delhi.

———. 1997. Fertility and Mortality Indicators. Registrar General, India, New Delhi.

Sankaranarayanan, K.C., and M. Meera Bhai. 1994. 'Industrial Development of Kerala – Problems and Prospects'. In B.A. Prakash, ed., *Kerala's Economy: Performance, Problems, Prospects*. New Delhi: Sage.

Saradamoni, K. 1980. *Emergence of a Slave Caste: Pulayas of Kerala*. New Delhi: People's Publishing House.

———. 1981. *Divided Poor: Study of a Kerala Village*. New Delhi: Ajanta Publications.

Sathyamurthy, T.V. 1985. *India since Independence: Studies in the Development of the Power of the State. Volume 1: Centre-State Relations, The Case of Kerala.* Delhi: Ajanta.

Sen, Abhijit. 1991. 'Shocks and Instabilities in an Agriculture-constrained Economy: India 1964–85'. In Jan Breman and Sudipto Mundle, eds, *Rural Transformation in India.* Delhi: Oxford University Press, 1991.

Sen, Amartya. 1993. 'The Economics of Life and Death'. *Scientific American* 268(5), May: 40–47.

———. 1997. 'Radical Needs and Moderate Reforms'. In Jean Drèze and Amartya Sen, eds, *Indian Development: Selected Regional Perspectives.* New Delhi: Oxford University Press: 1–32.

Sessions, G., ed. 1995. *Deep Ecology for the 21st Century: Readings on the Philosophy and Practice of the New Environmentalism.* Boston, Mass.: Shambhala.

Shaw, P. 1998. *Agenda for Change: New Education Policy, Choice and Competition.* New Delhi: Rajiv Gandhi Institute for Contemporary Studies.

Shiva Kumar, A.K. 1991. 'UNDP's Human Development Index: A Computation for Indian States'. *Economic and Political Weekly* 26(21): 3343–5

———. 1996. 'UNDP's Gender-Related Development Index: A Computation for Indian States'. *Economic and Political Weekly* 31(14): 887–95.

Soman, C.R., Malati Damodaran, S. Rajasree, V. Ramankutty and K. Vijayakuma. 1990. 'High Morbidity and Low Mortality: The Experience of Urban Pre-School Children in Kerala'. *Journal of Tropical Paediatrics* 37: 17–141.

Shrum, Wesley. 1996. *Research Capacity for Sustainable Development: Report of a Field Study in Ghana, Kenya, and Kerala (India).* The Hague: RAWOO, Advisory Council for Scientific Research in Development Problems.

———. 1997. 'View From Afar: "Visible" Productivity of Scientists in the Developing World'. *Scientometrics* 40: 215–35.

Shrum, W., and Y. Shenhav. 1995. 'Science and Technology in Less Developed Countries'. In Sheila Jasanoff, Gerald Markle, James Peterson and Trevor Pinch, eds, *Handbook of Science, Technology, and Society.* Newbury Park, Calif.: Sage.

Shrum, Wesley and John J. Beggs. 1997. 'Methodology for Studying Research Networks in the Developing World: Generating Information for Science and Technology Policy'. *Knowledge and Policy* 9: 62–85.

Simon, Julian L. 1996. *Ultimate Resource.* Princeton, N.J.: Princeton University Press.

Singh, Sohan, John E. Gordon and John B. Wyon. 1962. 'Medical Care in Fatal Illnesses of a Rural Punjab Population'. *Indian Journal of Medical Research* 50(6): 865–80.

Singh, Manjit. 1991. *Labour Process in the Unorganised Industry: A Case Study of the Garment Industry.* New Delhi: Manohar Publications.

Sooryamoorthy, R. 1997. *Consumption to Consumerism in the Context of Kerala.* New Delhi: Classical Publishing Co.

Sreekumar T.T. 1990. 'Neither Rural Nor Urban'. *Economic and Political Weekly* 25(37), 15 September.

———. 1993. 'Urban Process in Kerala, 1900–1981'. Trivandrum: Centre for Development Studies.

Srinivasan, K., and A. Shariff, 1997. *Towards Population and Development Goals.* New Delhi: Oxford University Press and UNFPA.

Steer, A., and E. Lutz. 1993. 'Measuring Environmentally Sustainable Development'. *Finance and Development*, December 1993: 20–23.

Stepan, Alfred. 1978. *The State and Society: Peru in Comparative Perspective.* Princeton, N.J.: Princeton University Press.

Subrahmanian, K.K. 1994. 'Some Facets of the Manufacturing Industry in Kerala'.

In B.A. Prakash, ed., *Kerala's Economy: Performance, Problems, Prospects*. New Delhi: Sage: 237–58.

Subrahmanyam, Sanjay. 1986. 'Aspects of State Formation in South India and Southeast Asia, 1500–1650'. *Indian Economic and Social History Review* 23(4): 357–77.

Subramony, Dhanalakshmy. 1994. 'A Profile of Urban Poverty: The Case of Domestic Servants in Thiruvananthapuram City'. Paper presented at the First International Congress on Kerala Studies, Thiruvananthapuram, 27–29 August.

Swaminathan, Madhura. 1999. 'The Public Distribution System in India'. Manuscript, Mumbai: Indira Gandhi Institute of Development Research.

Swaminathan, Madhura and V.K. Ramachandran. 1999. 'New Data on Calorie Intakes'. *Frontline*, Chennai, 16(5), 27 February–12 March.

Swaminathan, Madhura, and Vikas Rawal. 1999. 'Primary Education'. In Kirit S. Parikh, ed., *India Development Report 1999*. New Delhi: Oxford University Press.

Tambiah, S.J. 1986. *Sri Lanka: Ethnic Fratricide and the Dismantling of Democracy*. Chicago: University of Chicago Press.

———. 1992. *Buddhism Betrayed? Religion, Politics and Violence in Sri Lanka*. Chicago: University of Chicago Press.

Thampy, M.M. 1994. 'Development of Organised Small-scale Industries: Some Issues'. In B.A. Prakash, ed. *Kerala's Economy: Performance, Problems, Prospects*. New Delhi: Sage: 279–97.

Thapar, Romila. 1989. 'Imagined Religious Communities? Ancient History and the Modern Search for a Hindu Identity'. *Modern Asian Studies* 23(2): 209–31.

Tharamangalam, Joseph. 1998a. 'The Perils of Social Development without Economic Growth: The Development Debacle of Kerala, India'. *Bulletin of Concerned Asian Scholars* 30(1): 23–34.

———. 1998b. 'A Rejoinder'. *Bulletin of Concerned Asian Scholars* 30(4): 47–52.

Thomas, E.J. 1989. 'Socio-Economic Factors Influencing Educational Standards in a Marginalised Community'. MPhil dissertation, Jawaharlal Nehru University, New Delhi.

———. 1994. 'Emerging Trends in Kerala Society'. *Kerala Sociologist* 22: 7–10.

Thomas Isaac, T.M. 1982. 'Class Struggle and Structural Changes: Coir Mat and Matting Industry in Kerala: 1950–1980'. *Economic and Political Weekly* 17(31): PE13–29.

———. 1983a. 'Class Struggle and Transition to Specifically Capitalist Forms of Production: Some Conclusions of a Study of the Coir Industry in Kerala'. *Social Scientist* 11(12): 35–58.

———. 1983b. 'The Emergence of Radical Working Class Movement in Alleppey'. Working Paper No. 175, Centre for Development Studies, Trivandrum.

———. 1984. 'Class Struggle and Industrial Structure: A Study of the Coir Weaving Industry in Kerala, 1859–1980'. PhD thesis, Jawaharlal Nehru University, New Delhi.

———. 1985. 'From Caste Consciousness to Class-consciousness: Alleppey Coir Workers during the Inter-war Period'. *Economic and Political Weekly* 20(4): PE5–18.

———. 1986. 'An Introduction to the Study of Agrarian Relations in Kerala'. In *Golden Jubilee Souvenir of the Kerala Karshaka Samity* [Malayalam Text]. Cochin: Kerala Karshaka Samity: 113–25.

———. 1992. 'Economic Consequences of the Gulf Crisis: A Study of India with Special Reference to Kerala'. In Piyasiri Wickramasekara, ed., *The Gulf Crisis and*

South Asia: Studies on the Economic Impact. New Delhi: Asian Regional Team for Employment Promotion (ARTEP) of the United Nations Development Programme: 59–102.

———. 1994a. 'The Trend and Pattern of External Trade of Kerala'. In B.A. Prakash, ed., *Kerala's Economy: Performance, Problems, Prospects.* New Delhi: Sage: 368–93.

———. 1994b. 'The Left Movement in Kerala: Lessons of the Past and Challenges of the Present'. In A.K.G. Centre for Research and Studies, *International Congress on Kerala Studies*, Abstracts, Volume 1, Thiruvananthapuram.

———. 1997. 'Economic Consequences of Gulf Migration'. In K.C. Zachariah and S. Irudaya Rajan, eds, *Kerala's Demographic Transition.* New Delhi: Sage.

———. 1998. 'Decentralisation, Democracy and Development'. Paper given to workshop on Civil Society, Authoritarianism and Globalization, Stockholm, 18–20 September.

Thomas Isaac, T.M., with Richard W. Franke. 1999. 'Local Democracy and Local Development: The People's Campaign for Decentralized Planning in Kerala'. Unpublished manuscript.

Thomas Isaac, T.M., and Harilal, K.N. 1997. 'Planning for Empowerment: People's Campaign for Decentralised Planning Kerala'. *Economic and Political Weekly* 32(1–2): 53–8.

Thomas Isaac, T.M., and S. Mohana Kumar. 1991. 'Kerala Elections, 1991: Lessons and Non-Lessons'. *Economic and Political Weekly* 26(47): 2691–704.

Thomas Isaac, T.M., and Michael Tharakan. 1986. 'Sree Narayana Movement in Travancore. 1988–1939: A Study of Social Basis and Ideological Reproduction', Working Paper No. 214, Centre for Development Studies, Trivandrum.

———. 1995. 'Kerala: Towards a New Agenda'. *Economic and Political Weekly* 30(31–32): 1993–2004.

Thomas Isaac, T.M., Richard W. Franke and M.P. Parameswaran. 1997. 'From Anti-feudalism to Sustainable Development: The Kerala People's Science Movement'. *Bulletin of Concerned Asian Scholars* 29(3): 34–44.

Thomas Isaac, T.M., Richard W. Franke, and Pyaralal Raghavan. 1998. *Democracy at Work in an Indian Industrial Cooperative: The Story of Kerala Dinesh Beedi.* Ithaca, N.Y.: Cornell University Press.

Thorp, Rosemary. 1993. Review of Magnus Blomstrom and Patricio Meller, eds, *Diverging Paths: Comparing a Century of Scandinavian and Latin American Economic Development* (Washington D.C.: Inter American Development Bank, 1991). *Economic Journal* 103: 420.

Timberg, Thomas. 1981. 'Regions in Indian Development'. *Pacific Affairs* 53(4): 643–50.

Törnquist, Olle. 1989. *What's Wrong with Marxism? Volume I: On Capitalists and State in India and Indonesia.* New Delhi: Manohar.

———. 1991a. *What's Wrong with Marxism? Volume II: On Peasants and Workers in India and Indonesia.* New Delhi: Manohar.

———. 1991b. 'Communists and Democracy: Two Indian Cases and One Debate'. *Bulletin of Concerned Asian Scholars* 23(2).

———. 1996. 'Marginal Notes on Impressive Attempts'. Paper given to the International Conference on Kerala, New Delhi, 9–11 December 1996.

———. 1998a. 'Making Democratisation Work: from Civil Society and Social Capital to Political Inclusion and Politicisation – Theoretical Reflections on Concrete Cases in Indonesia, Kerala, and the Philippines'. In L. Rudebeck and

O. Törnquist with V. Rojas, *Democratisation in the Third World. Concrete Cases in Comparative and Theoretical Perspective*. London: Macmillan.

———. 1998b. 'Beyond Romanticism – Remarkable Popular Reorganising. Comment on Tharamangalam'. *Bulletin of Concerned Asian Scholars* 30(4): 43–4.

———. 1999. *Politics and Development. A Critical Introduction*. London, Thousand Oaks and New Delhi: Sage.

Törnquist, Olle, with P.K. Michael Tharakan. 1995. *The Next Left? Democratisation and Attempts to Renew the Radical Political Development Project: The Case of Kerala*. Copenhagen: Nordic Institute of Asian Studies, Report Series, No. 24.

Törnquist, Olle, and P.K. Michael Tharakan. 1996. 'Democratisation and Attempts to Renew the Radical Political Development Project: The Case of Kerala'. *Economic and Political Weekly* 31(28): 1847–58, 31(29): 1953–73, and 31(30): 2041–5.

Ukkuru, Mary P., Prema L. Jyothi Augustine and A. Sujatha. 1994. 'Working Pattern and Nutritional Profiles of Women Engaged in Stone Breaking'. Paper presented at the First International Congress on Kerala Studies, Thiruvananthapuram, 27–29 August.

UNCTAD (United Nations Conference on Trade and Development). 1997. *Handbook of International Trade and Statistics 1995*. Geneva: United Nations.

UNDP (United Nations Development Programme). 1990. *Human Development Report 1990*. New York: Oxford University Press.

———. 1995. *Human Development Report 1995*. New York: Oxford University Press.

———. 1996. *Human Development Report 1996*. New York: Oxford University Press.

———. 1997. *Human Development Report 1997*. New York: Oxford University Press.

———. 1998. *World Development Report 1998*. New York: Oxford University Press.

Vaidyanathan, K.E. 1989. 'Status of Women and Family Planning'. *Asia-Pacific Population Journal* 4(2): 3–18.

Variar, K. Sreedhara. 1969. *Marumakkathayam and Allied Systems of Law in the Kerala State*. Ernakulam.

Vasudevan Nair, P.K. 1995. 'Kerala Model Needs Follow Up'. *Hindu*, 18 September: 5.

Velayudhan, Meera. 1992. 'A Voice from the Women's Movement in Kerala: Meera Velayudhan in Conversation with Kalikutty Asatty'. *Women's Equality* 5(1), January–March: 34–3.

Véron, R. 1998. 'Markets, Environment and Development in South India: Cultivation and Marketing of Pineapple and Cashew in Kerala'. PhD thesis, University of Zurich.

Vijayasankar, P.S. 1986. 'The Urban Casual Labour Market in Kerala: A Study of Headload Workers in Trichur'. MPhil thesis, Centre for Development Studies, Trivandrum.

Vimala Kumari, T.K. 1991. *Infant Mortality Among Fishermen*. New Delhi: Discovery Publishing House.

Visaria, Pravin M. 1961. 'The Sex Ratio of the Population of India'. In *Census of India* Vol. I, Monograph No. 10. New Delhi: Office of the Registrar General.

Vishwanath, L.S. 1998. 'Efforts of the Colonial State to Suppress Female Infanticide: Use of Sacred Texts, Generation of Knowledge'. *Economic and Political Weekly* 33(19): 1104–12.

Wallich, Paul. 1995. 'A Mystery inside a Riddle inside an Enigma'. *Scientific American*, March: 37.

WCED (World Commission on Environment and Development). 1987. *Our Common Future*. New York: Oxford University Press.

Weiner, Myron. 1991. *The Child and the State in India*. Princeton, N.J.: Princeton University Press.

Wickremeratne, Ananda. 1995. *The Roots of Nationalism: Sri Lanka*. Colombo: Karunaratne & Sons.

WHO (World Health Organization). 1995. *World Health Report 1995: Bridging the Gaps*. Geneva: World Health Organization.

Woodcock, George. 1967. *Kerala: A Portrait of the Malabar Coast*. London: Faber & Faber.

World Bank. 1993. *The East Asian Miracle: Economic Growth and Public Policy*. New York: Oxford University Press.

———. 1994. *World Development Report 1994*. New York: Oxford University Press.

———. 1995. *World Development Report 1995: Workers in an Integrating World*. New York: Oxford University Press.

———. 1997. *World Development Report 1997: The State in a Changing World*, Oxford: Oxford University Press.

———. 1999. *World Development Report: Knowledge for Development*. New York: Oxford University Press.

WRI (World Resource Institute). 1994. *World Resources 1994–95*. New York and Oxford: Oxford University Press.

———. 1997. *World Resources 1996–97*. New York and Oxford: Oxford University Press.

Wyon, John B., and John E. Gordon. 1971. *The Khanna Study*. Cambridge, Mass.: Harvard University Press.

Yunus, Mohammad. 1997. 'Towards a Poverty Free World'. *Mainstream*, 23 August.

Zachariah, K.C. 1965. 'Migration and Population Growth in Kerala'. In R.S. Kurup and K.A. George, eds, *Population Growth in Kerala*. Trivandrum: Bureau of Economics and Statistics: 92–114.

———. 1994. 'Demographic Transition in Kerala: A Response to Official Policies and Programmes'. In *International Congress on Kerala Studies*, Abstracts, Volume 1, Thiruvananthapuram.

Zachariah, K.C., S. Irudaya Rajan, K. Navaneetham, P.S. Sarma, U.S. Mishra and P.S. Gopinathan Nair. 1992. *Demographic Transition in Kerala in the 1980s: Results of a Survey in Three Districts*. Thiruvananthapuram: Centre for Development Studies, and Ahmedabad: Gujarat Institute of Area Planning.

Zachariah, K.C., and Sulekha Patel. 1982. 'Trends and Determinants of Infant and Child Morbidity in Kerala'. Discussion Paper 82–2, Population and Human Resources Division, World Bank, Washington, D.C.

Zachariah, K.C., and S. Irudaya Rajan. 1997. *Kerala's Demographic Transition: Determinants and Consequences*. New Delhi: Sage.

Contributors

William M. Alexander is Emeritus Professor of World Food Politics at California Polytechnic State University, Santa Rosa.

Rex Casinader is a Research Associate at the Institute of Asian Studies, University of British Columbia, Vancouver.

Barbara H. Chasin is Professor of Sociology at Montclair State University, New Jersey.

Richard W. Franke is Professor of Anthropology at Montclair State University, New Jersey.

Patrick Heller is Assistant Professor of Sociology and International Affairs at Columbia University, New York.

K.P. Kannan is a Fellow at the Centre for Development Studies, Thiruvananthapuram, Kerala.

John Kurien is an Associate Fellow at the Centre for Development Studies, Thiruvananthapuram, Kerala.

M.P. Parameswaran is a retired nuclear physicist. A past president of Kerala Sastra Sahitya Parishad, he is now engaged in local-level planning through the KSSP.

Govindan Parayil teaches environmental studies, and science and technology studies in the Division of Social Science at the Hong Kong University of Science and Technology.

V.K. Ramachandran is Professor at the Indira Gandhi Institute of Development Research, Mumbai.

Sundar Ramanathaiyer is a PhD candidate in Development Studies at Edith Cowan University, Perth.

Wesley Shrum is Professor of Sociology at Louisiana State University, Baton Rouge.

Olle Törnquist is Professor pro tem of Politics and Development at the University of Oslo.

René Véron is a human geographer specializing in South Asian development studies. He is currently engaged in research on rural development in West Bengal and Bihar under the auspices of Cambridge and Keele Universities.

Index